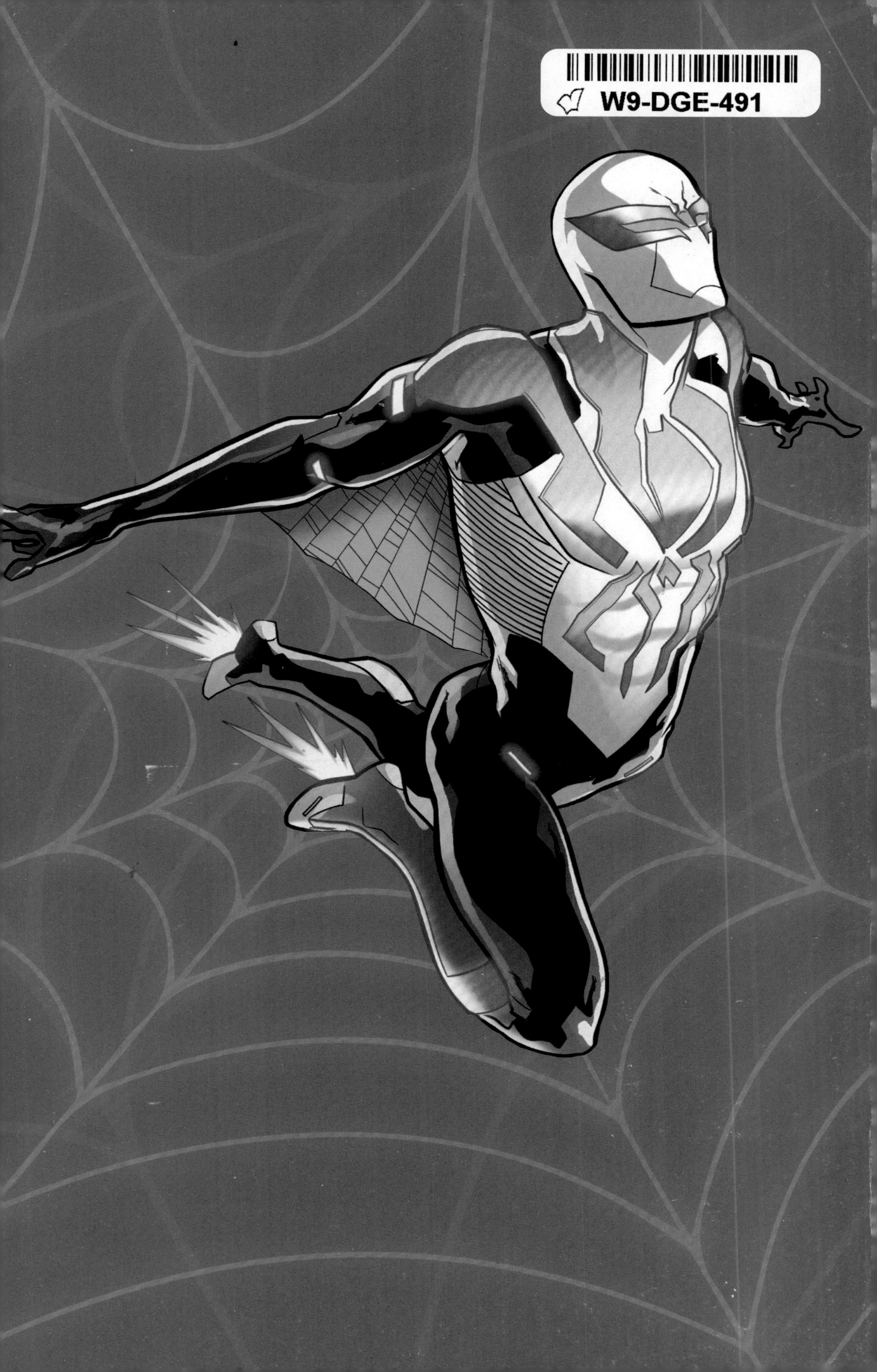

collection editor ALEX STARBUCK
associate editor SARAH BRUNSTAD
editor, special projects MARK D. BEAZLEY
senior editor, special projects JENNIFER GRÜNWALD
vp, production & special projects JEFF YOUNGQUIST
book design ADAM DEL RE

svp print, sales & marketing DAVID GABRIEL
editor in chief AXEL ALONSO
chief creative officer JOE QUESADA
publisher DAN BUCKLEY
executive producer ALAN FINE

SPIDER-MAN 2099 VOL. 4: GODS AND WOMEN. Contains material originally published in magazine form as SPIDER-MAN 2099 #6-10. First printing 2016. ISBN# 978-0-7851-9964-9. Published by MARVEL WORLDWIDE, INC., a subsidiary of MARVEL ENTERTAINMENT, LLC. OFFICE OF PUBLICATION: 135 West 50th Street, New York, NY 10020. Copyright © 2016 MARVEL No similarity between any of the names, characters, persons, and/or institutions in this magazine with those of any living or dead person or institution is intended, and any such similarity which may exist is purely coincidental. **Printed in Canada. ALAN FINE,** President, Marvel Entertainment; DAN BUCKLEY, President, TV, Publishing & Brand Management; JOE QUESADA, Chief Creative Officer; TOM BREVOORT, SVP of Publishing; DAVID BOGART, SVP of Business Affairs & Operations, Publishing & Partnership; C.B. CEBULSKI, VP of Brand Management & Development, Asia; DAVID GABRIEL, SVP of Sales & Marketing, Publishing; JEFF YOUNGQUIST, VP of Production & Special Projects; DAN CARR, Executive Director of Publishing Technology; ALEX MORALES, Director of Publishing Operations; SUSAN CRESPI, Production Manager; STAN LEE, Chairman Emeritus. For information regarding advertising in Marvel Comics or on Marvel.com, please contact Vit DeBellis, Integrated Sales Manager, at vdebellis@marvel.com. For Marvel subscription inquiries, please call 888-511-5480. **Manufactured between 6/3/2016 and 7/11/2016 by SOLISCO PRINTERS, SCOTT, QC, CANADA.**

10 9 8 7 6 5 4 3 2 1

FIGHTING CRIME BEFORE HIS TIME!

SPIDER-MAN 2099

GODS AND WOMEN

PETER DAVID
writer

WILL SLINEY
artist

RACHELLE ROSENBERG
with WIL QUINTANA [#7]
colorists

VC's CORY PETIT
letterer

FRANCESCO MATTINA
cover art

DEVIN LEWIS
editor

NICK LOWE
senior editor

SPIDER-MAN created by STAN LEE & STEVE DITKO

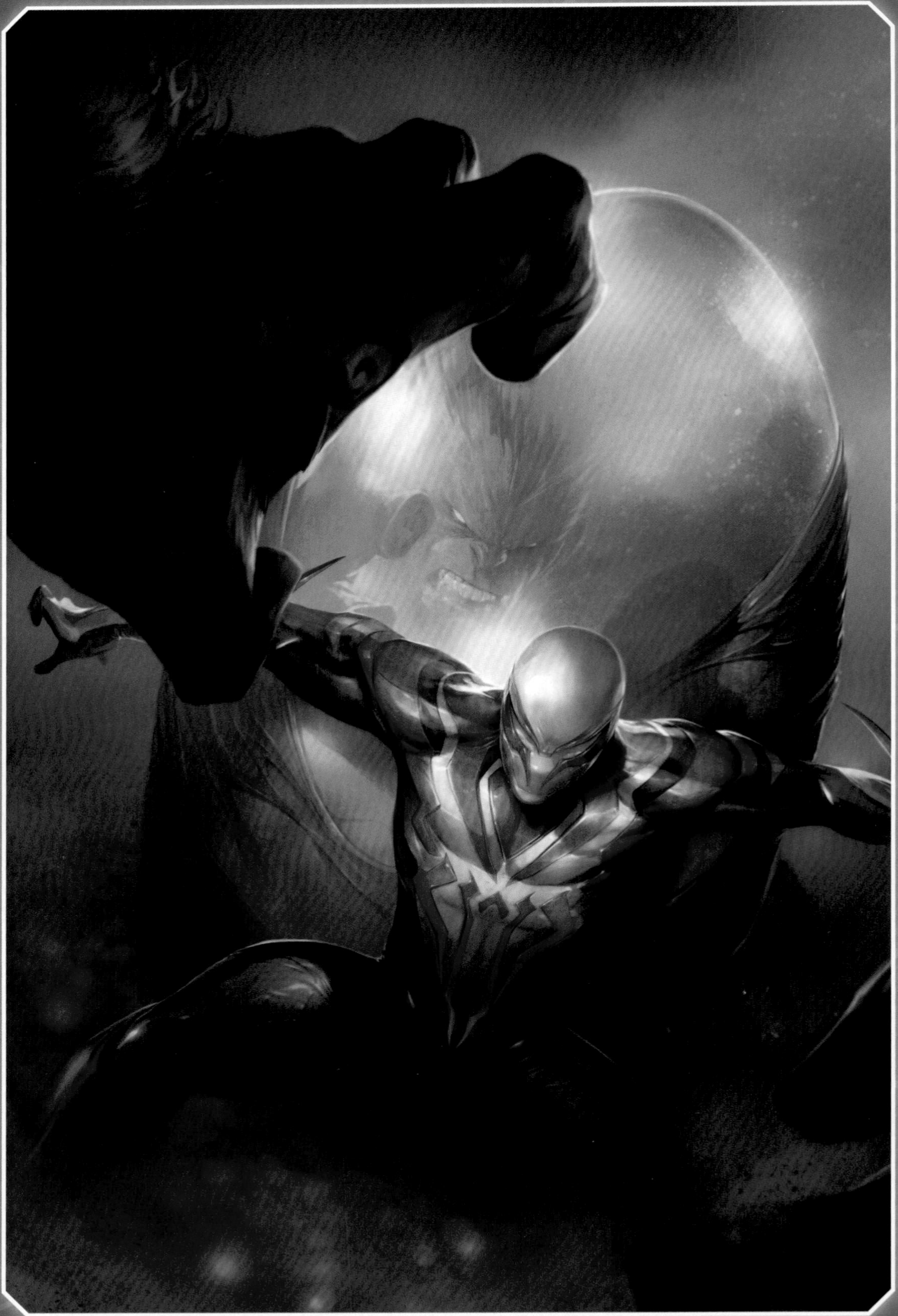

MIGUEL O'HARA WAS A YOUNG GENETICS GENIUS EMPLOYED AT THE MEGACORPORATION ALCHEMAX IN THE FUTURE CITY OF NUEVA YORK! ONE HIS EXPERIMENTS—TO REPLICATE THE POWERS OF THE PRESENT-DAY SPIDER-MAN—WAS TURNED AGAINST HIM AND REWROTE HIS DNA TO MAKE IT 50 PERCENT SPIDER! AFTER LEARNING HOW TO USE HIS AMAZING NEW ABILITIES, MIGUEL BECAME...

SPIDER-MAN 2099

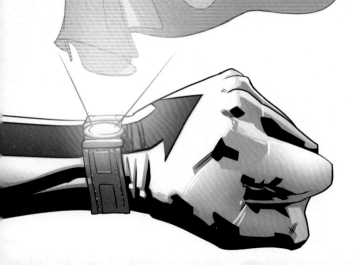

HI, I'M LYLA, MIGUEL O'HARA'S LYRATE, LIFE-FORM APPROXIMATION HOLOGRAPHIC ASSISTANT!

FOR YEARS, MIGUEL O'HARA WAS THE SPIDER-MAN OF THE YEAR OF 2099, BUT HE RECENTLY FOUND HIMSELF STRANDED IN YOUR PRESENT-DAY NEW YORK CITY! HE HAS FOUND AN ALLY IN PETER PARKER AND BECAME THE HEAD OF RESEARCH AND DEVELOPMENT FOR HIS TECH CONGLOMERATE PARKER INDUSTRIES.

ALSO STRANDED IN THE PRESENT AND WORKING AT PARKER INDUSTRIES IS ROBERTA MENDEZ, WHO IS ALSO THE CAPTAIN AMERICA OF THE YEAR 2099. ROBERTA'S MIND HAS BEEN SEPARATED INTO TWO CONSCIOUSNESSES-- ONE BEING THE CAPTAIN AMERICA PORTION OF HER MIND, THE OTHER HER CIVILIAN IDENTITY. AS ROBERTA, SHE HAS NO KNOWLEDGE OF HER AMAZING ABILITIES OR THAT THE TIME SHE LIVES IN IS NOT HER OWN.

MIGUEL HAS MADE MANY EFFORTS TO TRAVEL BACK HOME, BUT SOMETHING THAT HAS HAPPENED IN THE PRESENT DAY HAS DRASTICALLY AFFECTED HIS TIMELINE, AND THE NUEVA YORK HE AND CAPTAIN AMERICA CALLED HOME NO LONGER EXISTS!

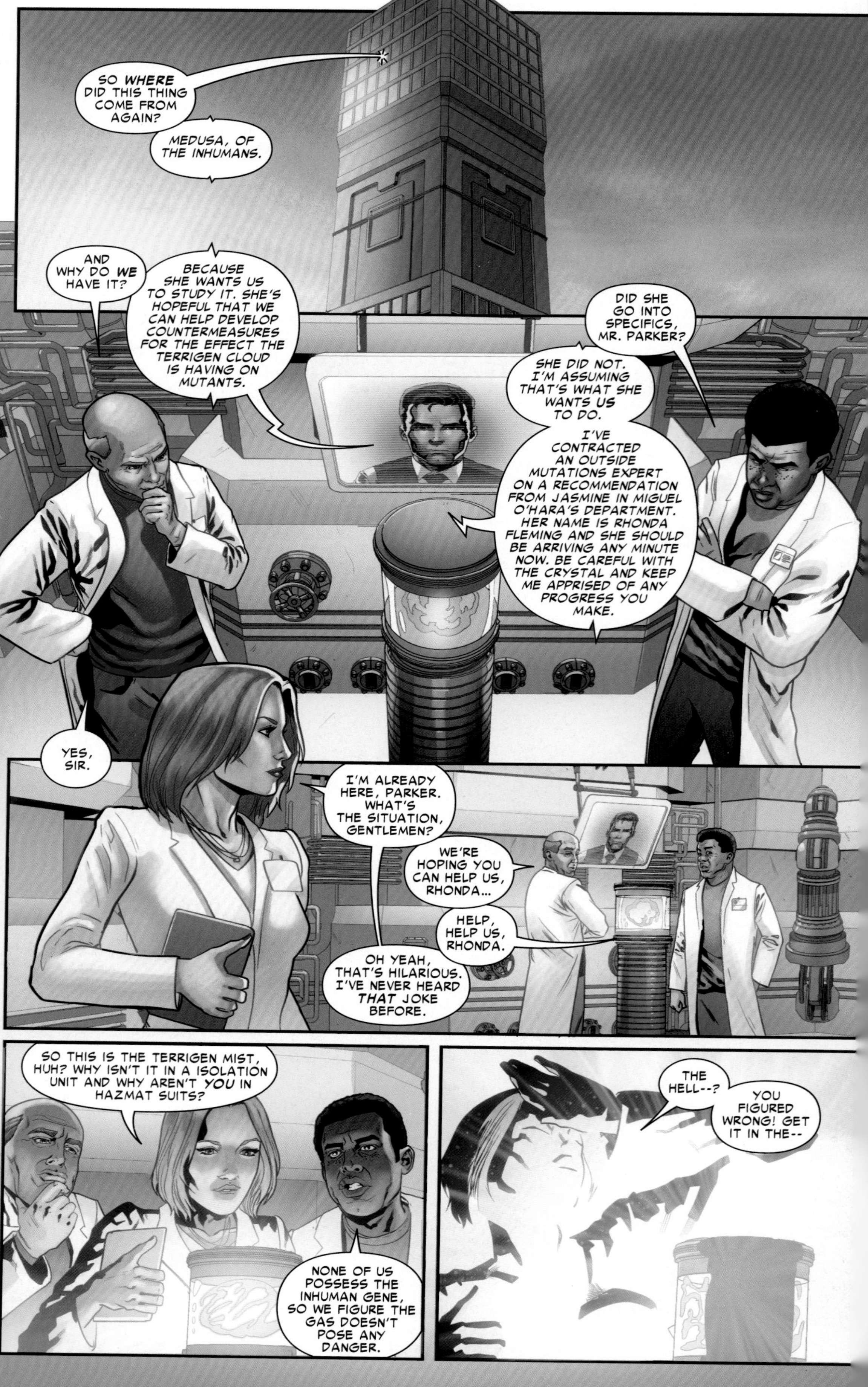
SO WHERE DID THIS THING COME FROM AGAIN?
MEDUSA, OF THE INHUMANS.
AND WHY DO WE HAVE IT?
BECAUSE SHE WANTS US TO STUDY IT. SHE'S HOPEFUL THAT WE CAN HELP DEVELOP COUNTERMEASURES FOR THE EFFECT THE TERRIGEN CLOUD IS HAVING ON MUTANTS.
DID SHE GO INTO SPECIFICS, MR. PARKER?
SHE DID NOT. I'M ASSUMING THAT'S WHAT SHE WANTS US TO DO.
I'VE CONTRACTED AN OUTSIDE MUTATIONS EXPERT ON A RECOMMENDATION FROM JASMINE IN MIGUEL O'HARA'S DEPARTMENT. HER NAME IS RHONDA FLEMING AND SHE SHOULD BE ARRIVING ANY MINUTE NOW. BE CAREFUL WITH THE CRYSTAL AND KEEP ME APPRISED OF ANY PROGRESS YOU MAKE.
YES, SIR.
I'M ALREADY HERE, PARKER. WHAT'S THE SITUATION, GENTLEMEN?
WE'RE HOPING YOU CAN HELP US, RHONDA...
HELP, HELP US, RHONDA.
OH YEAH, THAT'S HILARIOUS. I'VE NEVER HEARD THAT JOKE BEFORE.
SO THIS IS THE TERRIGEN MIST, HUH? WHY ISN'T IT IN A ISOLATION UNIT AND WHY AREN'T YOU IN HAZMAT SUITS?
NONE OF US POSSESS THE INHUMAN GENE, SO WE FIGURE THE GAS DOESN'T POSE ANY DANGER.
THE HELL--?
YOU FIGURED WRONG! GET IT IN THE--

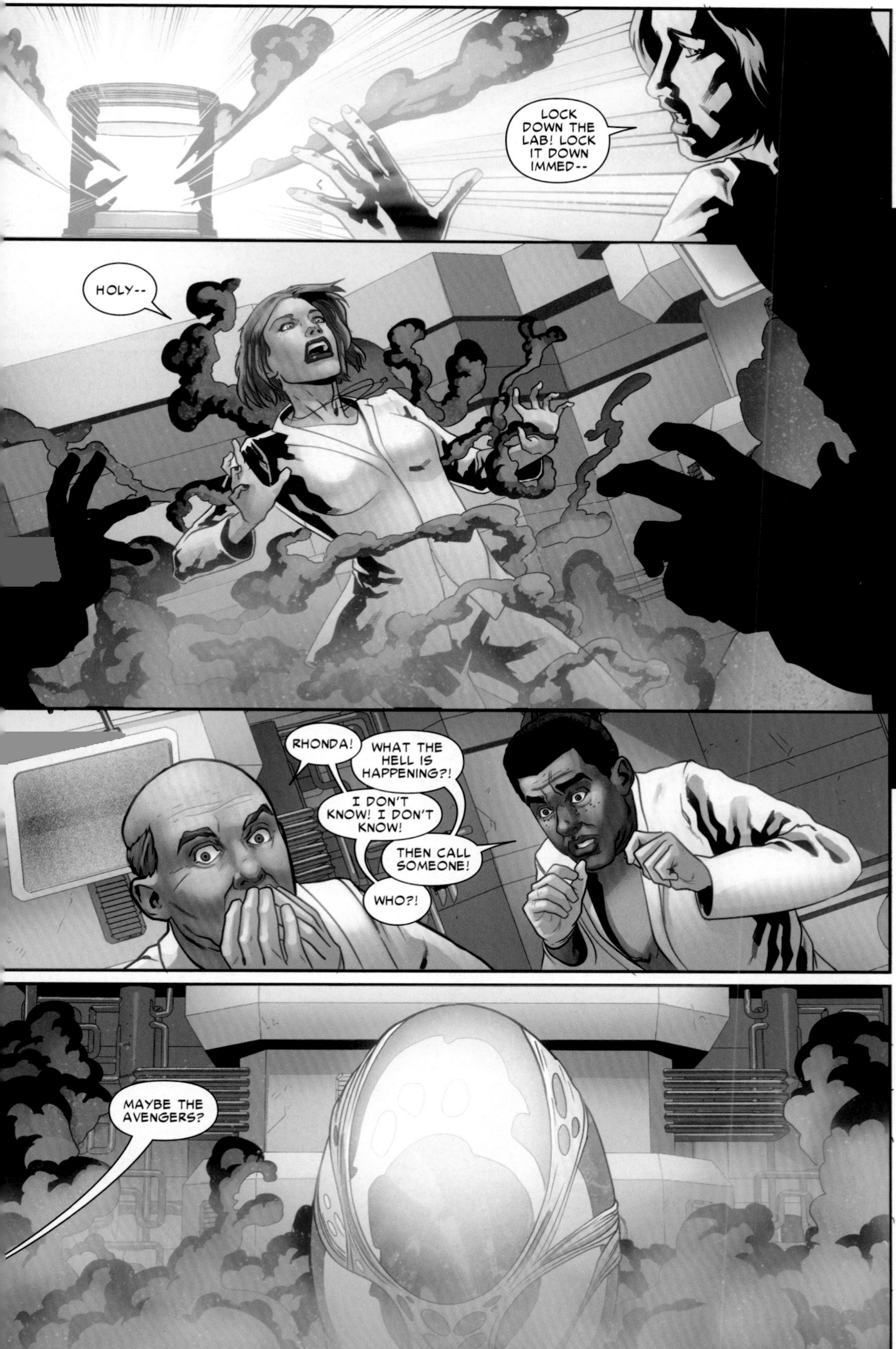
LOCK DOWN THE LAB! LOCK IT DOWN IMMED--
HOLY--
RHONDA!
WHAT THE HELL IS HAPPENING?!
I DON'T KNOW! I DON'T KNOW!
THEN CALL SOMEONE!
WHO?!
MAYBE THE AVENGERS?

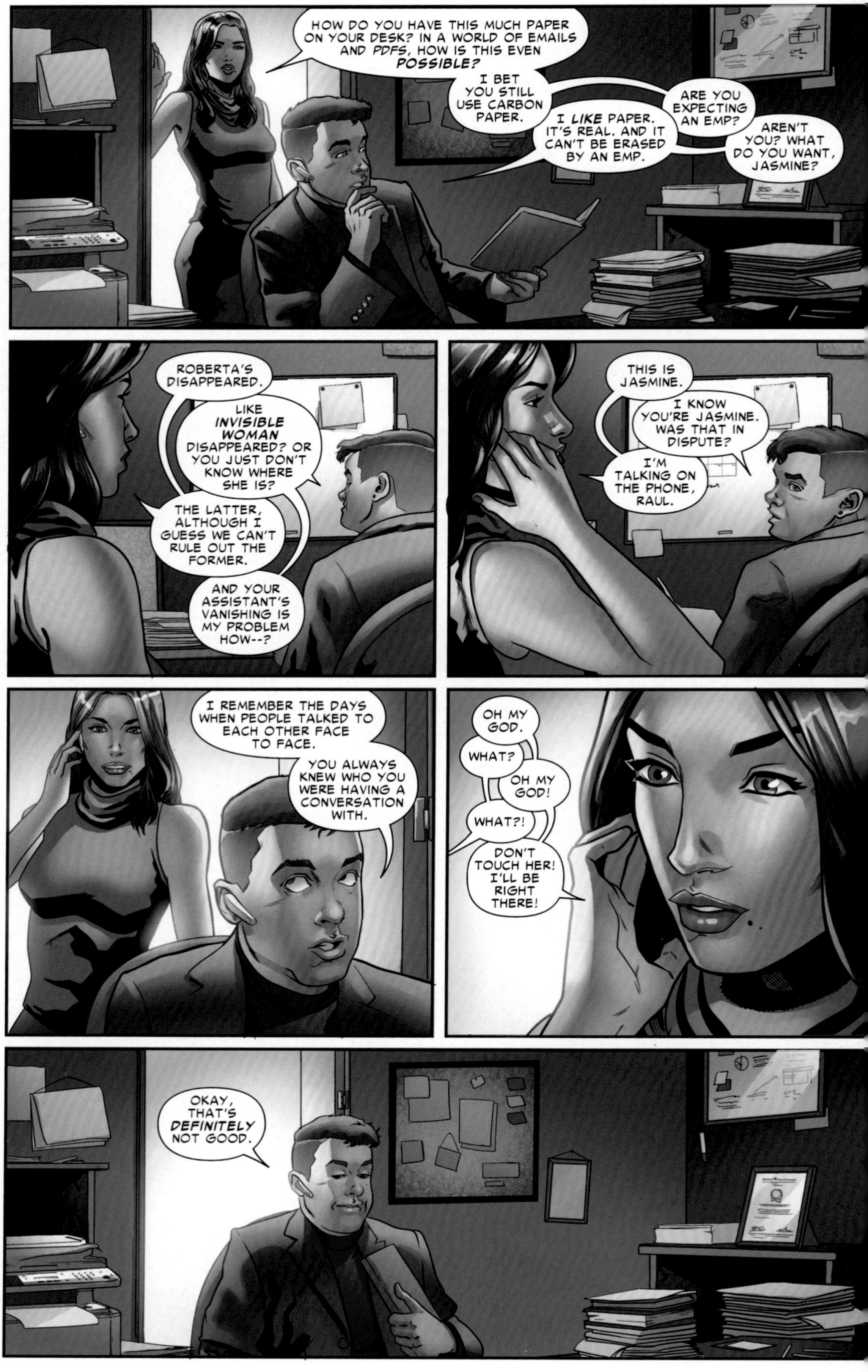

HOW DO YOU HAVE THIS MUCH PAPER ON YOUR DESK? IN A WORLD OF EMAILS AND PDFS, HOW IS THIS EVEN POSSIBLE?
I BET YOU STILL USE CARBON PAPER.
I LIKE PAPER. IT'S REAL. AND IT CAN'T BE ERASED BY AN EMP.
ARE YOU EXPECTING AN EMP?
AREN'T YOU? WHAT DO YOU WANT, JASMINE?
ROBERTA'S DISAPPEARED.
LIKE INVISIBLE WOMAN DISAPPEARED? OR YOU JUST DON'T KNOW WHERE SHE IS?
THE LATTER, ALTHOUGH I GUESS WE CAN'T RULE OUT THE FORMER.
AND YOUR ASSISTANT'S VANISHING IS MY PROBLEM HOW--?
THIS IS JASMINE.
I KNOW YOU'RE JASMINE. WAS THAT IN DISPUTE?
I'M TALKING ON THE PHONE, RAUL.
I REMEMBER THE DAYS WHEN PEOPLE TALKED TO EACH OTHER FACE TO FACE.
YOU ALWAYS KNEW WHO YOU WERE HAVING A CONVERSATION WITH.
OH MY GOD.
WHAT?
OH MY GOD!
WHAT?!
DON'T TOUCH HER! I'LL BE RIGHT THERE!
OKAY, THAT'S DEFINITELY NOT GOOD.

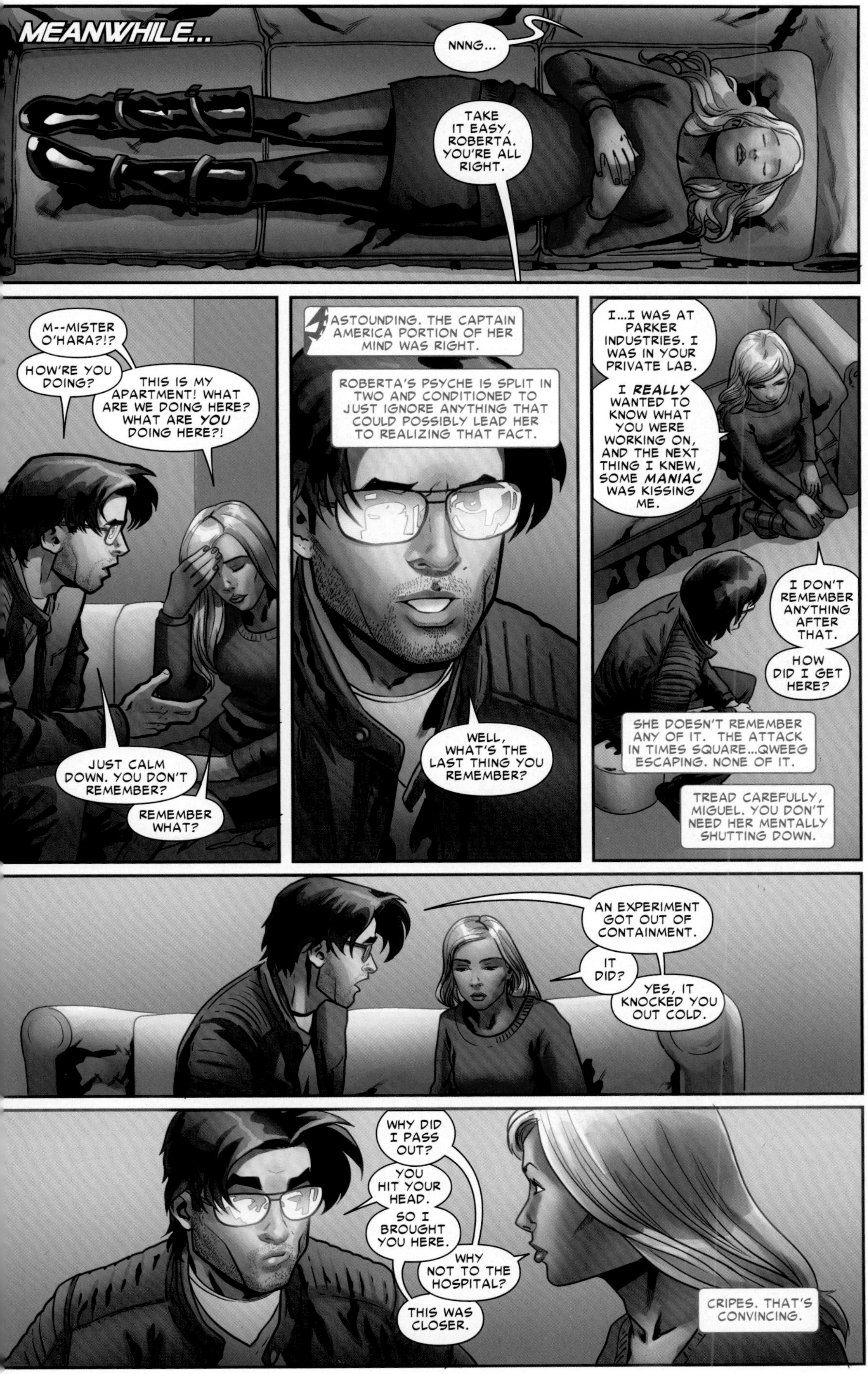
MEANWHILE...
NNNG...
TAKE IT EASY, ROBERTA. YOU'RE ALL RIGHT.
M--MISTER O'HARA?!?
HOW'RE YOU DOING?
THIS IS MY APARTMENT! WHAT ARE WE DOING HERE? WHAT ARE YOU DOING HERE?!
JUST CALM DOWN. YOU DON'T REMEMBER?
REMEMBER WHAT?
ASTOUNDING. THE CAPTAIN AMERICA PORTION OF HER MIND WAS RIGHT.
ROBERTA'S PSYCHE IS SPLIT IN TWO AND CONDITIONED TO JUST IGNORE ANYTHING THAT COULD POSSIBLY LEAD HER TO REALIZING THAT FACT.
WELL, WHAT'S THE LAST THING YOU REMEMBER?
I...I WAS AT PARKER INDUSTRIES. I WAS IN YOUR PRIVATE LAB.
I REALLY WANTED TO KNOW WHAT YOU WERE WORKING ON, AND THE NEXT THING I KNEW, SOME MANIAC WAS KISSING ME.
I DON'T REMEMBER ANYTHING AFTER THAT.
HOW DID I GET HERE?
SHE DOESN'T REMEMBER ANY OF IT. THE ATTACK IN TIMES SQUARE...QWEEG ESCAPING. NONE OF IT.
TREAD CAREFULLY, MIGUEL. YOU DON'T NEED HER MENTALLY SHUTTING DOWN.
AN EXPERIMENT GOT OUT OF CONTAINMENT.
IT DID?
YES, IT KNOCKED YOU OUT COLD.
WHY DID I PASS OUT?
YOU HIT YOUR HEAD.
SO I BROUGHT YOU HERE.
WHY NOT TO THE HOSPITAL?
THIS WAS CLOSER.
CRIPES. THAT'S CONVINCING.

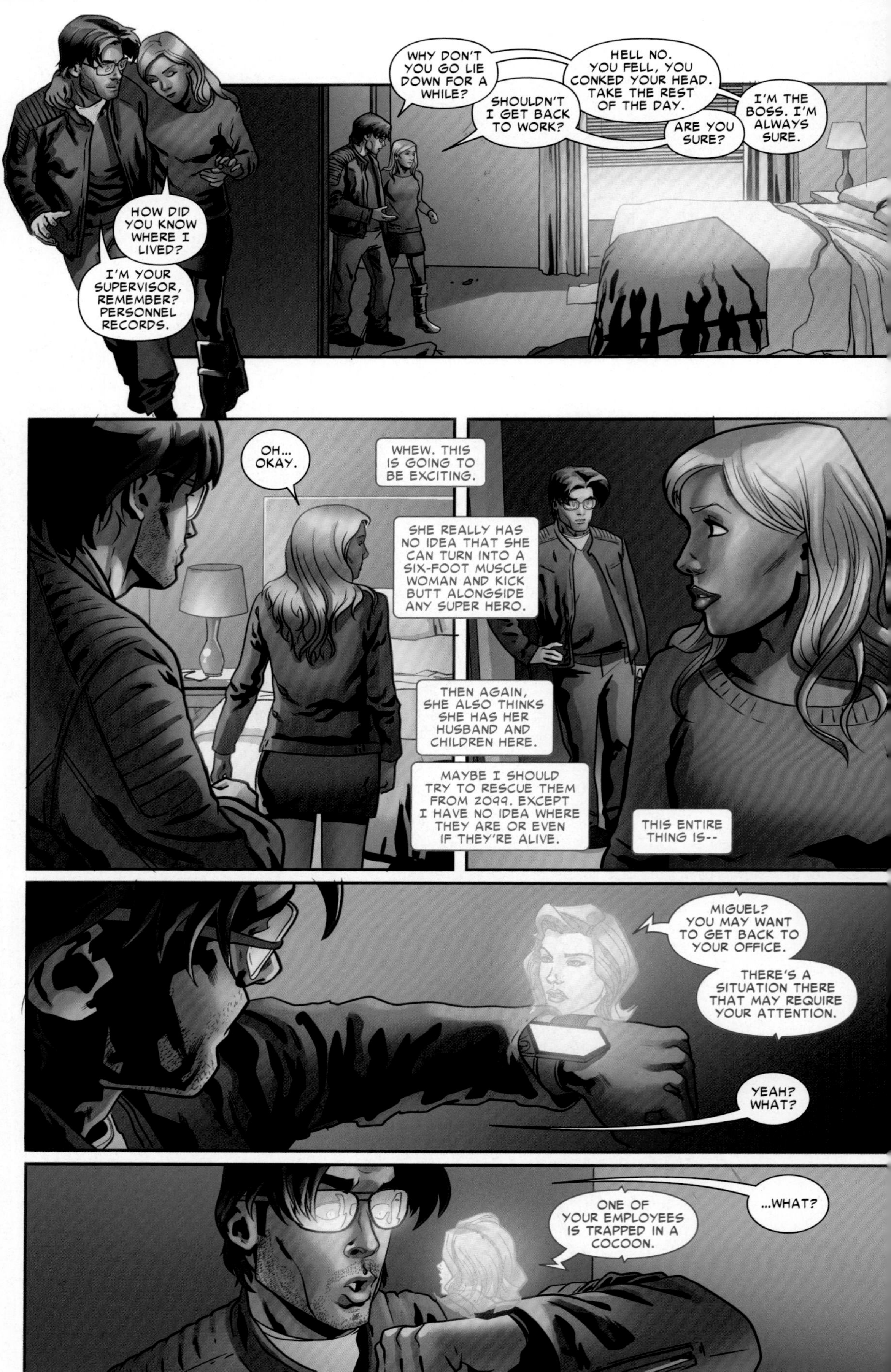
HOW DID YOU KNOW WHERE I LIVED?
I'M YOUR SUPERVISOR, REMEMBER? PERSONNEL RECORDS.
WHY DON'T YOU GO LIE DOWN FOR A WHILE?
SHOULDN'T I GET BACK TO WORK?
HELL NO. YOU FELL, YOU CONKED YOUR HEAD. TAKE THE REST OF THE DAY.
ARE YOU SURE?
I'M THE BOSS. I'M ALWAYS SURE.
OH... OKAY.
WHEW. THIS IS GOING TO BE EXCITING.
SHE REALLY HAS NO IDEA THAT SHE CAN TURN INTO A SIX-FOOT MUSCLE WOMAN AND KICK BUTT ALONGSIDE ANY SUPER HERO.
THEN AGAIN, SHE ALSO THINKS SHE HAS HER HUSBAND AND CHILDREN HERE.
MAYBE I SHOULD TRY TO RESCUE THEM FROM 2099. EXCEPT I HAVE NO IDEA WHERE THEY ARE OR EVEN IF THEY'RE ALIVE.
THIS ENTIRE THING IS--
MIGUEL? YOU MAY WANT TO GET BACK TO YOUR OFFICE.
THERE'S A SITUATION THERE THAT MAY REQUIRE YOUR ATTENTION.
YEAH? WHAT?
ONE OF YOUR EMPLOYEES IS TRAPPED IN A COCOON.
...WHAT?

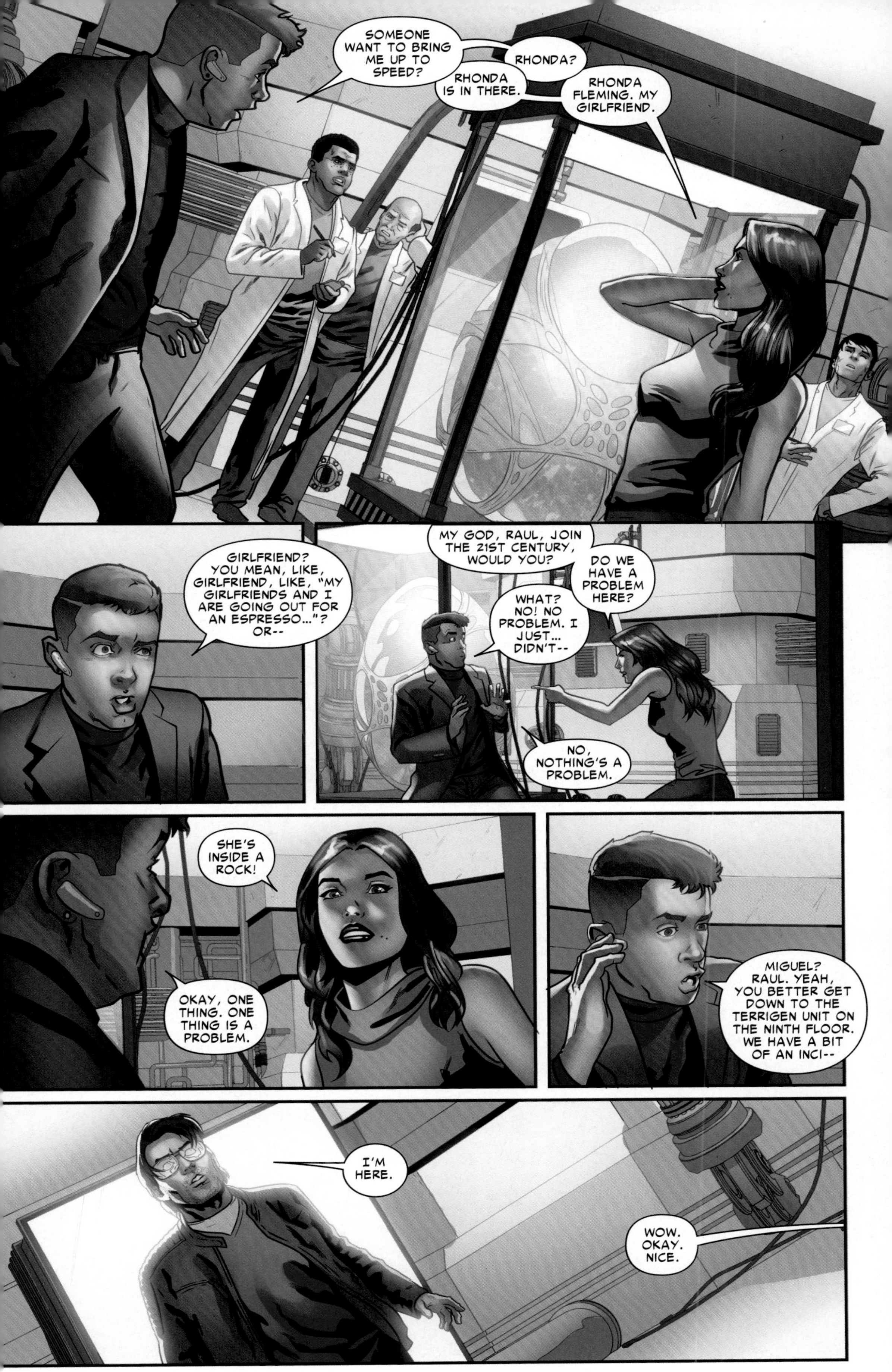
SOMEONE WANT TO BRING ME UP TO SPEED?
RHONDA IS IN THERE.
RHONDA?
RHONDA FLEMING. MY GIRLFRIEND.
GIRLFRIEND? YOU MEAN, LIKE, GIRLFRIEND, LIKE, "MY GIRLFRIENDS AND I ARE GOING OUT FOR AN ESPRESSO..."? OR--
MY GOD, RAUL, JOIN THE 21ST CENTURY, WOULD YOU?
DO WE HAVE A PROBLEM HERE?
WHAT? NO! NO PROBLEM. I JUST... DIDN'T--
NO, NOTHING'S A PROBLEM.
SHE'S INSIDE A ROCK!
OKAY, ONE THING. ONE THING IS A PROBLEM.
MIGUEL? RAUL. YEAH, YOU BETTER GET DOWN TO THE TERRIGEN UNIT ON THE NINTH FLOOR. WE HAVE A BIT OF AN INCI--
I'M HERE.
WOW. OKAY. NICE.

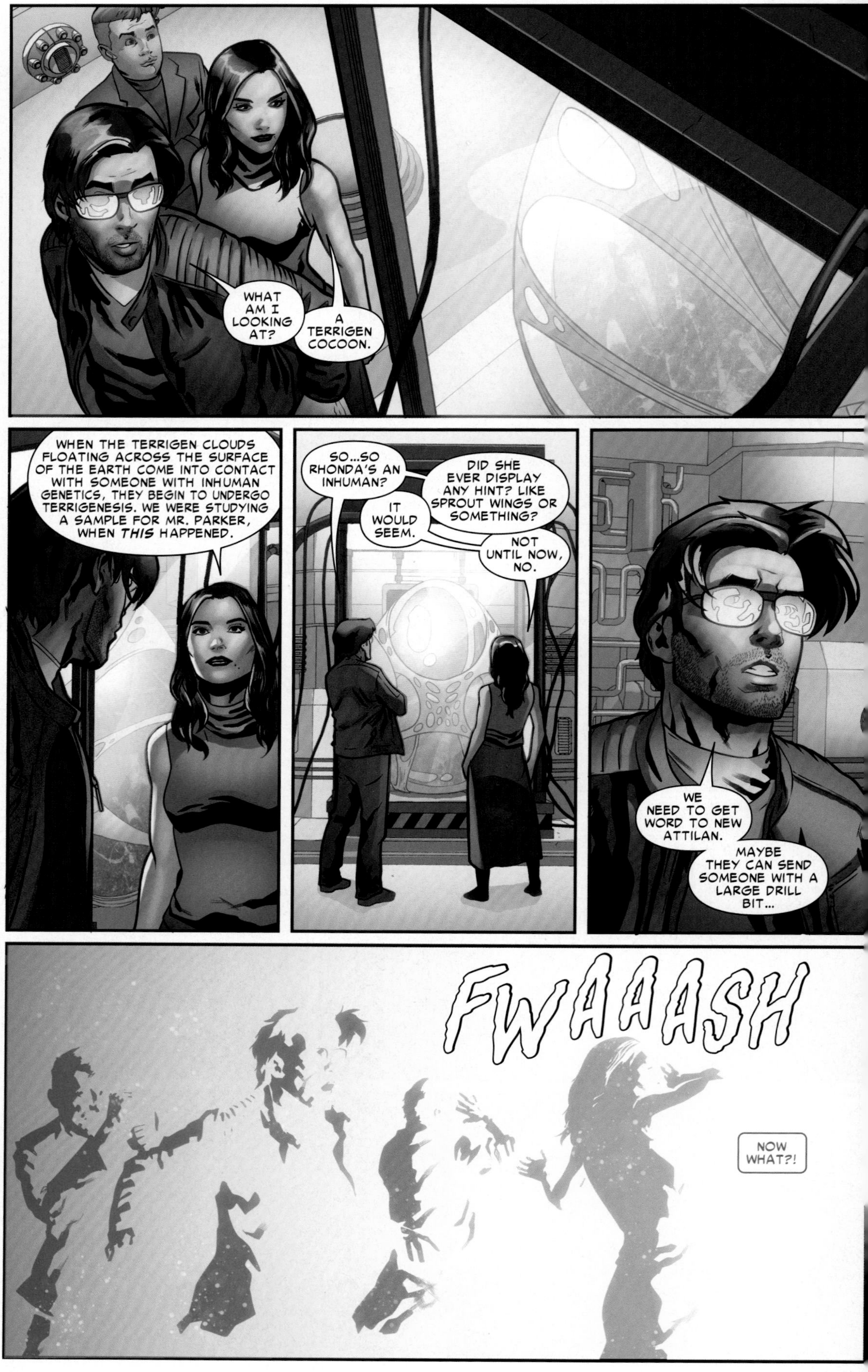
WHAT AM I LOOKING AT?
A TERRIGEN COCOON.
WHEN THE TERRIGEN CLOUDS FLOATING ACROSS THE SURFACE OF THE EARTH COME INTO CONTACT WITH SOMEONE WITH INHUMAN GENETICS, THEY BEGIN TO UNDERGO TERRIGENESIS. WE WERE STUDYING A SAMPLE FOR MR. PARKER, WHEN *THIS* HAPPENED.
SO...SO RHONDA'S AN INHUMAN?
IT WOULD SEEM.
DID SHE EVER DISPLAY ANY HINT? LIKE SPROUT WINGS OR SOMETHING?
NOT UNTIL NOW, NO.
WE NEED TO GET WORD TO NEW ATTILAN.
MAYBE THEY CAN SEND SOMEONE WITH A LARGE DRILL BIT...
FWAAASH
NOW WHAT?!

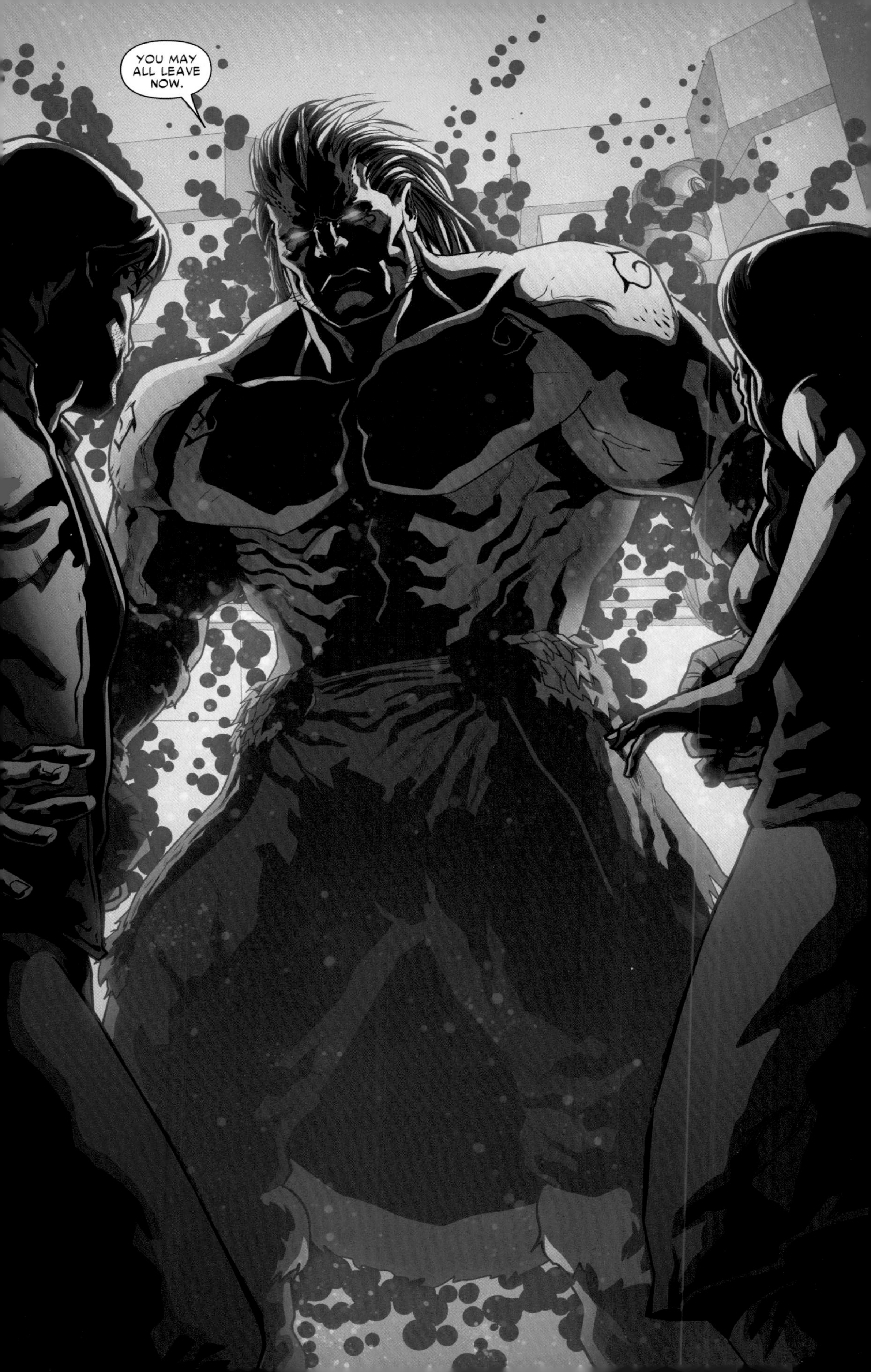
YOU MAY ALL LEAVE NOW.

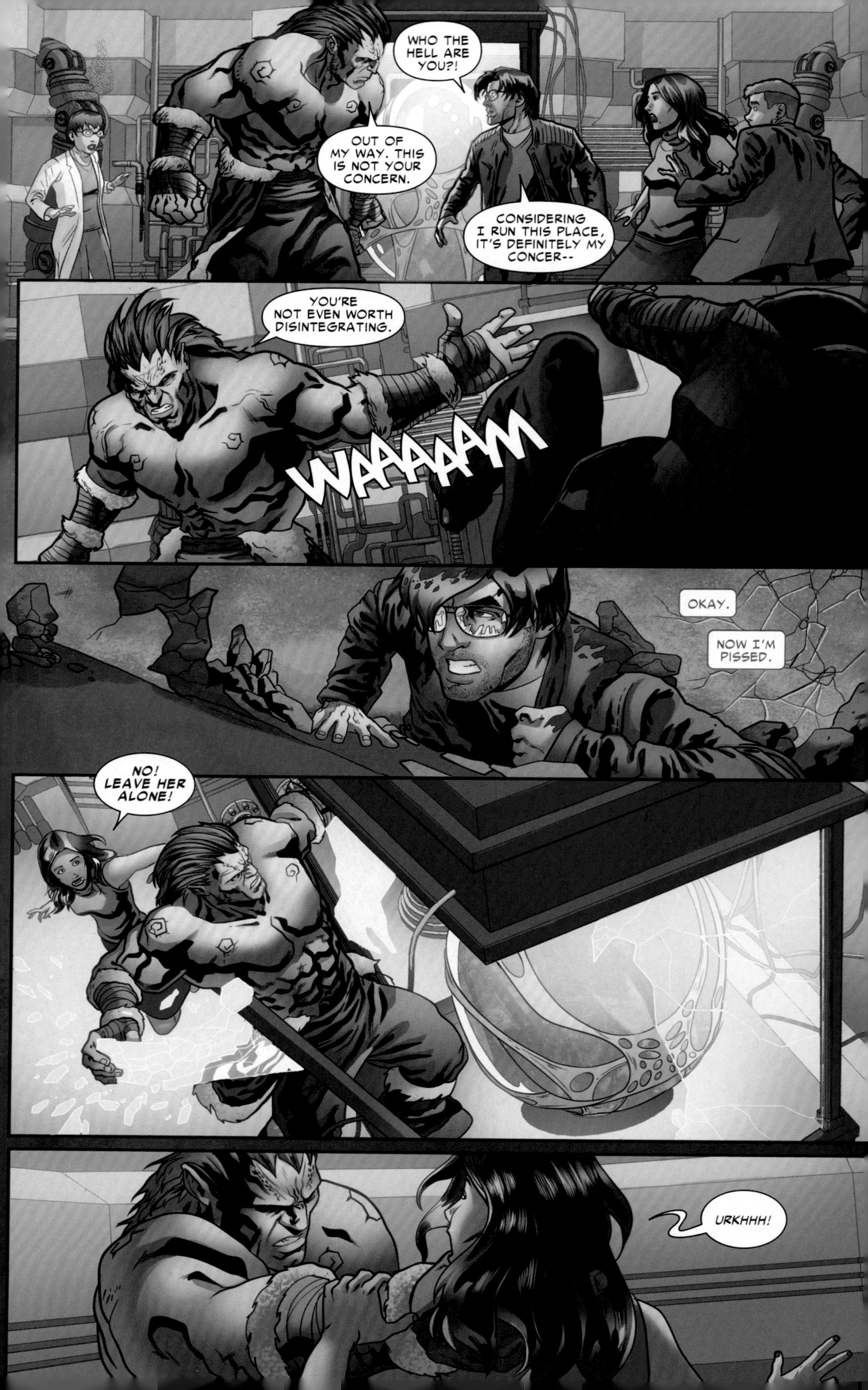
WHO THE HELL ARE YOU?!
OUT OF MY WAY. THIS IS NOT YOUR CONCERN.
CONSIDERING I RUN THIS PLACE, IT'S DEFINITELY MY CONCER--
YOU'RE NOT EVEN WORTH DISINTEGRATING.
WAAAAAM
OKAY.
NOW I'M PISSED.
NO! LEAVE HER ALONE!
URKHHH!

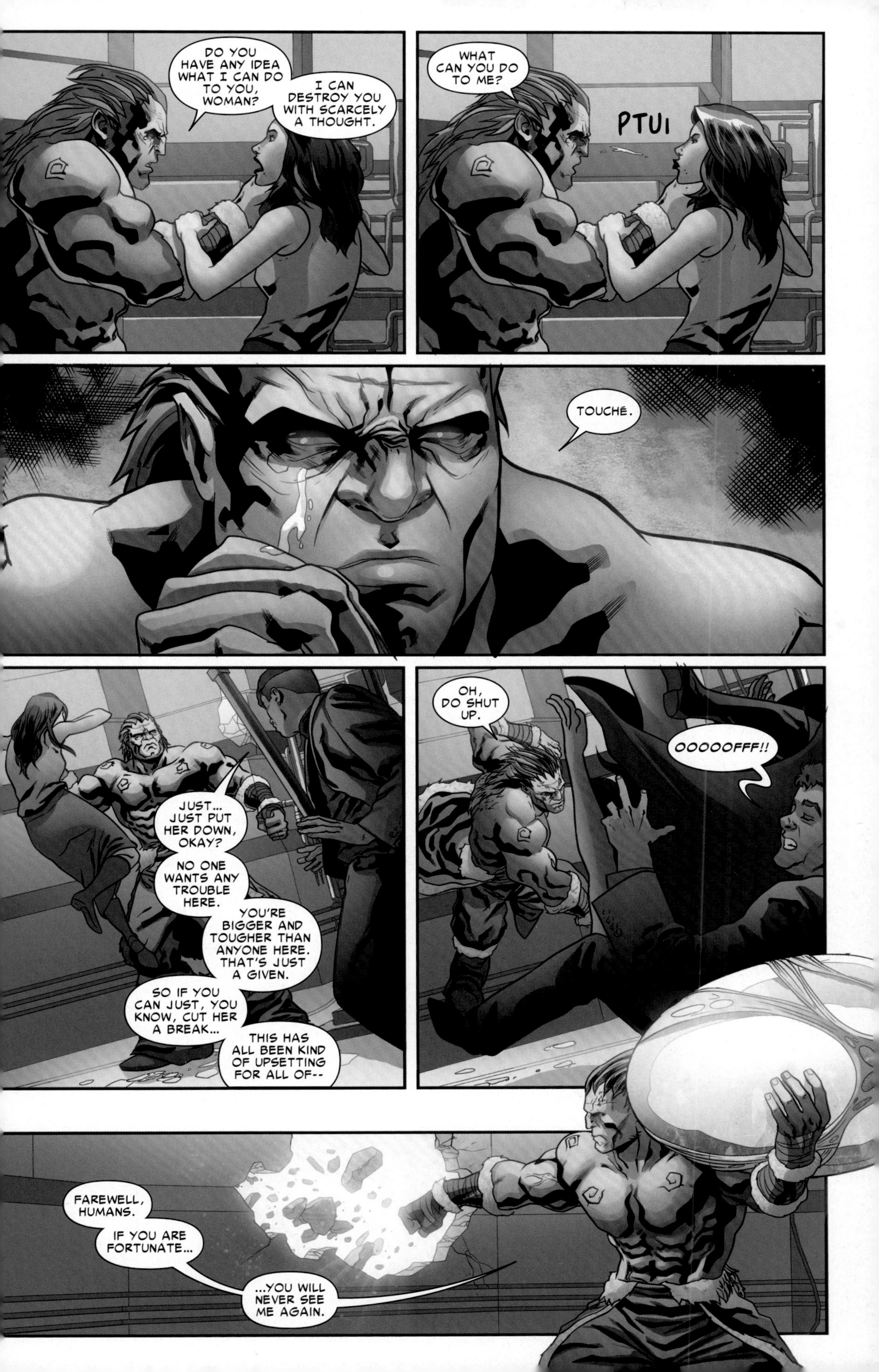
DO YOU HAVE ANY IDEA WHAT I CAN DO TO YOU, WOMAN?
I CAN DESTROY YOU WITH SCARCELY A THOUGHT.
WHAT CAN YOU DO TO ME?
PTUI
TOUCHÉ.
JUST... JUST PUT HER DOWN, OKAY?
NO ONE WANTS ANY TROUBLE HERE.
YOU'RE BIGGER AND TOUGHER THAN ANYONE HERE. THAT'S JUST A GIVEN.
SO IF YOU CAN JUST, YOU KNOW, CUT HER A BREAK...
THIS HAS ALL BEEN KIND OF UPSETTING FOR ALL OF--
OH, DO SHUT UP.
OOOOOFFF!!
FAREWELL, HUMANS.
IF YOU ARE FORTUNATE...
...YOU WILL NEVER SEE ME AGAIN.

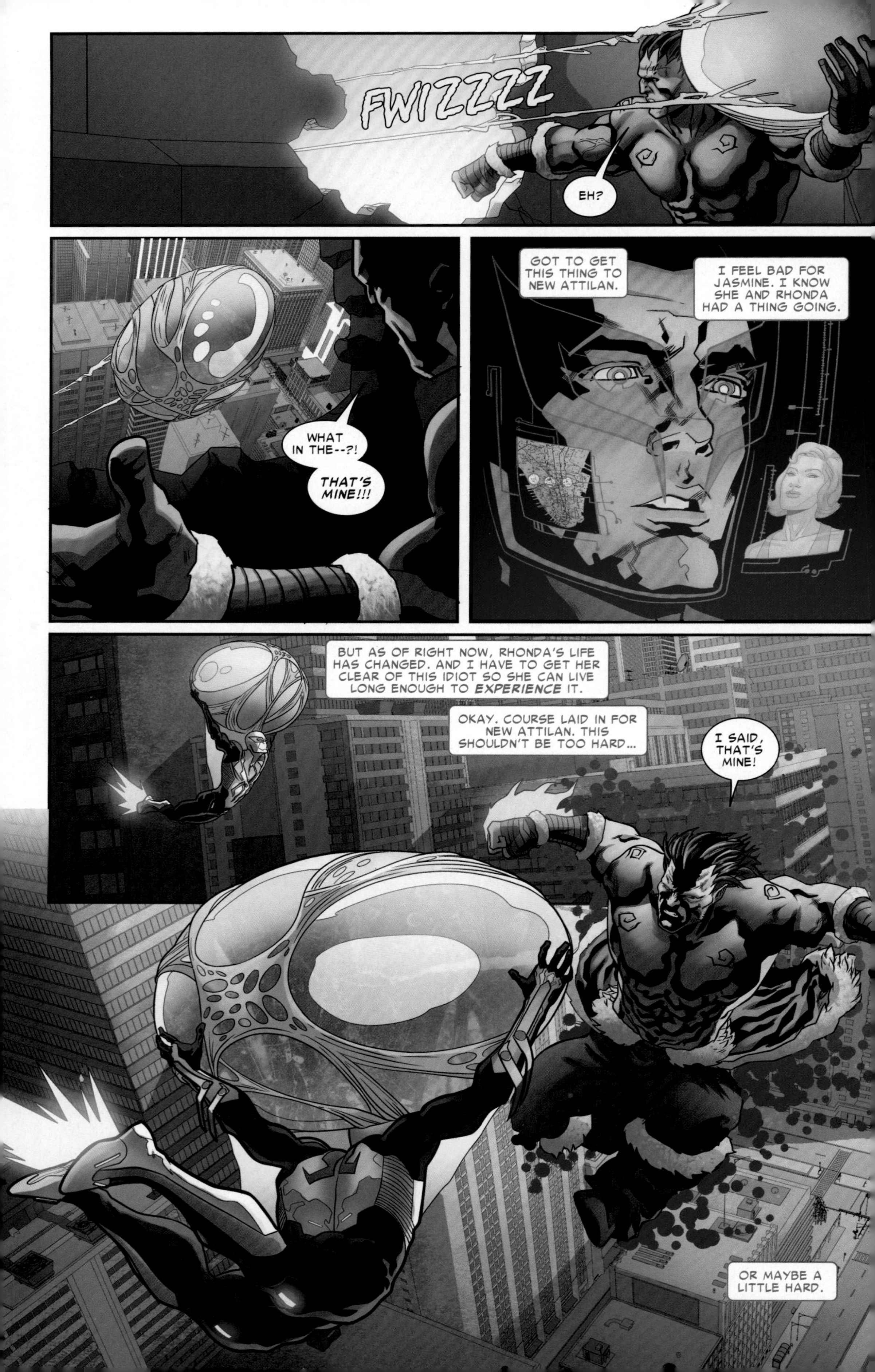
FWIZZZZ
EH?
WHAT IN THE--?!
THAT'S MINE!!!
GOT TO GET THIS THING TO NEW ATTILAN.
I FEEL BAD FOR JASMINE. I KNOW SHE AND RHONDA HAD A THING GOING.
BUT AS OF RIGHT NOW, RHONDA'S LIFE HAS CHANGED. AND I HAVE TO GET HER CLEAR OF THIS IDIOT SO SHE CAN LIVE LONG ENOUGH TO EXPERIENCE IT.
OKAY. COURSE LAID IN FOR NEW ATTILAN. THIS SHOULDN'T BE TOO HARD...
I SAID, THAT'S MINE!
OR MAYBE A LITTLE HARD.

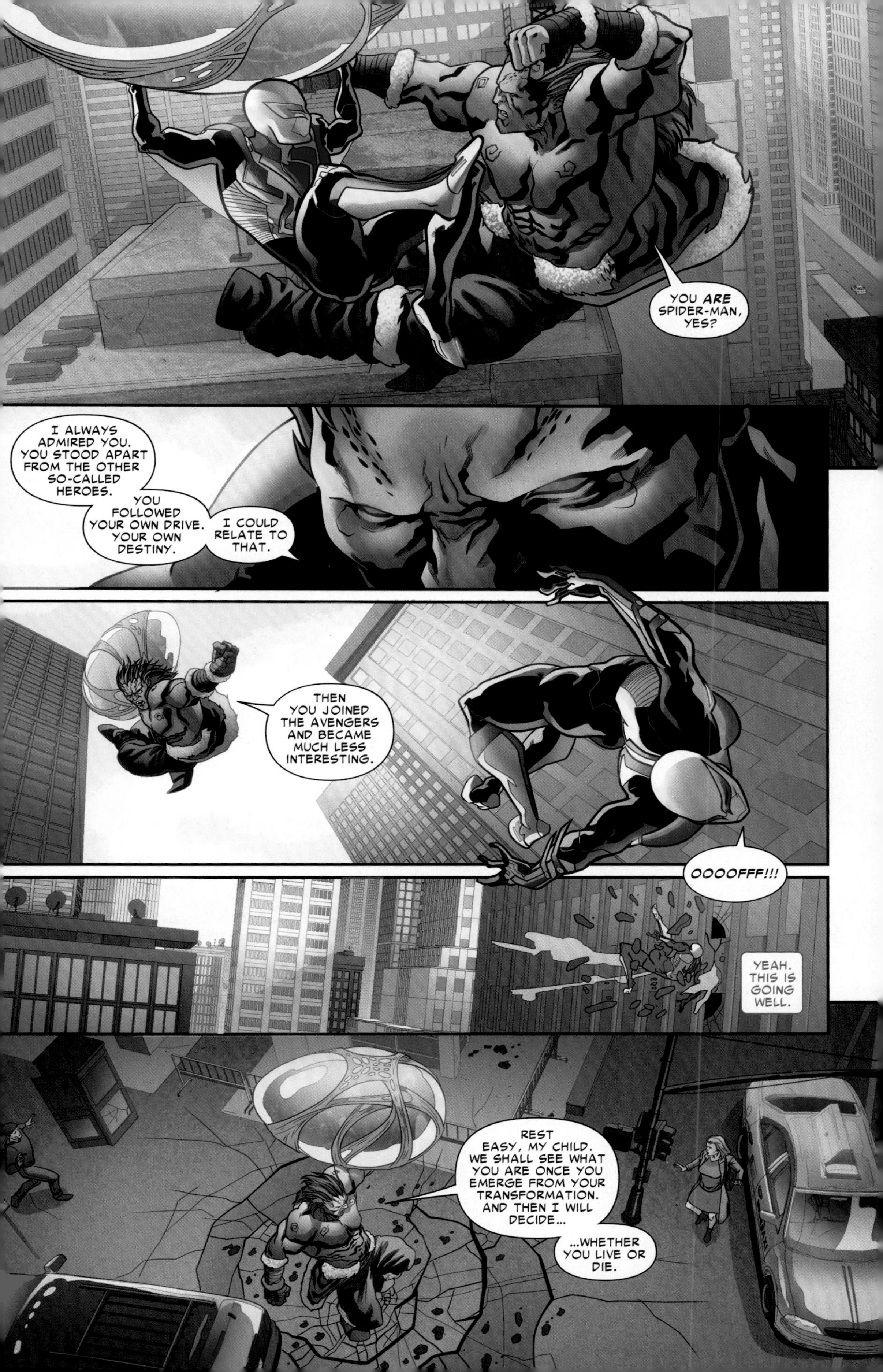
YOU ARE SPIDER-MAN, YES?
I ALWAYS ADMIRED YOU. YOU STOOD APART FROM THE OTHER SO-CALLED HEROES.
YOU FOLLOWED YOUR OWN DRIVE. YOUR OWN DESTINY.
I COULD RELATE TO THAT.
THEN YOU JOINED THE AVENGERS AND BECAME MUCH LESS INTERESTING.
OOOOFFF!!!
YEAH. THIS IS GOING WELL.
REST EASY, MY CHILD. WE SHALL SEE WHAT YOU ARE ONCE YOU EMERGE FROM YOUR TRANSFORMATION. AND THEN I WILL DECIDE...
...WHETHER YOU LIVE OR DIE.

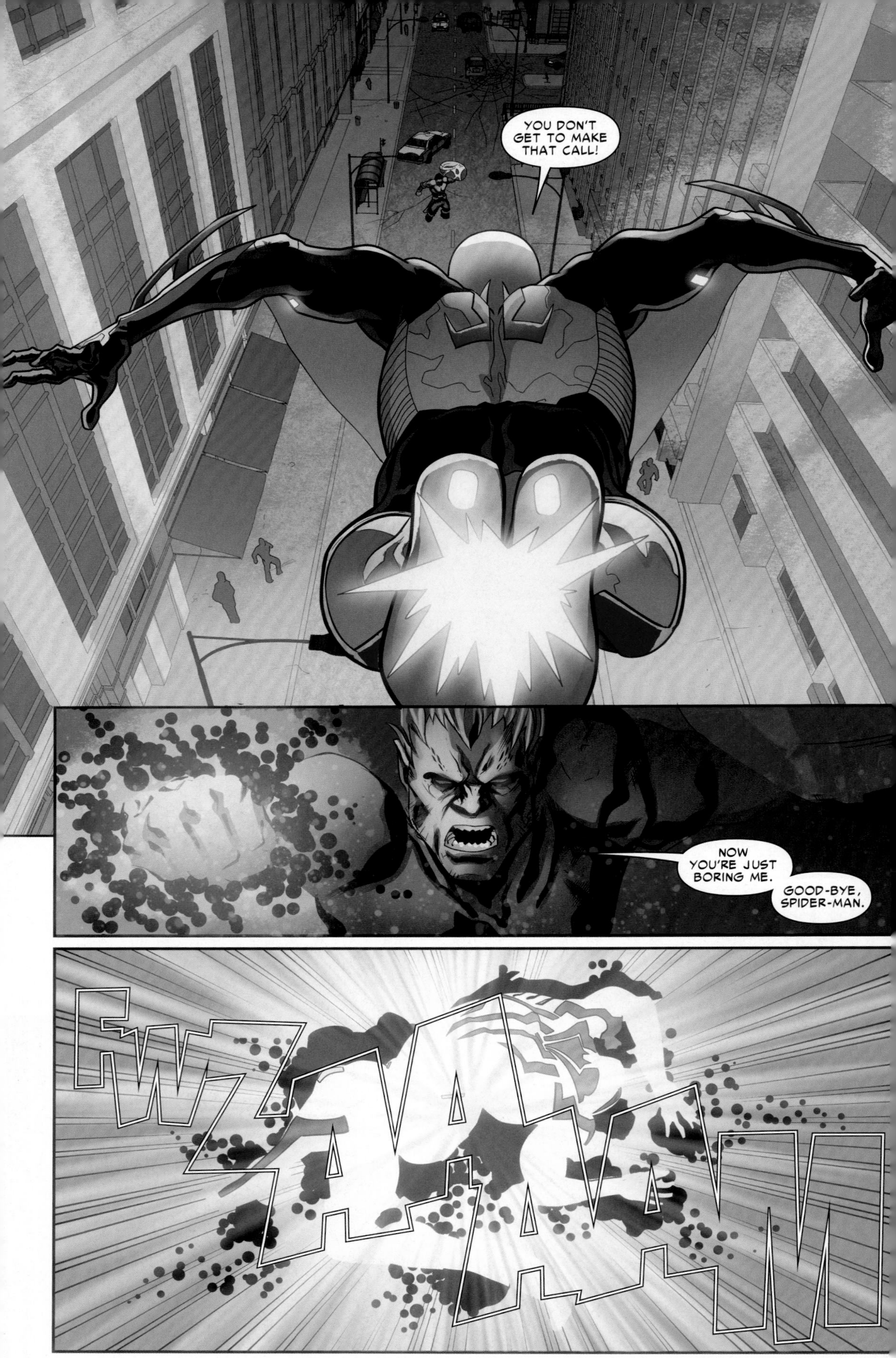
YOU DON'T GET TO MAKE THAT CALL!
NOW YOU'RE JUST BORING ME.
GOOD-BYE, SPIDER-MAN.
FWZAAAAAM

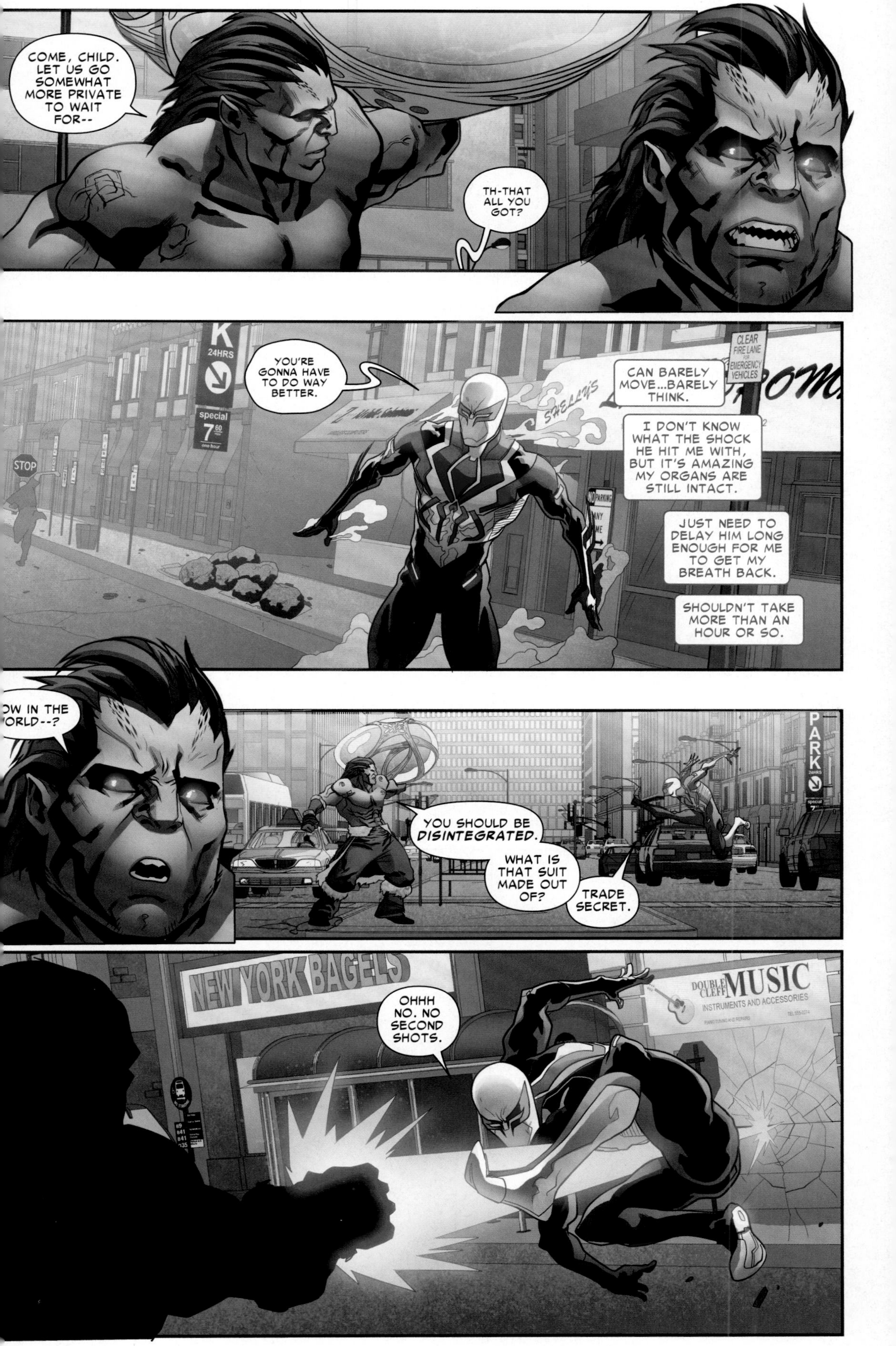
COME, CHILD. LET US GO SOMEWHAT MORE PRIVATE TO WAIT FOR--
TH-THAT ALL YOU GOT?
YOU'RE GONNA HAVE TO DO WAY BETTER.
CAN BARELY MOVE...BARELY THINK.
I DON'T KNOW WHAT THE SHOCK HE HIT ME WITH, BUT IT'S AMAZING MY ORGANS ARE STILL INTACT.
JUST NEED TO DELAY HIM LONG ENOUGH FOR ME TO GET MY BREATH BACK.
SHOULDN'T TAKE MORE THAN AN HOUR OR SO.
OW IN THE ORLD--?
YOU SHOULD BE *DISINTEGRATED*.
WHAT IS THAT SUIT MADE OUT OF?
TRADE SECRET.
OHHH NO. NO SECOND SHOTS.
NEW YORK BAGELS
DOUBLE CLEFF MUSIC INSTRUMENTS AND ACCESSORIES
PARK 24HRS
CLEAR FIRE LANE FOR EMERGENCY VEHICLES
STOP

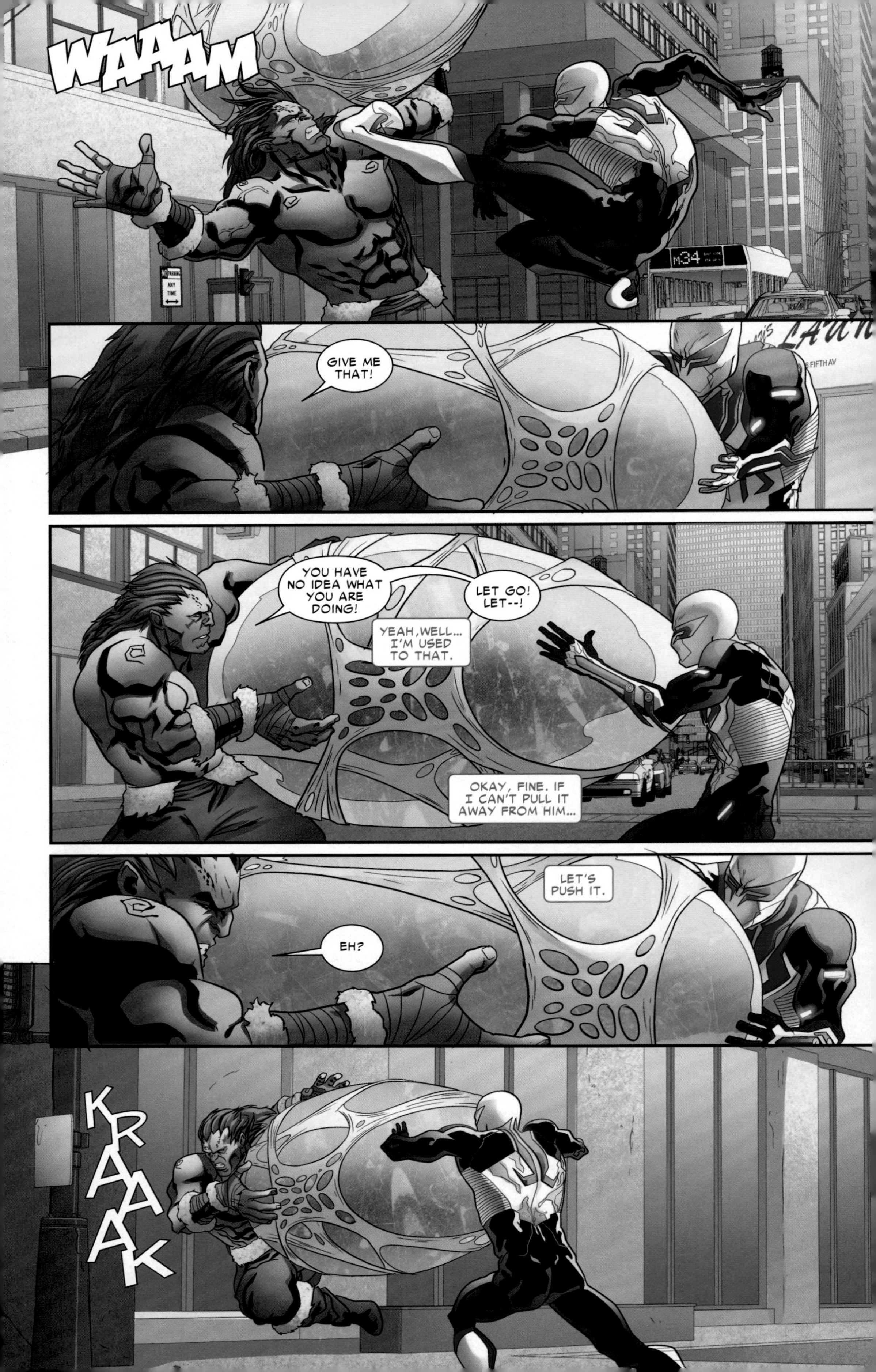
WAAAM
M34
NO PARKING ANY TIME
GIVE ME THAT!
YOU HAVE NO IDEA WHAT YOU ARE DOING!
LET GO! LET--!
YEAH, WELL... I'M USED TO THAT.
OKAY, FINE. IF I CAN'T PULL IT AWAY FROM HIM...
LET'S PUSH IT.
EH?
KRAAAK

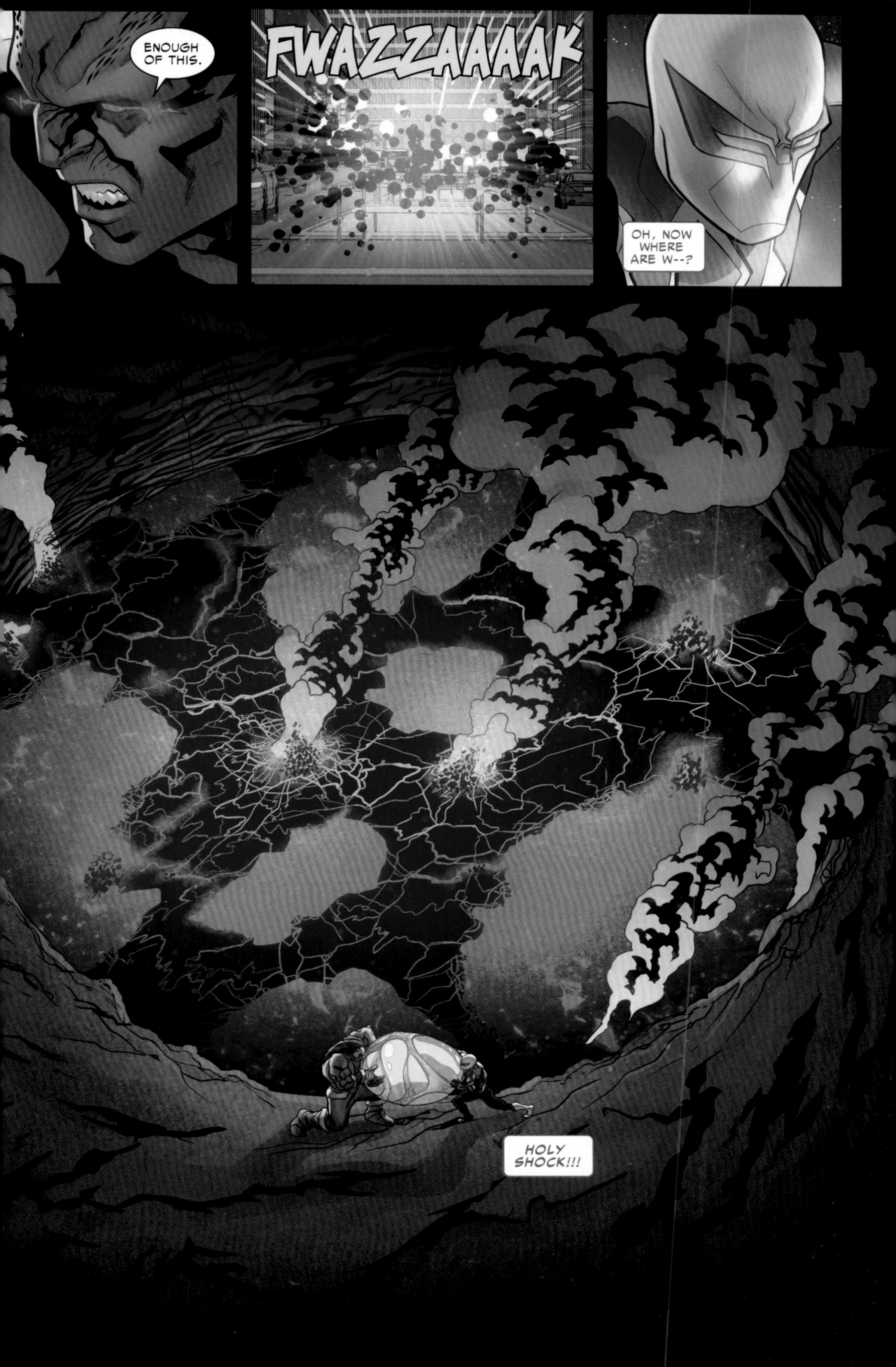
ENOUGH OF THIS.
FWAZZAAAAK
OH, NOW WHERE ARE W--?
HOLY SHOCK!!!

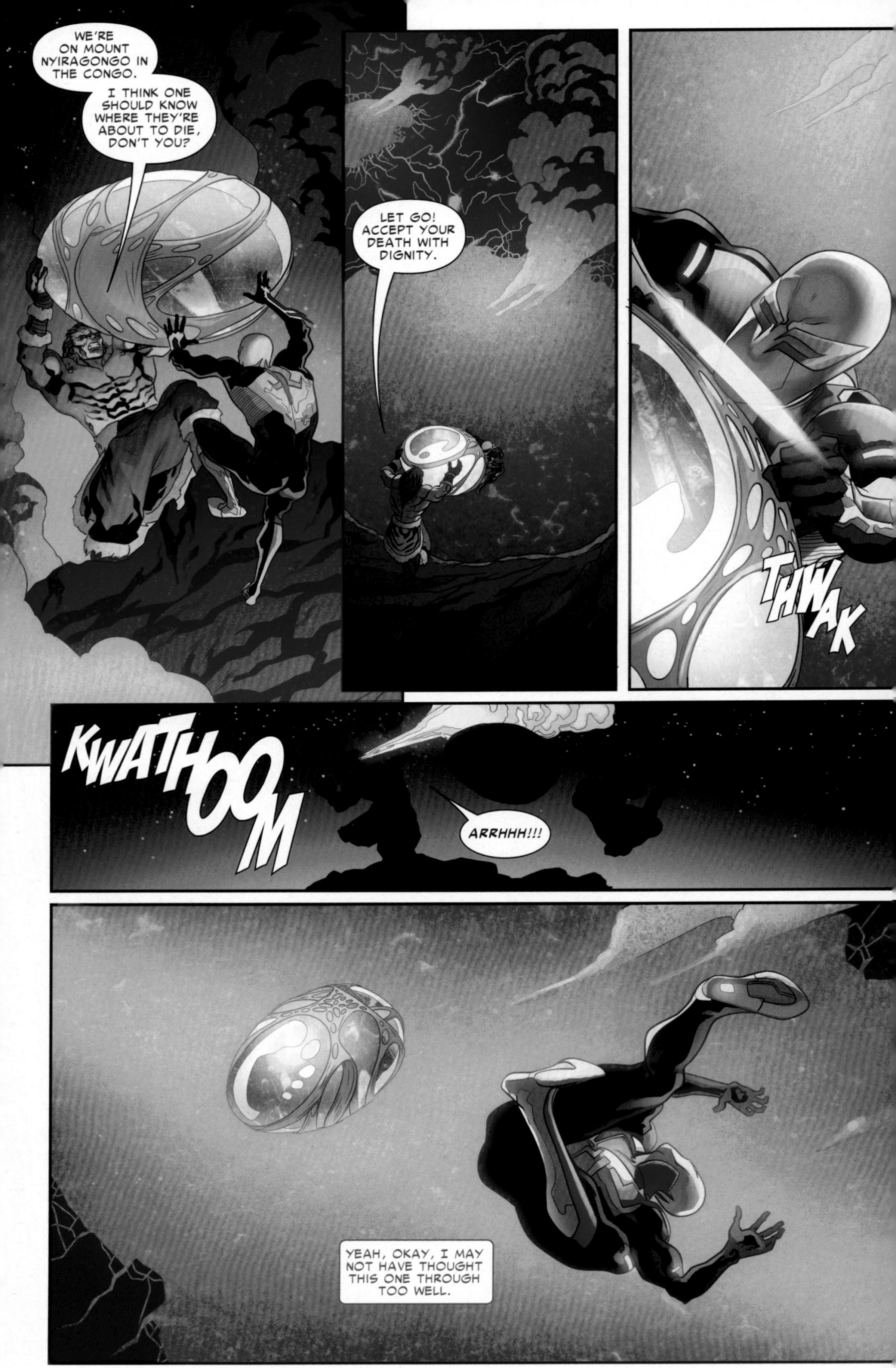
WE'RE ON MOUNT NYIRAGONGO IN THE CONGO.
I THINK ONE SHOULD KNOW WHERE THEY'RE ABOUT TO DIE, DON'T YOU?
LET GO! ACCEPT YOUR DEATH WITH DIGNITY.
THWAK
KWATHOOM
ARRHHH!!!
YEAH, OKAY, I MAY NOT HAVE THOUGHT THIS ONE THROUGH TOO WELL.

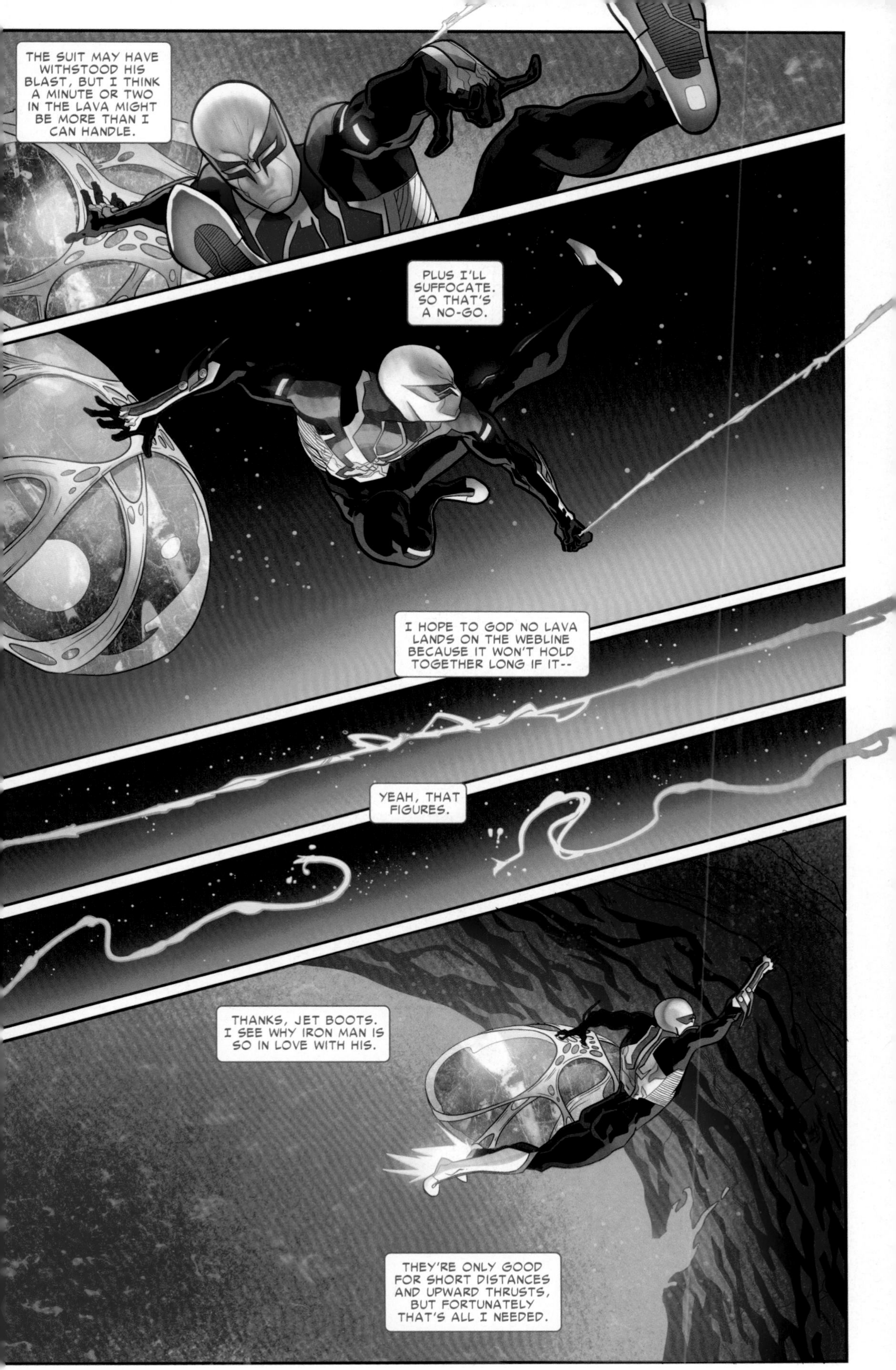
THE SUIT MAY HAVE WITHSTOOD HIS BLAST, BUT I THINK A MINUTE OR TWO IN THE LAVA MIGHT BE MORE THAN I CAN HANDLE.
PLUS I'LL SUFFOCATE. SO THAT'S A NO-GO.
I HOPE TO GOD NO LAVA LANDS ON THE WEBLINE BECAUSE IT WON'T HOLD TOGETHER LONG IF IT--
YEAH, THAT FIGURES.
THANKS, JET BOOTS. I SEE WHY IRON MAN IS SO IN LOVE WITH HIS.
THEY'RE ONLY GOOD FOR SHORT DISTANCES AND UPWARD THRUSTS, BUT FORTUNATELY THAT'S ALL I NEEDED.

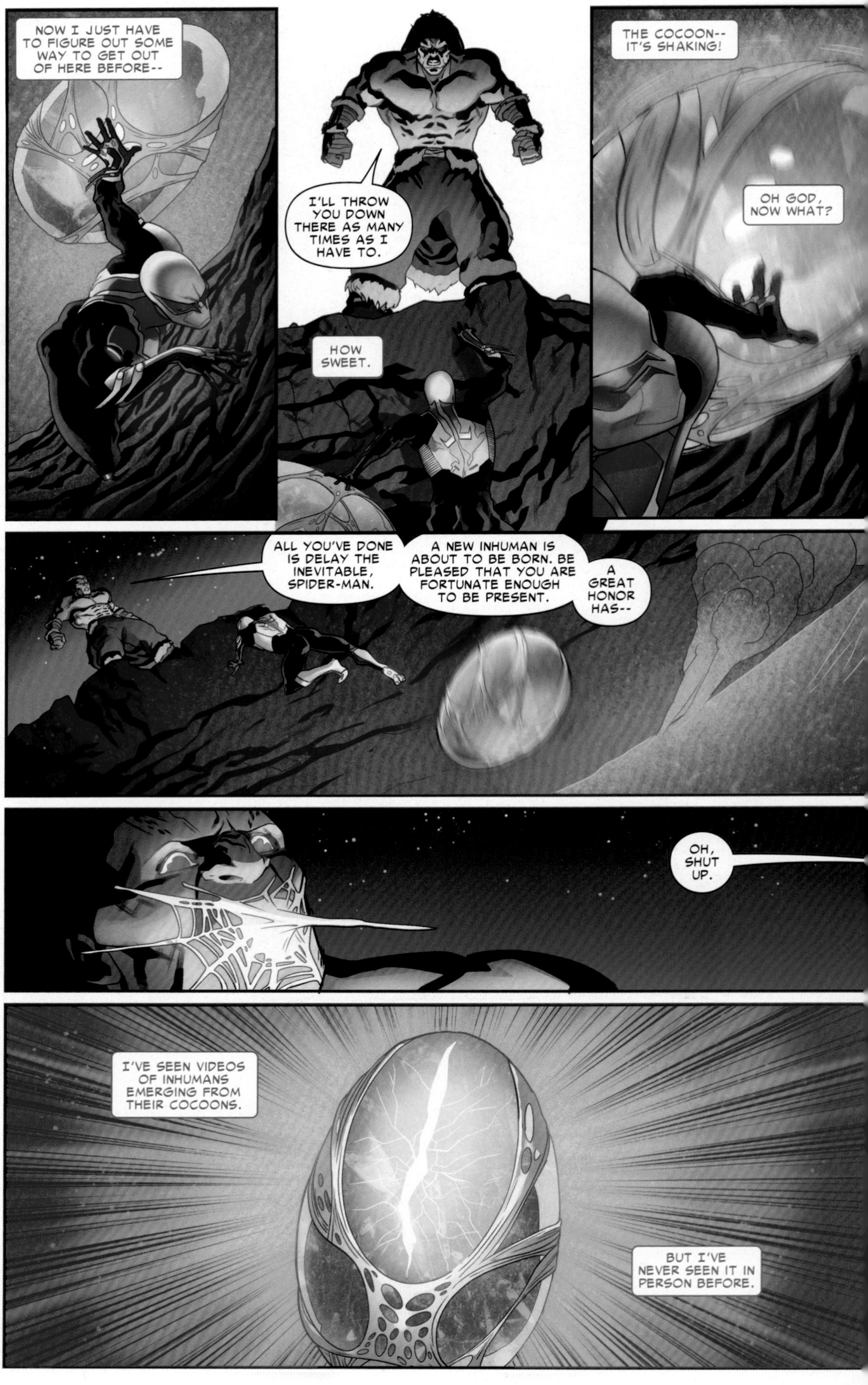
NOW I JUST HAVE TO FIGURE OUT SOME WAY TO GET OUT OF HERE BEFORE--
I'LL THROW YOU DOWN THERE AS MANY TIMES AS I HAVE TO.
HOW SWEET.
THE COCOON-- IT'S SHAKING!
OH GOD, NOW WHAT?
ALL YOU'VE DONE IS DELAY THE INEVITABLE, SPIDER-MAN.
A NEW INHUMAN IS ABOUT TO BE BORN. BE PLEASED THAT YOU ARE FORTUNATE ENOUGH TO BE PRESENT.
A GREAT HONOR HAS--
OH, SHUT UP.
I'VE SEEN VIDEOS OF INHUMANS EMERGING FROM THEIR COCOONS.
BUT I'VE NEVER SEEN IT IN PERSON BEFORE.

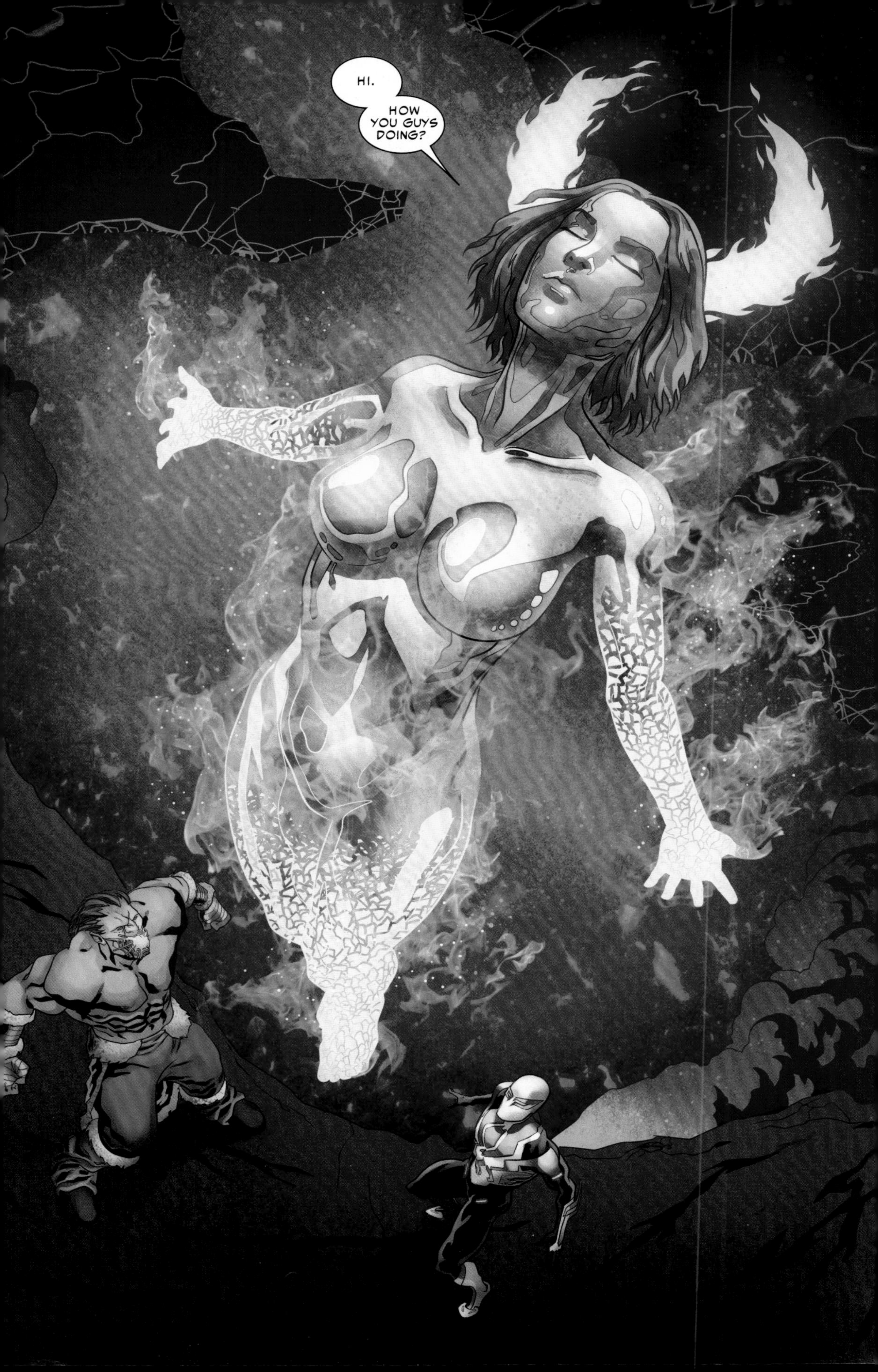
HI.
HOW YOU GUYS DOING?

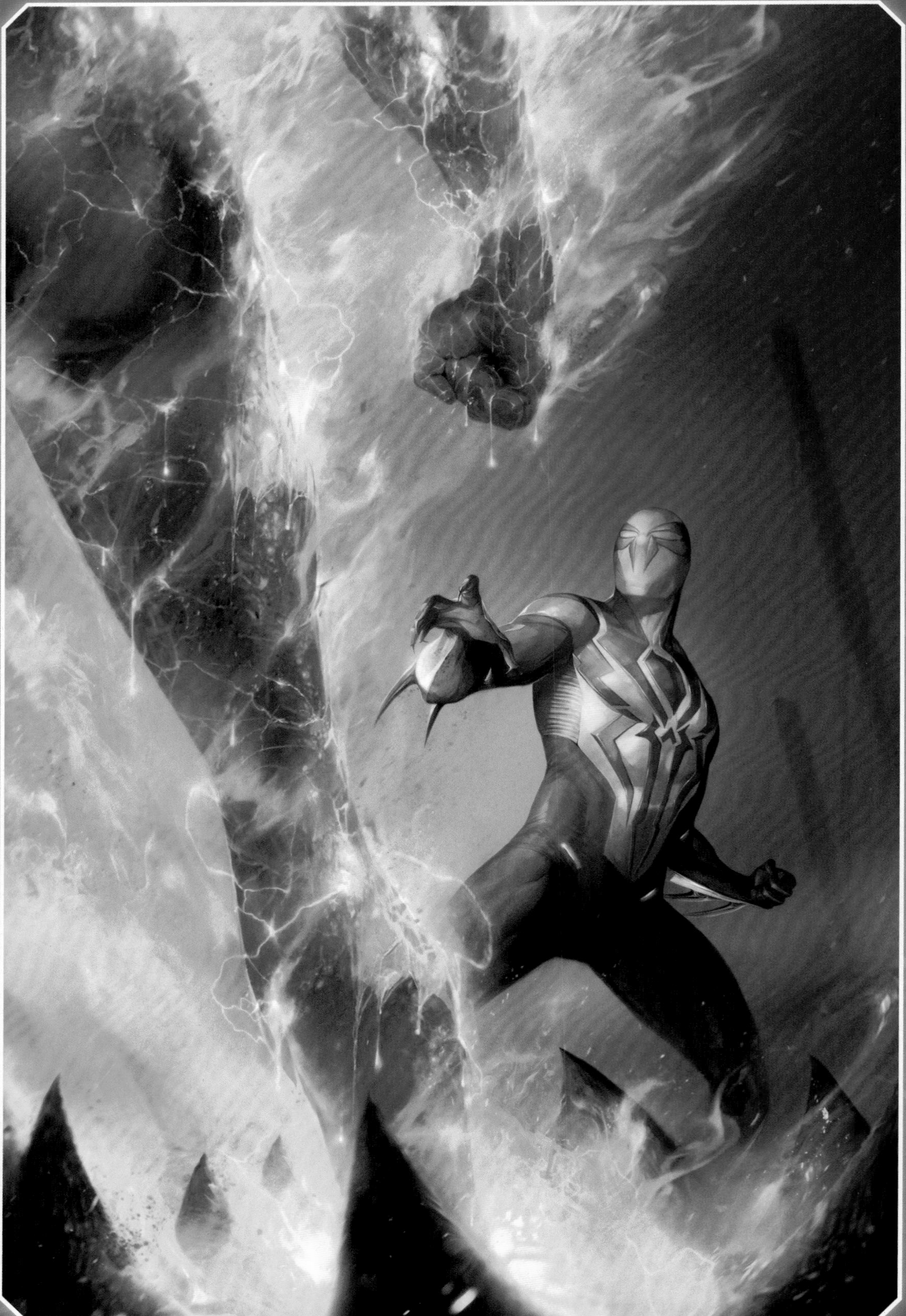

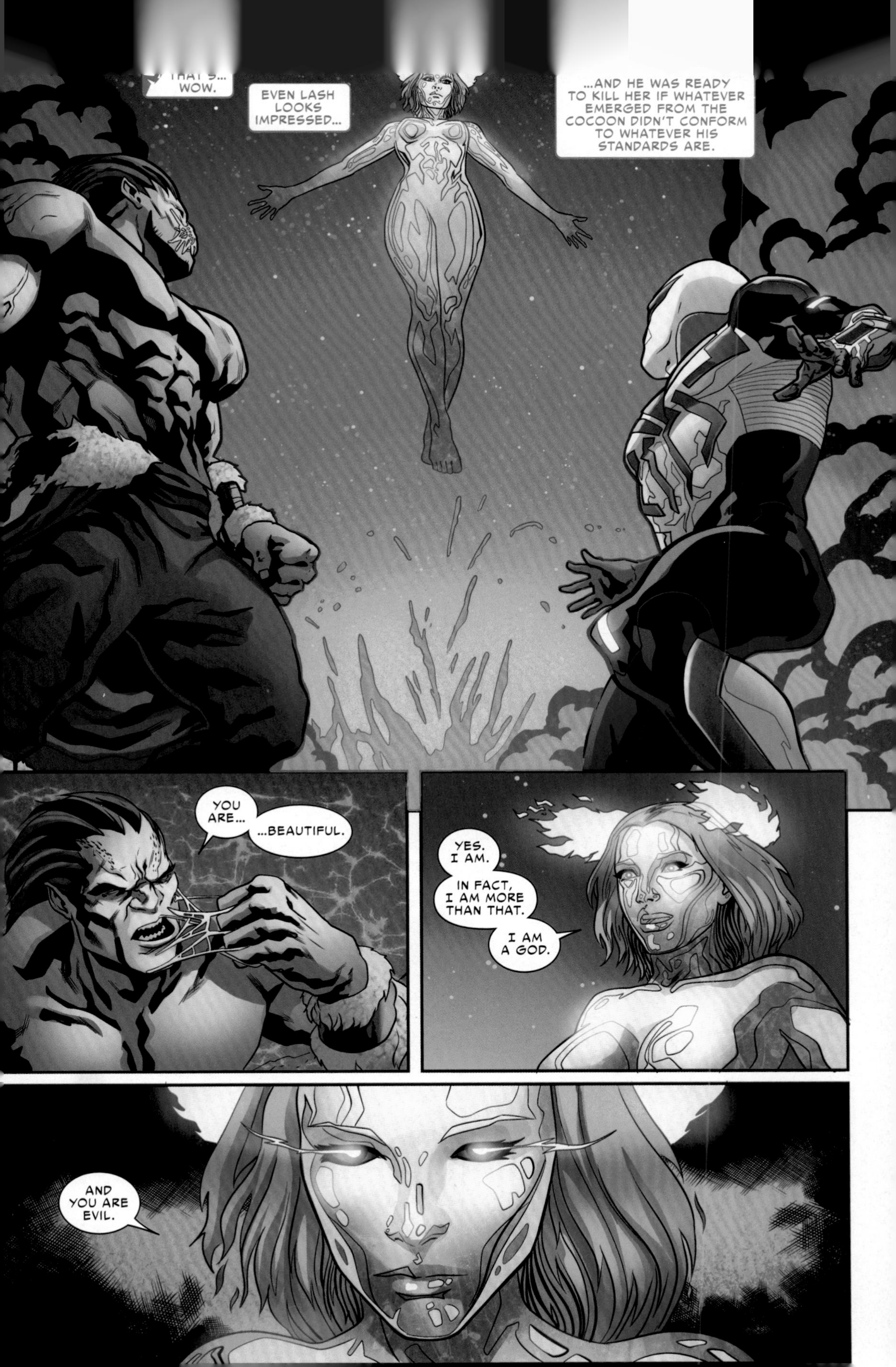

WOW.
EVEN LASH LOOKS IMPRESSED...
...AND HE WAS READY TO KILL HER IF WHATEVER EMERGED FROM THE COCOON DIDN'T CONFORM TO WHATEVER HIS STANDARDS ARE.
YOU ARE...
...BEAUTIFUL.
YES. I AM.
IN FACT, I AM MORE THAN THAT.
I AM A GOD.
AND YOU ARE EVIL.

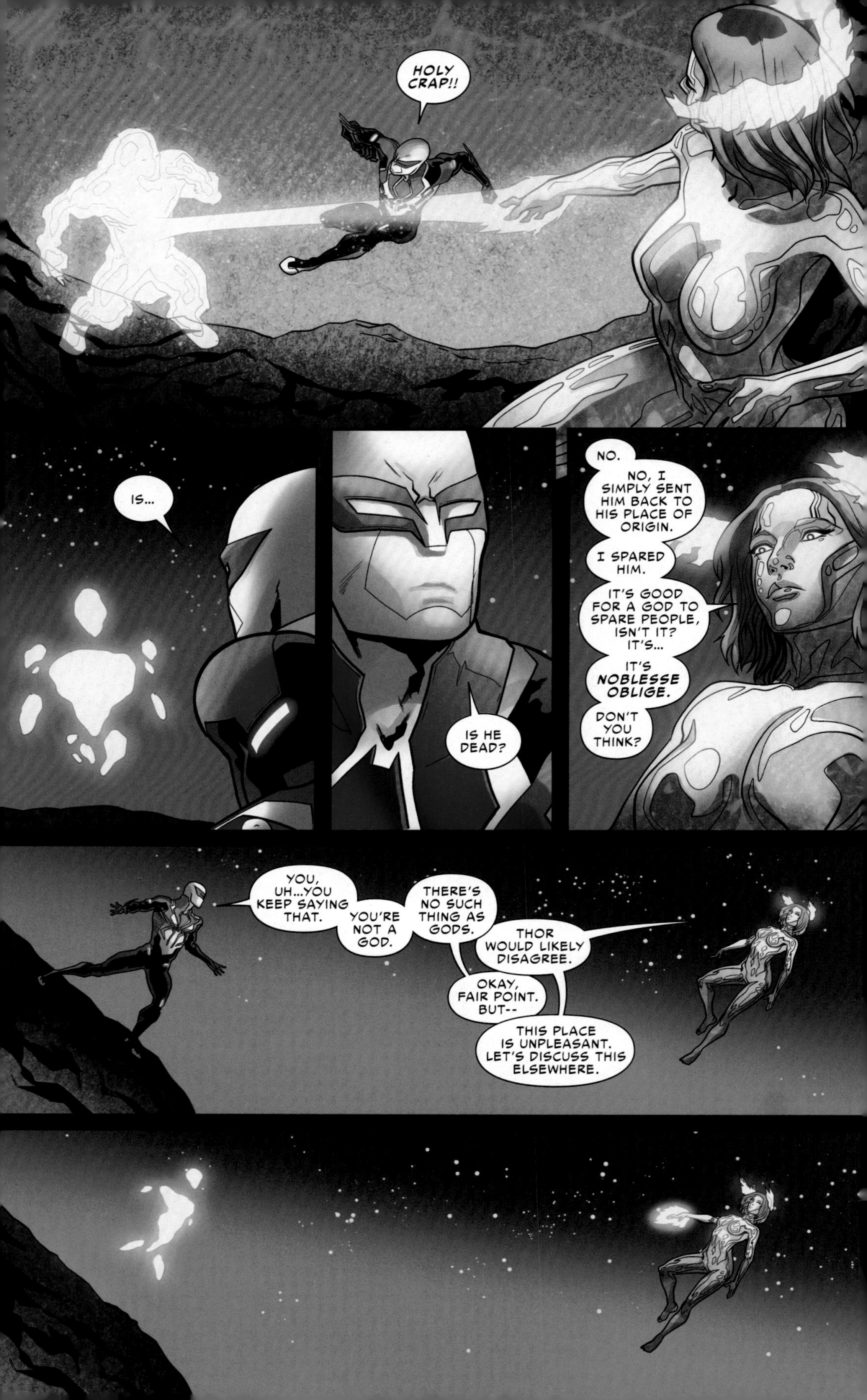
HOLY CRAP!!
IS...
IS HE DEAD?
NO.
NO, I SIMPLY SENT HIM BACK TO HIS PLACE OF ORIGIN.
I SPARED HIM.
IT'S GOOD FOR A GOD TO SPARE PEOPLE, ISN'T IT? IT'S...
IT'S NOBLESSE OBLIGE.
DON'T YOU THINK?
YOU, UH...YOU KEEP SAYING THAT.
YOU'RE NOT A GOD.
THERE'S NO SUCH THING AS GODS.
THOR WOULD LIKELY DISAGREE.
OKAY, FAIR POINT. BUT--
THIS PLACE IS UNPLEASANT. LET'S DISCUSS THIS ELSEWHERE.

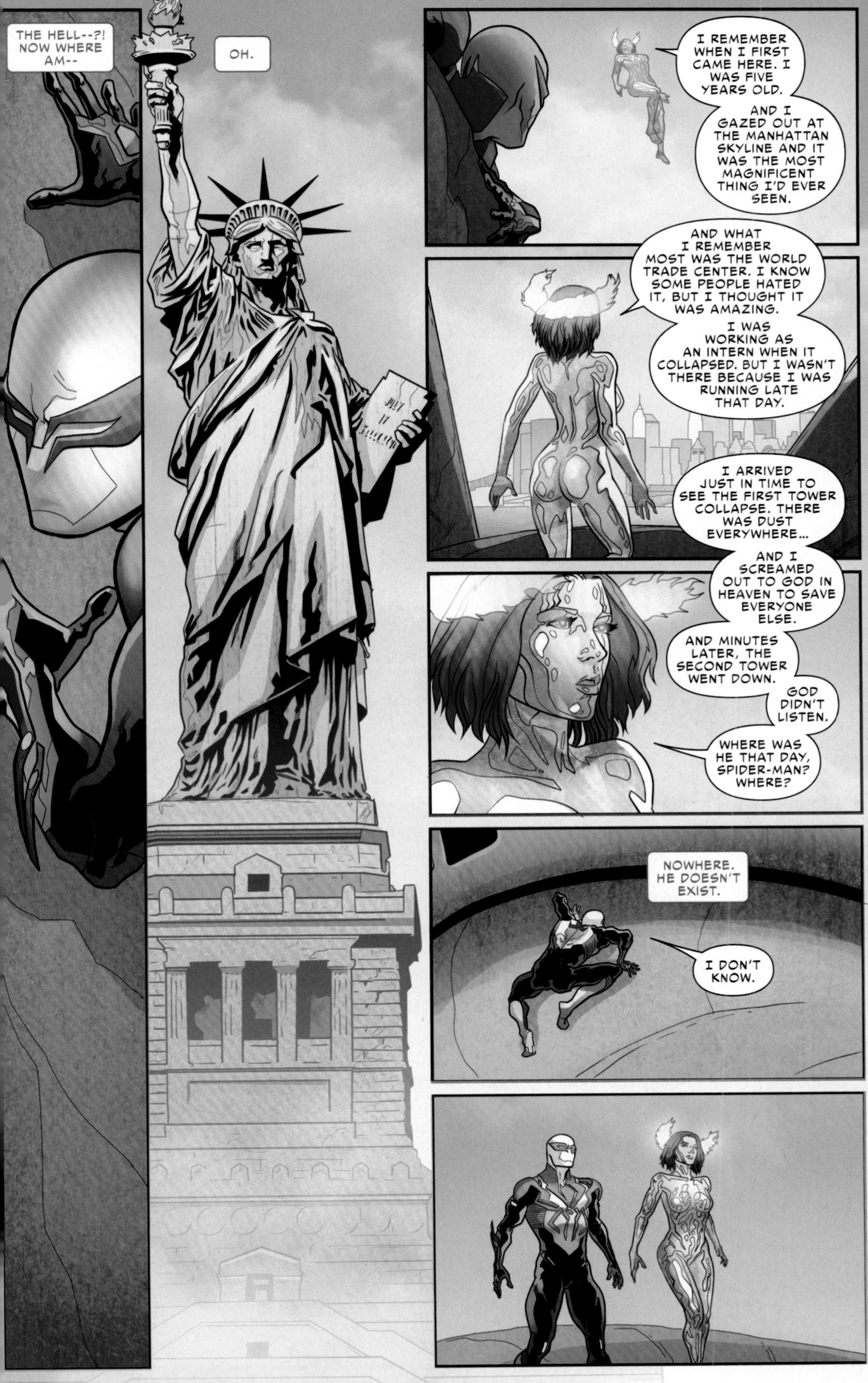
THE HELL--?! NOW WHERE AM--
OH.
I REMEMBER WHEN I FIRST CAME HERE. I WAS FIVE YEARS OLD.
AND I GAZED OUT AT THE MANHATTAN SKYLINE AND IT WAS THE MOST MAGNIFICENT THING I'D EVER SEEN.
AND WHAT I REMEMBER MOST WAS THE WORLD TRADE CENTER. I KNOW SOME PEOPLE HATED IT, BUT I THOUGHT IT WAS AMAZING.
I WAS WORKING AS AN INTERN WHEN IT COLLAPSED. BUT I WASN'T THERE BECAUSE I WAS RUNNING LATE THAT DAY.
I ARRIVED JUST IN TIME TO SEE THE FIRST TOWER COLLAPSE. THERE WAS DUST EVERYWHERE...
AND I SCREAMED OUT TO GOD IN HEAVEN TO SAVE EVERYONE ELSE.
AND MINUTES LATER, THE SECOND TOWER WENT DOWN.
GOD DIDN'T LISTEN.
WHERE WAS HE THAT DAY, SPIDER-MAN? WHERE?
NOWHERE. HE DOESN'T EXIST.
I DON'T KNOW.

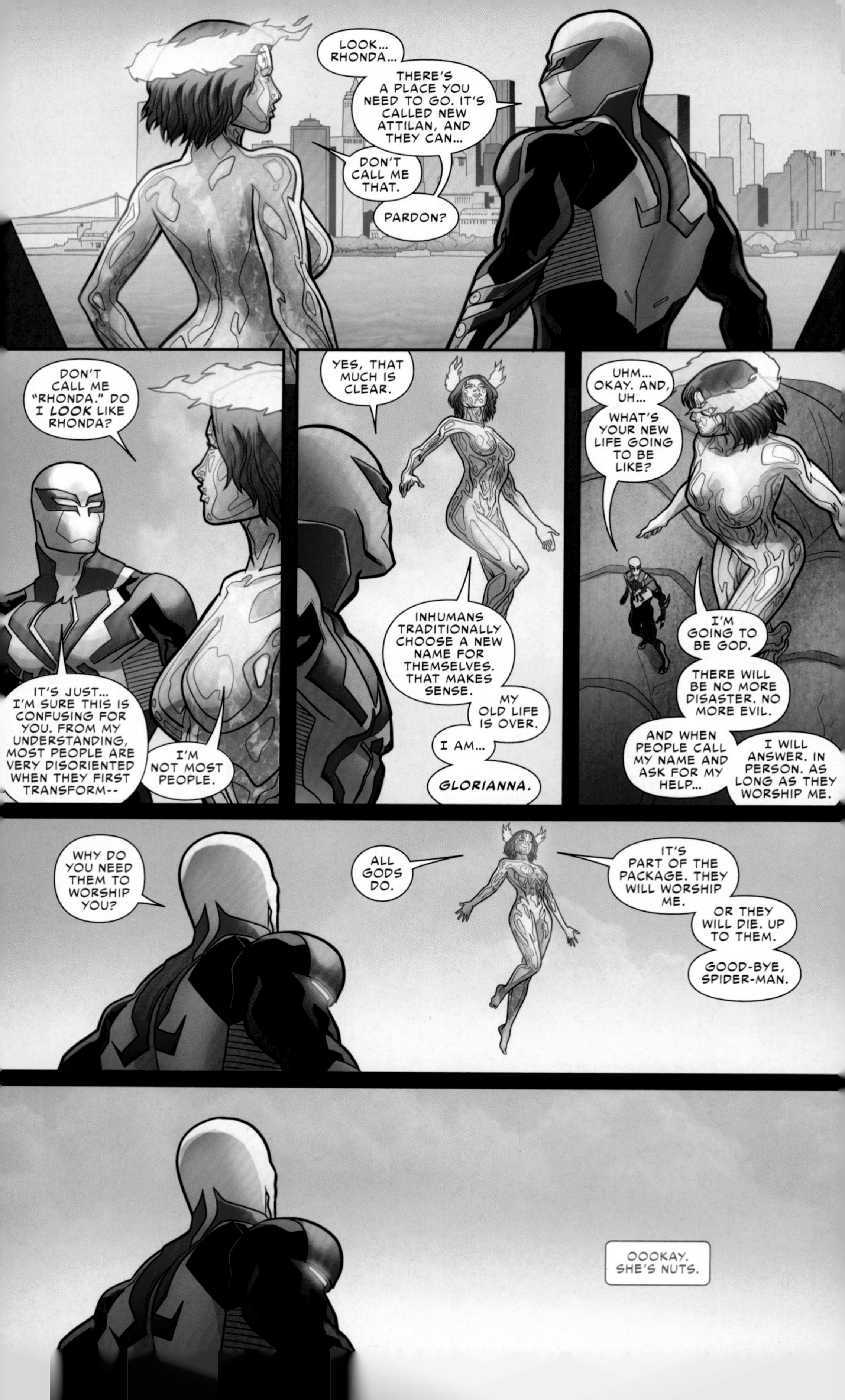
LOOK... RHONDA...
THERE'S A PLACE YOU NEED TO GO. IT'S CALLED NEW ATTILAN, AND THEY CAN...
DON'T CALL ME THAT.
PARDON?
DON'T CALL ME "RHONDA." DO I LOOK LIKE RHONDA?
IT'S JUST... I'M SURE THIS IS CONFUSING FOR YOU. FROM MY UNDERSTANDING, MOST PEOPLE ARE VERY DISORIENTED WHEN THEY FIRST TRANSFORM--
I'M NOT MOST PEOPLE.
YES, THAT MUCH IS CLEAR.
INHUMANS TRADITIONALLY CHOOSE A NEW NAME FOR THEMSELVES. THAT MAKES SENSE.
MY OLD LIFE IS OVER.
I AM...
GLORIANNA.
UHM... OKAY. AND, UH...
WHAT'S YOUR NEW LIFE GOING TO BE LIKE?
I'M GOING TO BE GOD.
THERE WILL BE NO MORE DISASTER. NO MORE EVIL.
AND WHEN PEOPLE CALL MY NAME AND ASK FOR MY HELP...
I WILL ANSWER. IN PERSON. AS LONG AS THEY WORSHIP ME.
WHY DO YOU NEED THEM TO WORSHIP YOU?
ALL GODS DO.
IT'S PART OF THE PACKAGE. THEY WILL WORSHIP ME.
OR THEY WILL DIE. UP TO THEM.
GOOD-BYE, SPIDER-MAN.
OOOKAY. SHE'S NUTS.

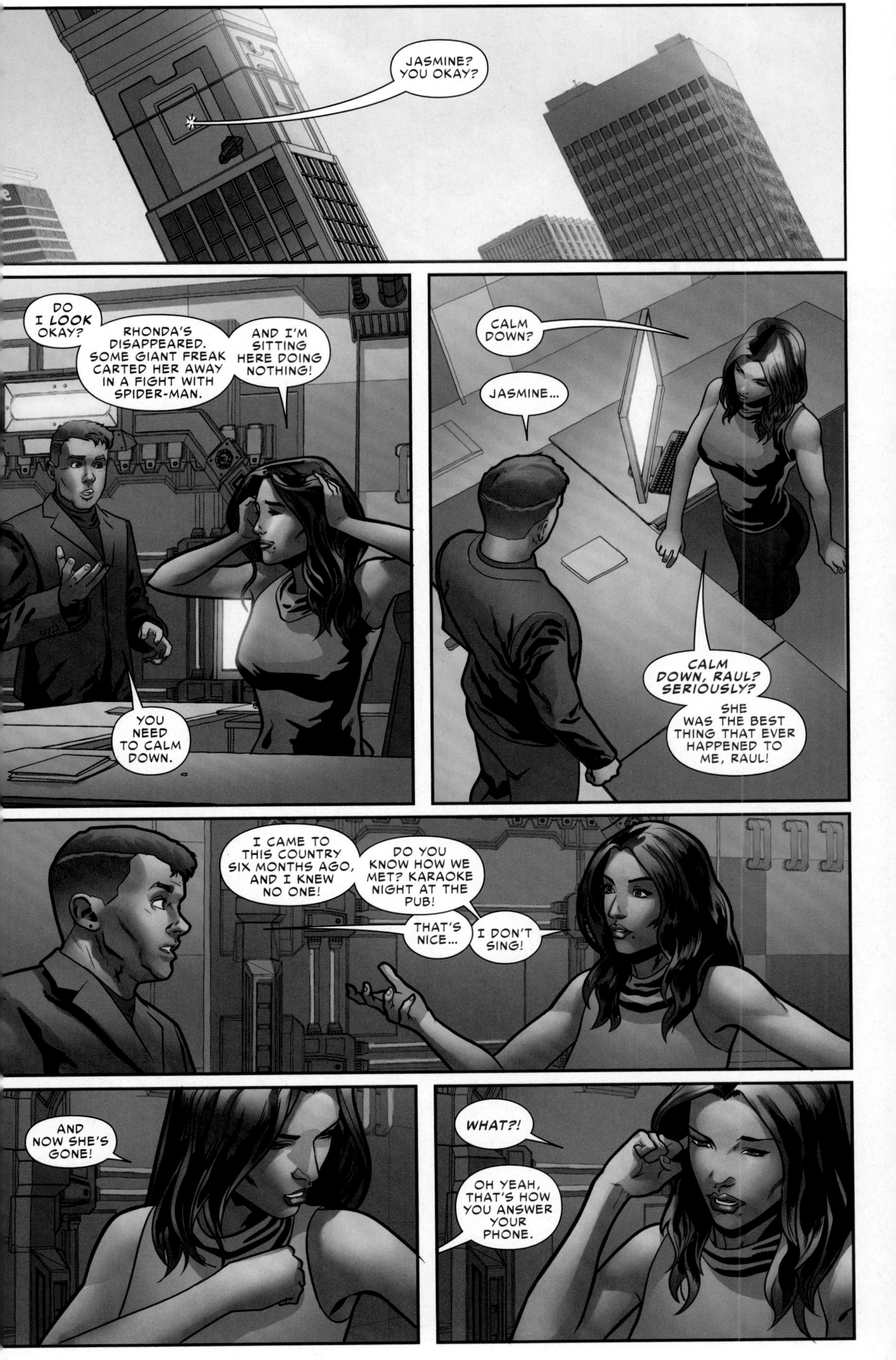
JASMINE? YOU OKAY?
DO I *LOOK* OKAY?
RHONDA'S DISAPPEARED. SOME GIANT FREAK CARTED HER AWAY IN A FIGHT WITH SPIDER-MAN.
AND I'M SITTING HERE DOING NOTHING!
YOU NEED TO CALM DOWN.
CALM DOWN?
JASMINE...
CALM DOWN, RAUL? SERIOUSLY?
SHE WAS THE BEST THING THAT EVER HAPPENED TO ME, RAUL!
I CAME TO THIS COUNTRY SIX MONTHS AGO, AND I KNEW NO ONE!
DO YOU KNOW HOW WE MET? KARAOKE NIGHT AT THE PUB!
THAT'S NICE...
I DON'T SING!
AND NOW SHE'S GONE!
WHAT?!
OH YEAH, THAT'S HOW YOU ANSWER YOUR PHONE.

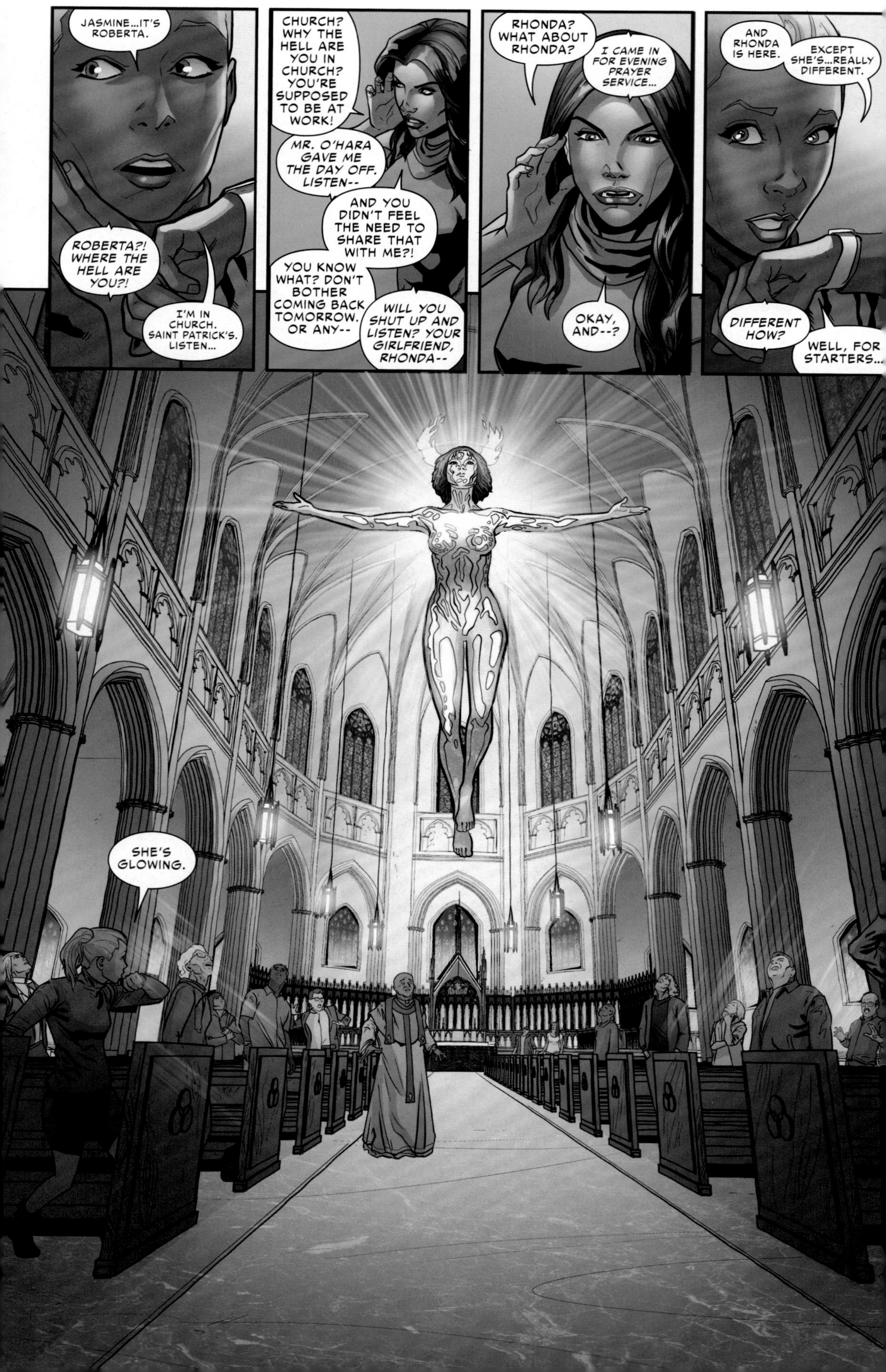
JASMINE...IT'S ROBERTA.
ROBERTA?! WHERE THE HELL ARE YOU?!
I'M IN CHURCH. SAINT PATRICK'S. LISTEN...
CHURCH? WHY THE HELL ARE YOU IN CHURCH? YOU'RE SUPPOSED TO BE AT WORK!
MR. O'HARA GAVE ME THE DAY OFF. LISTEN--
AND YOU DIDN'T FEEL THE NEED TO SHARE THAT WITH ME?!
YOU KNOW WHAT? DON'T BOTHER COMING BACK TOMORROW. OR ANY--
WILL YOU SHUT UP AND LISTEN? YOUR GIRLFRIEND, RHONDA--
RHONDA? WHAT ABOUT RHONDA?
I CAME IN FOR EVENING PRAYER SERVICE...
OKAY, AND--?
AND RHONDA IS HERE.
EXCEPT SHE'S...REALLY DIFFERENT.
DIFFERENT HOW?
WELL, FOR STARTERS...
SHE'S GLOWING.

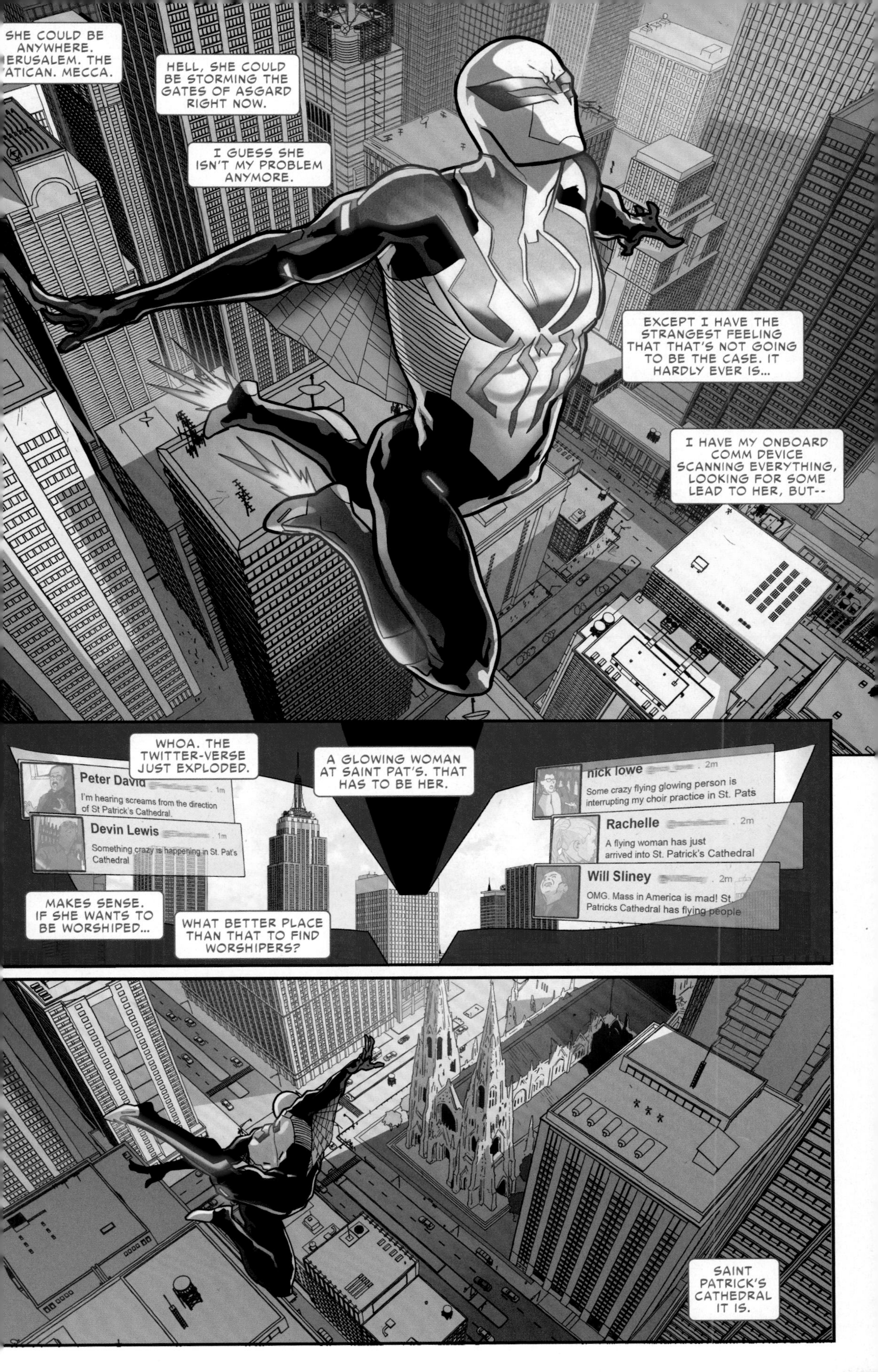
SHE COULD BE ANYWHERE. ERUSALEM. THE ATICAN. MECCA.
HELL, SHE COULD BE STORMING THE GATES OF ASGARD RIGHT NOW.
I GUESS SHE ISN'T MY PROBLEM ANYMORE.
EXCEPT I HAVE THE STRANGEST FEELING THAT THAT'S NOT GOING TO BE THE CASE. IT HARDLY EVER IS...
I HAVE MY ONBOARD COMM DEVICE SCANNING EVERYTHING, LOOKING FOR SOME LEAD TO HER, BUT--
WHOA. THE TWITTER-VERSE JUST EXPLODED.
Peter David 1m
I'm hearing screams from the direction of St Patrick's Cathedral.
Devin Lewis 1m
Something crazy is happening in St. Pat's Cathedral
A GLOWING WOMAN AT SAINT PAT'S. THAT HAS TO BE HER.
nick lowe 2m
Some crazy flying glowing person is interrupting my choir practice in St. Pats
Rachelle 2m
A flying woman has just arrived into St. Patrick's Cathedral
Will Sliney 2m
OMG. Mass in America is mad! St. Patricks Cathedral has flying people
MAKES SENSE. IF SHE WANTS TO BE WORSHIPED...
WHAT BETTER PLACE THAN THAT TO FIND WORSHIPERS?
SAINT PATRICK'S CATHEDRAL IT IS.

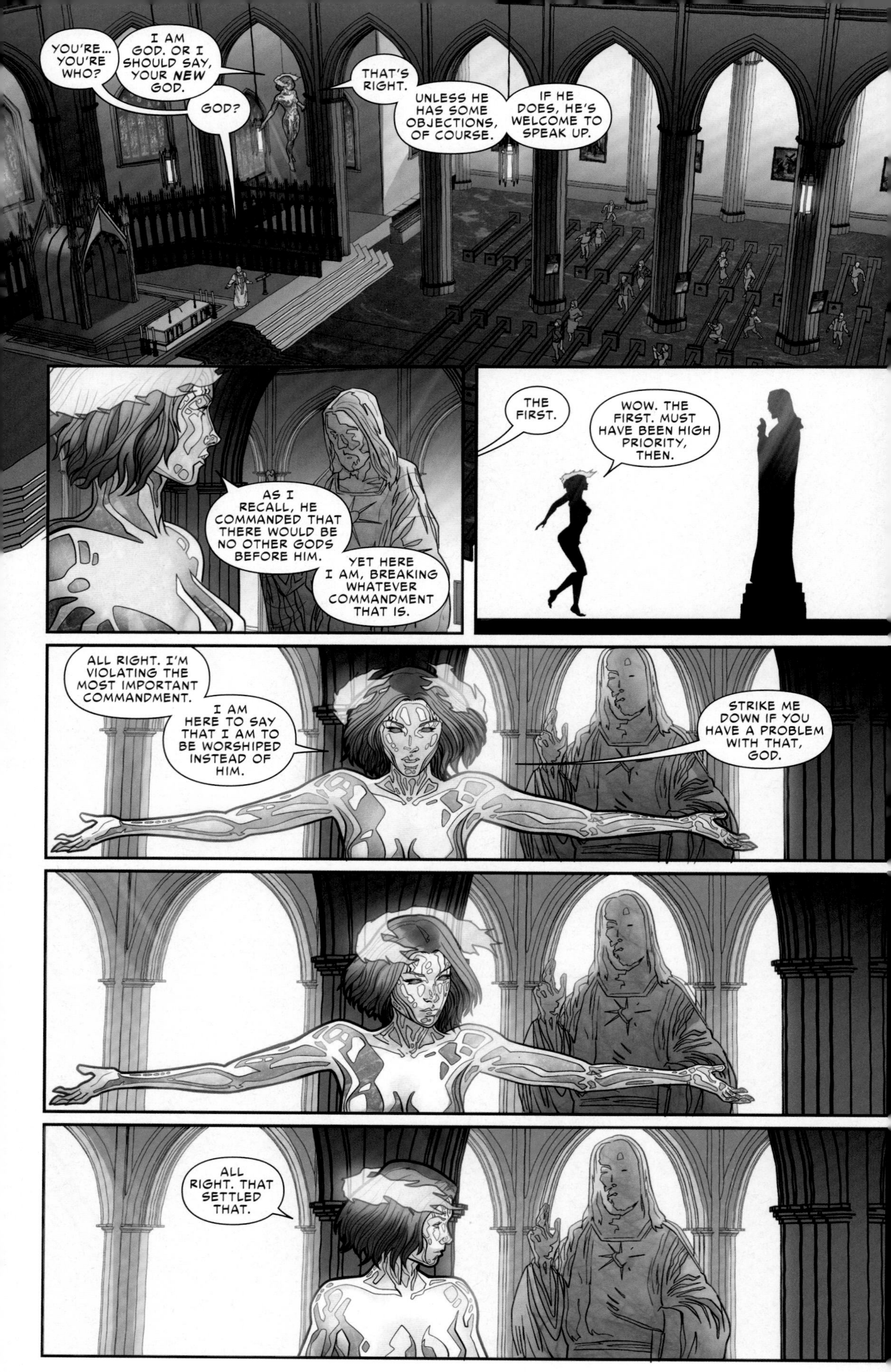
YOU'RE... YOU'RE WHO?
I AM GOD. OR I SHOULD SAY, YOUR NEW GOD.
GOD?
THAT'S RIGHT.
UNLESS HE HAS SOME OBJECTIONS, OF COURSE.
IF HE DOES, HE'S WELCOME TO SPEAK UP.
AS I RECALL, HE COMMANDED THAT THERE WOULD BE NO OTHER GODS BEFORE HIM.
YET HERE I AM, BREAKING WHATEVER COMMANDMENT THAT IS.
THE FIRST.
WOW. THE FIRST. MUST HAVE BEEN HIGH PRIORITY, THEN.
ALL RIGHT. I'M VIOLATING THE MOST IMPORTANT COMMANDMENT.
I AM HERE TO SAY THAT I AM TO BE WORSHIPED INSTEAD OF HIM.
STRIKE ME DOWN IF YOU HAVE A PROBLEM WITH THAT, GOD.
ALL RIGHT. THAT SETTLED THAT.

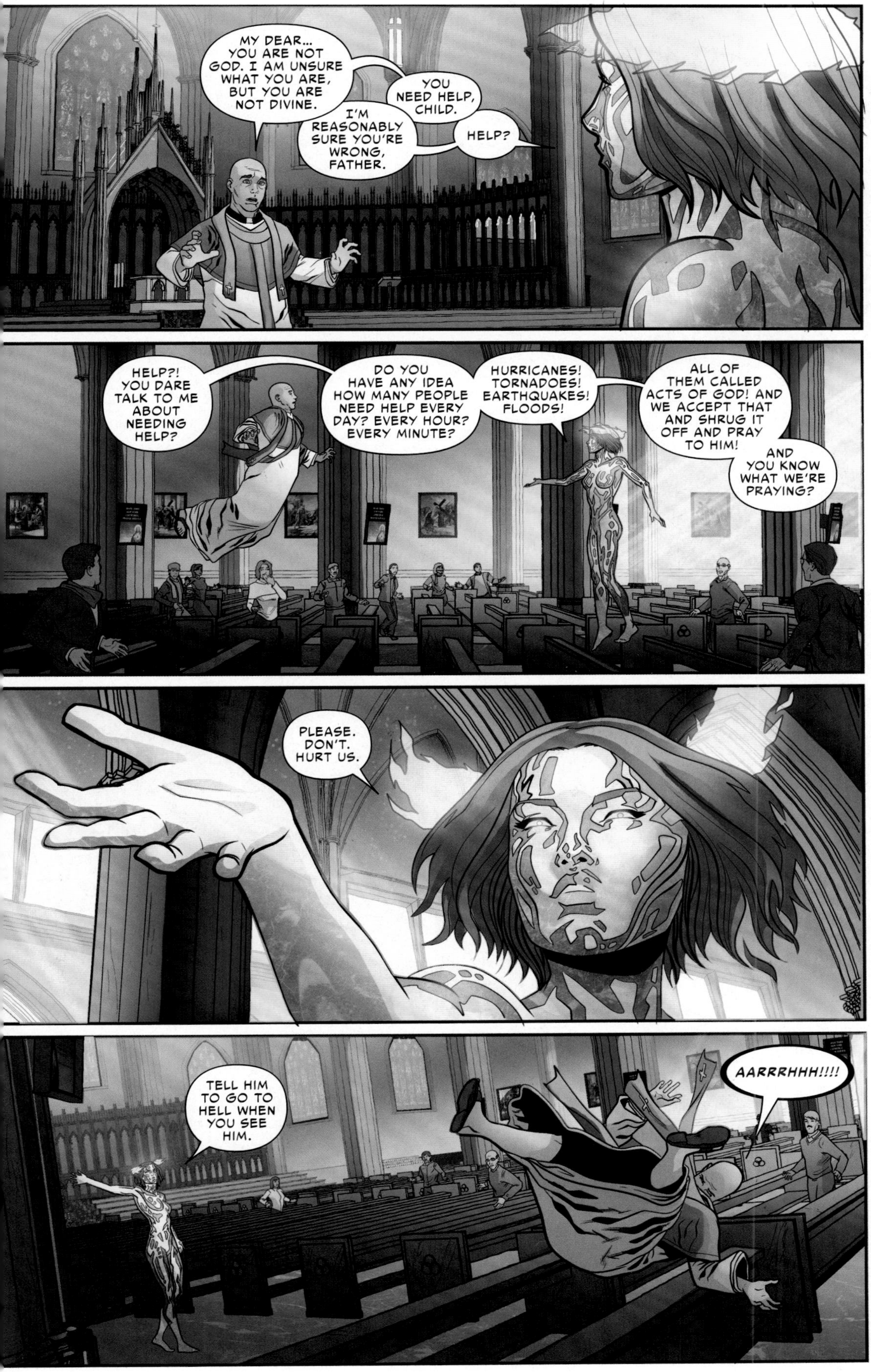
MY DEAR... YOU ARE NOT GOD. I AM UNSURE WHAT YOU ARE, BUT YOU ARE NOT DIVINE.
YOU NEED HELP, CHILD.
HELP?
I'M REASONABLY SURE YOU'RE WRONG, FATHER.
HELP?! YOU DARE TALK TO ME ABOUT NEEDING HELP?
DO YOU HAVE ANY IDEA HOW MANY PEOPLE NEED HELP EVERY DAY? EVERY HOUR? EVERY MINUTE?
HURRICANES! TORNADOES! EARTHQUAKES! FLOODS!
ALL OF THEM CALLED ACTS OF GOD! AND WE ACCEPT THAT AND SHRUG IT OFF AND PRAY TO HIM!
AND YOU KNOW WHAT WE'RE PRAYING?
PLEASE. DON'T. HURT US.
TELL HIM TO GO TO HELL WHEN YOU SEE HIM.
AARRRHHH!!!!

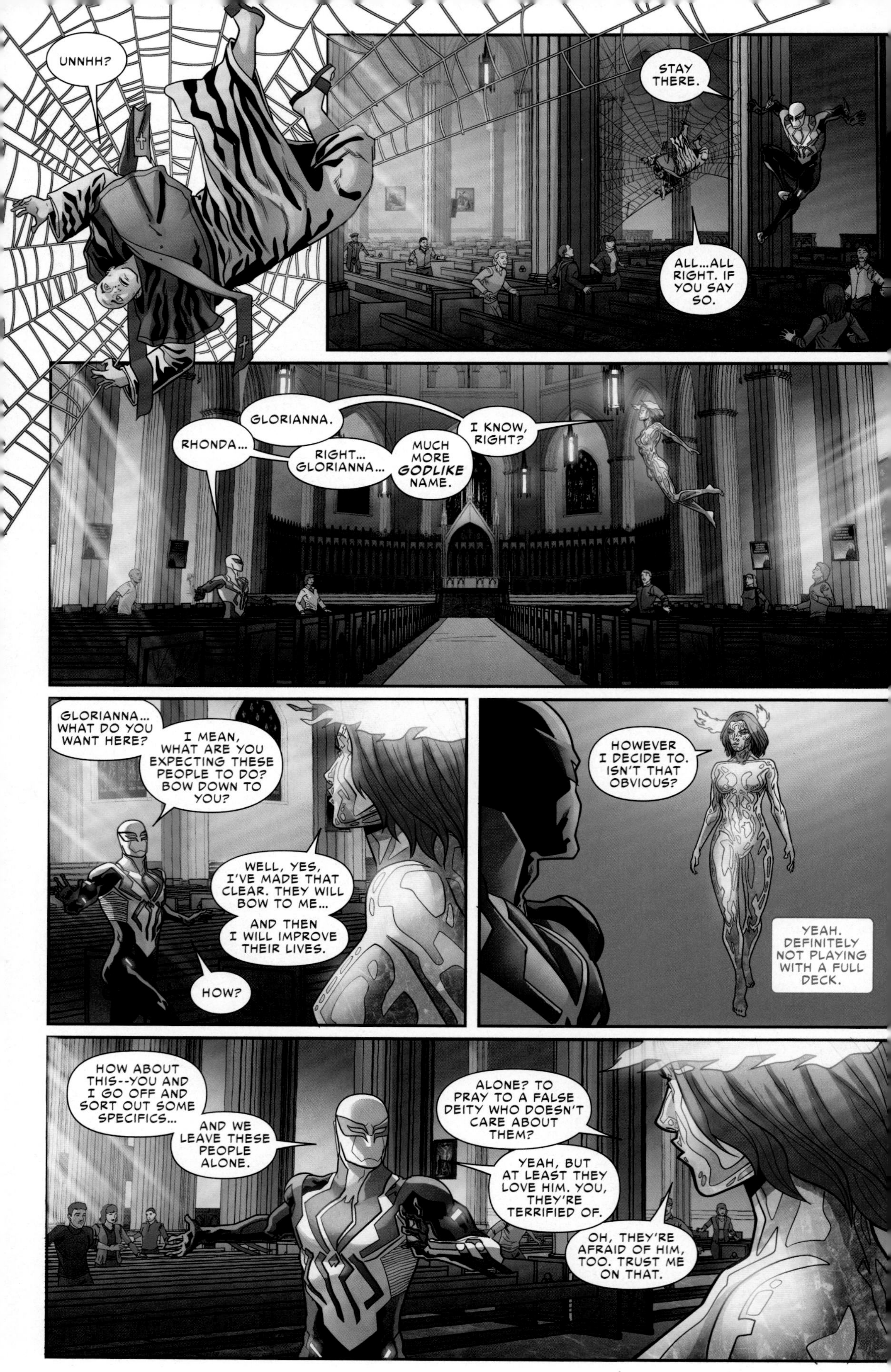
UNNHH?
STAY THERE.
ALL...ALL RIGHT. IF YOU SAY SO.
RHONDA...
GLORIANNA.
RIGHT... GLORIANNA...
I KNOW, RIGHT?
MUCH MORE GODLIKE NAME.
GLORIANNA... WHAT DO YOU WANT HERE?
I MEAN, WHAT ARE YOU EXPECTING THESE PEOPLE TO DO? BOW DOWN TO YOU?
WELL, YES, I'VE MADE THAT CLEAR. THEY WILL BOW TO ME...
AND THEN I WILL IMPROVE THEIR LIVES.
HOW?
HOWEVER I DECIDE TO. ISN'T THAT OBVIOUS?
YEAH. DEFINITELY NOT PLAYING WITH A FULL DECK.
HOW ABOUT THIS--YOU AND I GO OFF AND SORT OUT SOME SPECIFICS...
AND WE LEAVE THESE PEOPLE ALONE.
ALONE? TO PRAY TO A FALSE DEITY WHO DOESN'T CARE ABOUT THEM?
YEAH, BUT AT LEAST THEY LOVE HIM. YOU, THEY'RE TERRIFIED OF.
OH, THEY'RE AFRAID OF HIM, TOO. TRUST ME ON THAT.

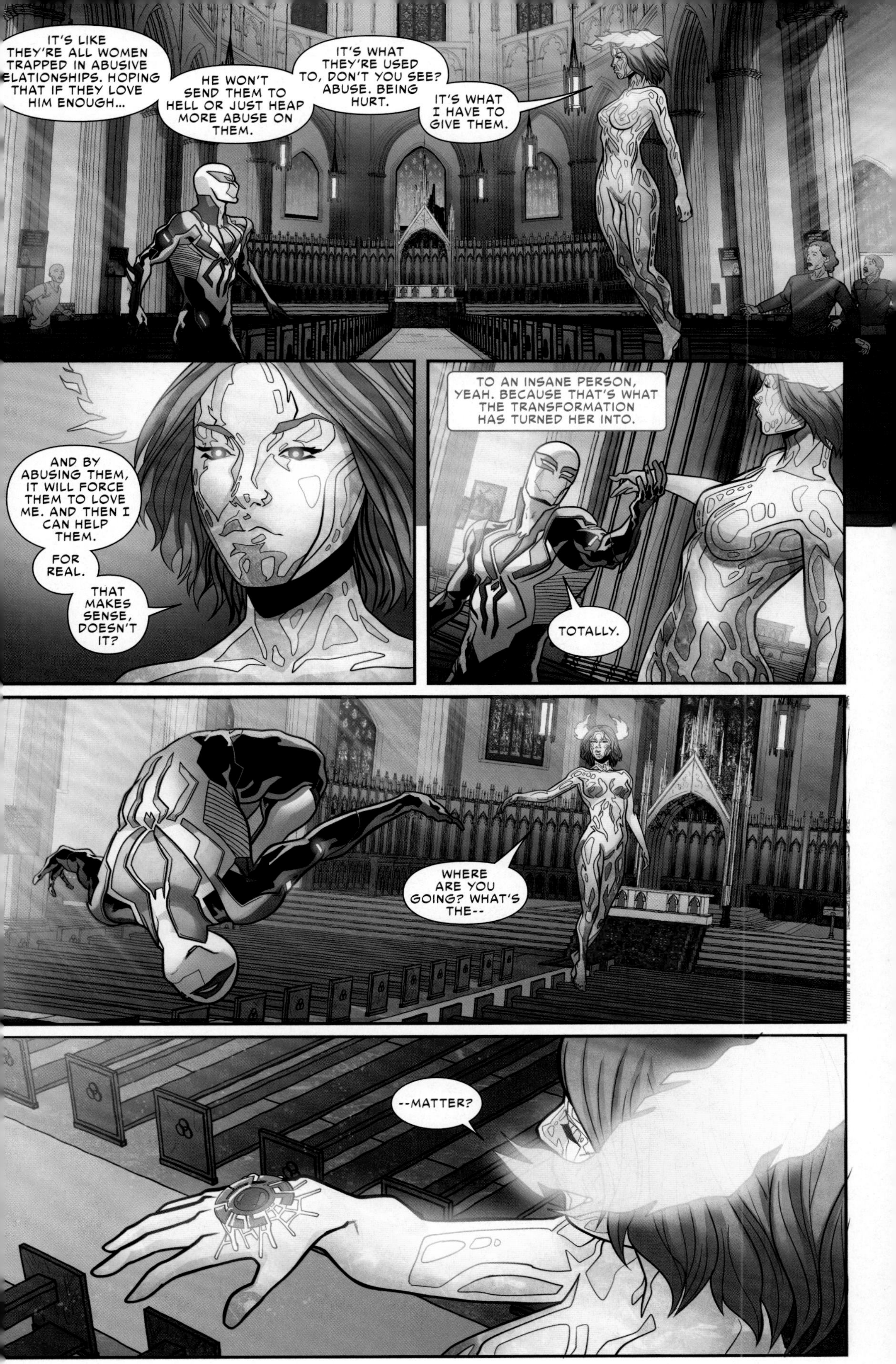
IT'S LIKE THEY'RE ALL WOMEN TRAPPED IN ABUSIVE ELATIONSHIPS. HOPING THAT IF THEY LOVE HIM ENOUGH...
HE WON'T SEND THEM TO HELL OR JUST HEAP MORE ABUSE ON THEM.
IT'S WHAT THEY'RE USED TO, DON'T YOU SEE? ABUSE. BEING HURT.
IT'S WHAT I HAVE TO GIVE THEM.
AND BY ABUSING THEM, IT WILL FORCE THEM TO LOVE ME. AND THEN I CAN HELP THEM.
FOR REAL.
THAT MAKES SENSE, DOESN'T IT?
TO AN INSANE PERSON, YEAH. BECAUSE THAT'S WHAT THE TRANSFORMATION HAS TURNED HER INTO.
TOTALLY.
WHERE ARE YOU GOING? WHAT'S THE--
--MATTER?

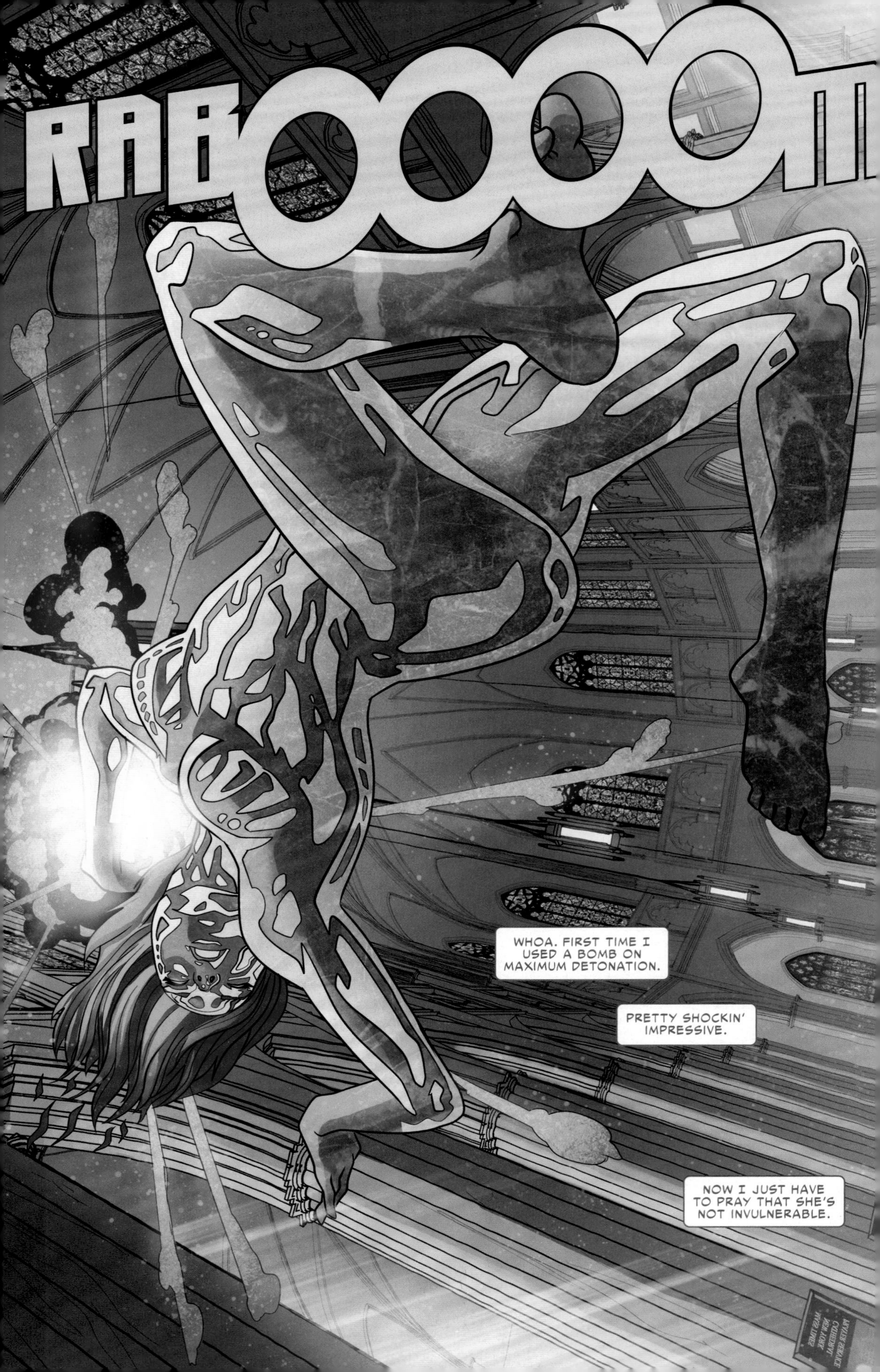
RABOOOOM
WHOA. FIRST TIME I USED A BOMB ON MAXIMUM DETONATION.
PRETTY SHOCKIN' IMPRESSIVE.
NOW I JUST HAVE TO PRAY THAT SHE'S NOT INVULNERABLE.

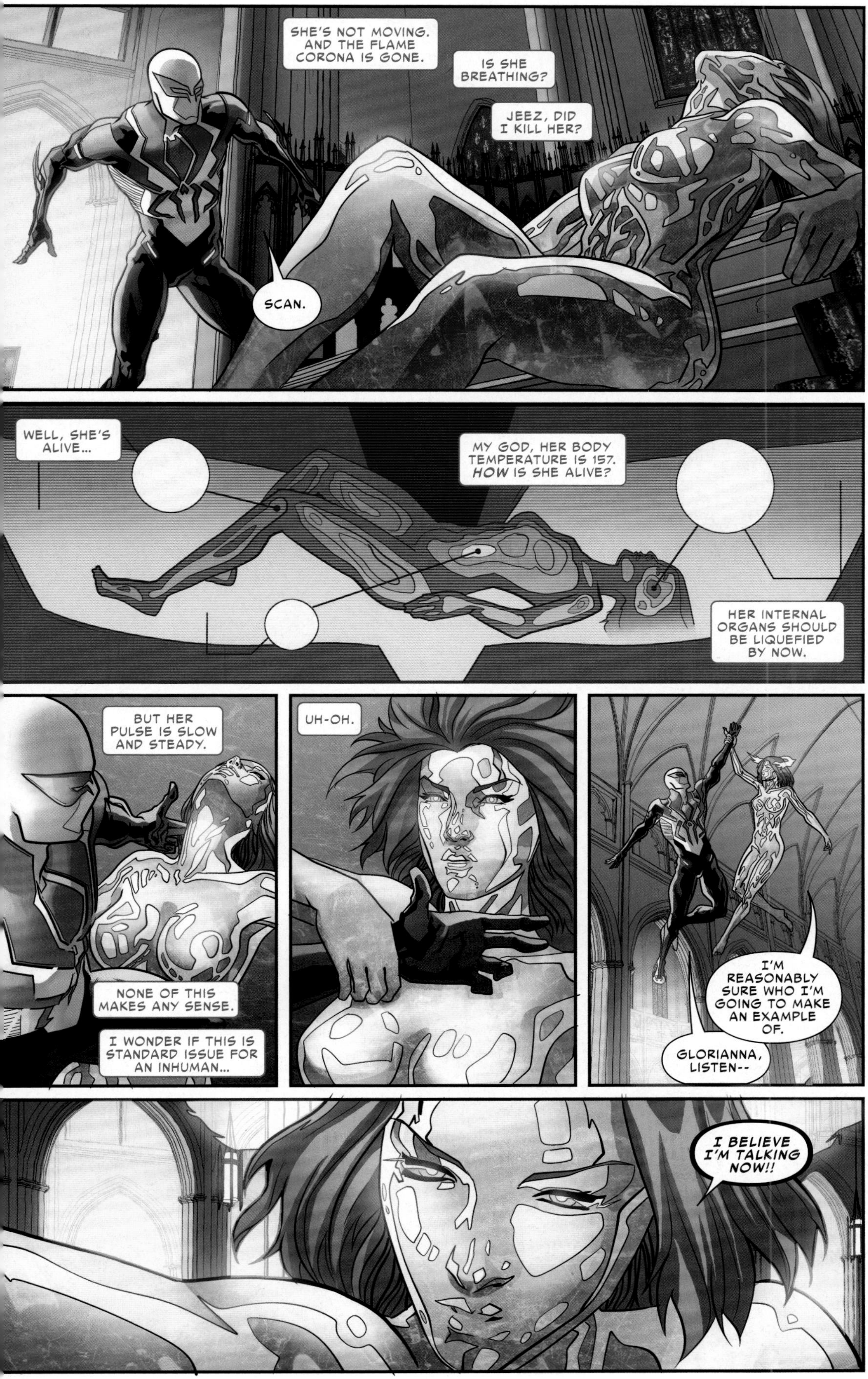
SHE'S NOT MOVING. AND THE FLAME CORONA IS GONE.
IS SHE BREATHING?
JEEZ, DID I KILL HER?
SCAN.
WELL, SHE'S ALIVE...
MY GOD, HER BODY TEMPERATURE IS 157. HOW IS SHE ALIVE?
HER INTERNAL ORGANS SHOULD BE LIQUEFIED BY NOW.
BUT HER PULSE IS SLOW AND STEADY.
NONE OF THIS MAKES ANY SENSE.
I WONDER IF THIS IS STANDARD ISSUE FOR AN INHUMAN...
UH-OH.
I'M REASONABLY SURE WHO I'M GOING TO MAKE AN EXAMPLE OF.
GLORIANNA, LISTEN--
I BELIEVE I'M TALKING NOW!!

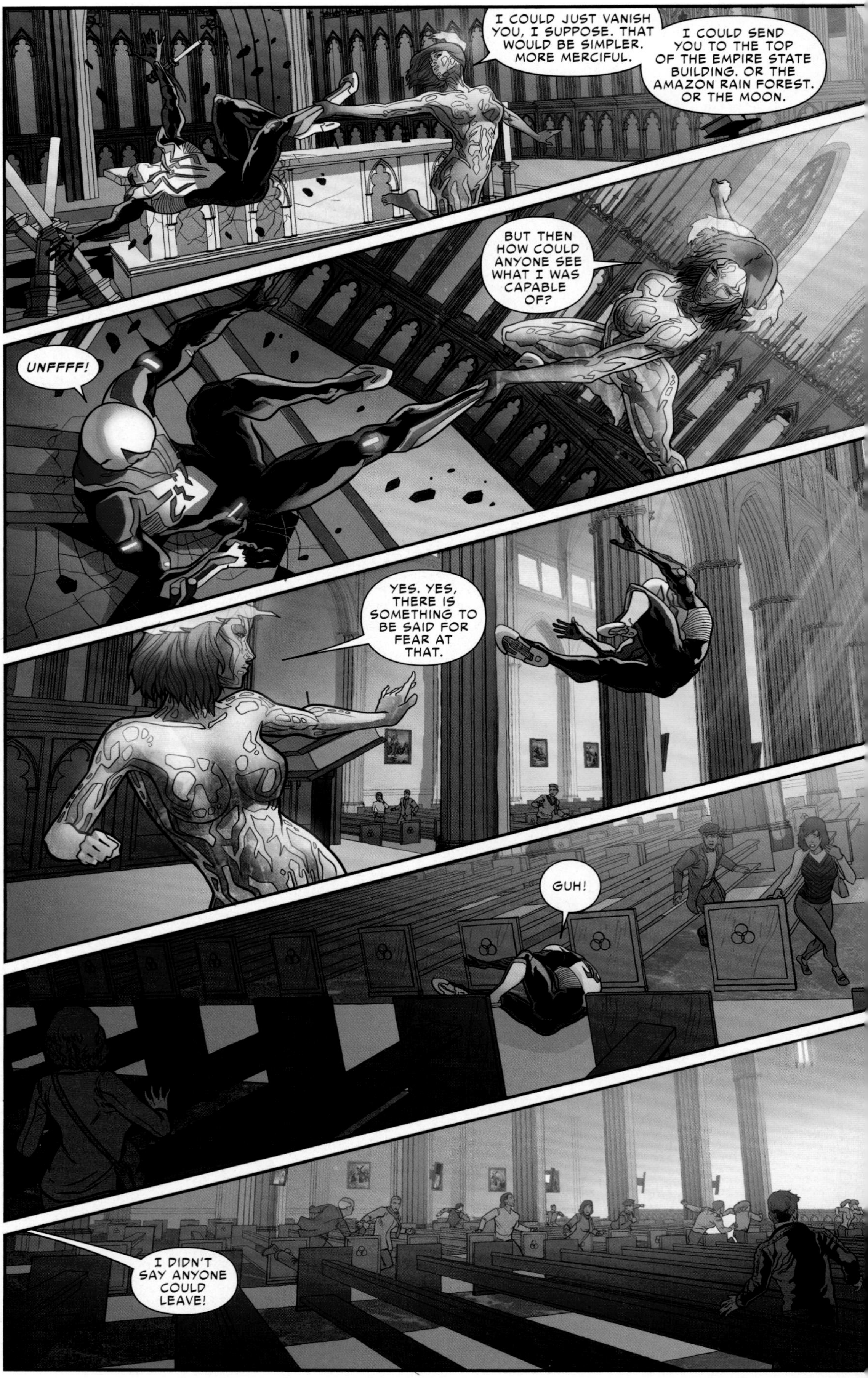
I COULD JUST VANISH YOU, I SUPPOSE. THAT WOULD BE SIMPLER. MORE MERCIFUL.
I COULD SEND YOU TO THE TOP OF THE EMPIRE STATE BUILDING. OR THE AMAZON RAIN FOREST. OR THE MOON.
BUT THEN HOW COULD ANYONE SEE WHAT I WAS CAPABLE OF?
UNFFFF!
YES. YES, THERE IS SOMETHING TO BE SAID FOR FEAR AT THAT.
GUH!
I DIDN'T SAY ANYONE COULD LEAVE!

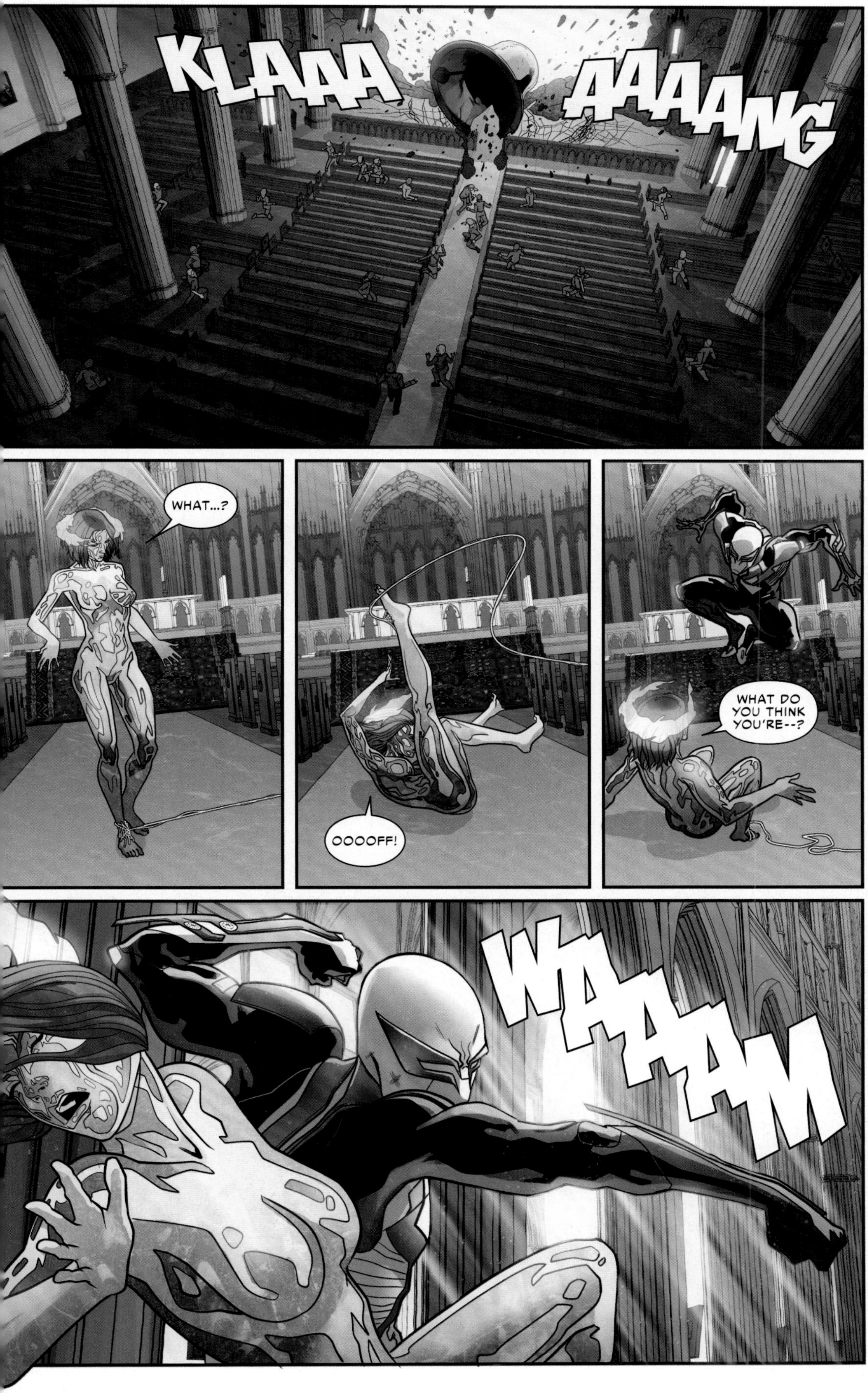
KLAAAAAAAANG
WHAT...?
OOOOFF!
WHAT DO YOU THINK YOU'RE--?
WAAAAM

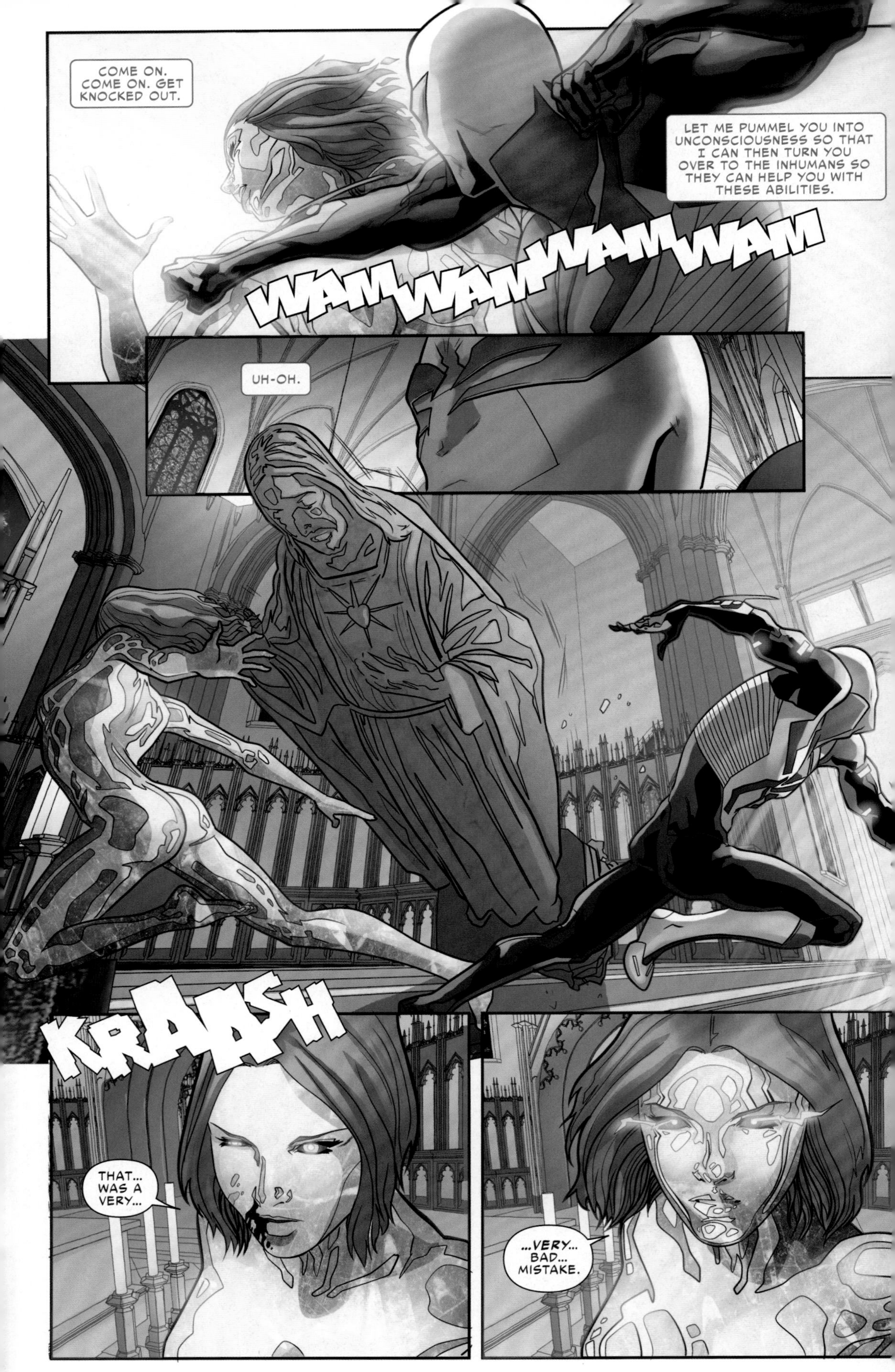

COME ON. COME ON. GET KNOCKED OUT.
LET ME PUMMEL YOU INTO UNCONSCIOUSNESS SO THAT I CAN THEN TURN YOU OVER TO THE INHUMANS SO THEY CAN HELP YOU WITH THESE ABILITIES.
WAM WAM WAM WAM
UH-OH.
KRAASH
THAT... WAS A VERY...
...VERY... BAD... MISTAKE.

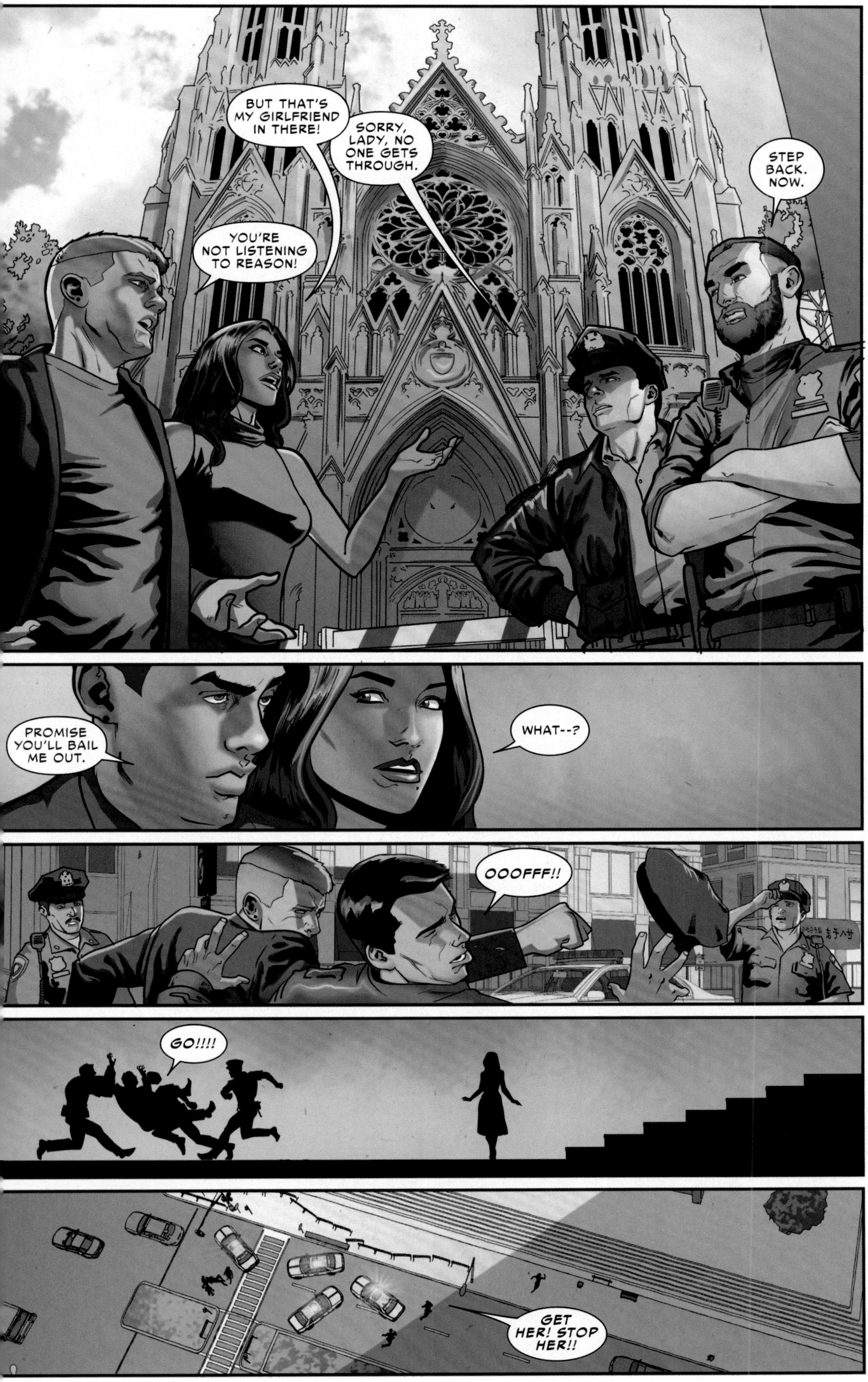
BUT THAT'S MY GIRLFRIEND IN THERE!
YOU'RE NOT LISTENING TO REASON!
SORRY, LADY, NO ONE GETS THROUGH.
STEP BACK. NOW.
PROMISE YOU'LL BAIL ME OUT.
WHAT--?
OOOFFF!!
GO!!!!
GET HER! STOP HER!!

ENOUGH'S ENOUGH. YOU'VE GOT TO ATTACK.

YEAH, IT'LL BLOW OUR IDENTITY, BUT WE CAN'T WAIT ANYMORE.

I...

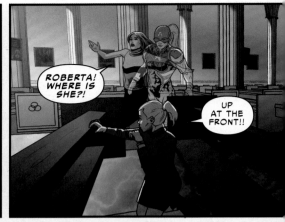

ROBERTA! WHERE IS SHE?!

UP AT THE FRONT!!

YOUR COSTUME IS QUITE STURDY, SPIDER-MAN.

BUT IF WE PUMMEL THE OUTSIDE HARD ENOUGH, I SUSPECT THE MAN INSIDE WILL BE EFFECTIVELY KILLED.

LET'S TEST THAT THEORY.

RHONDA! NO! N--!!!

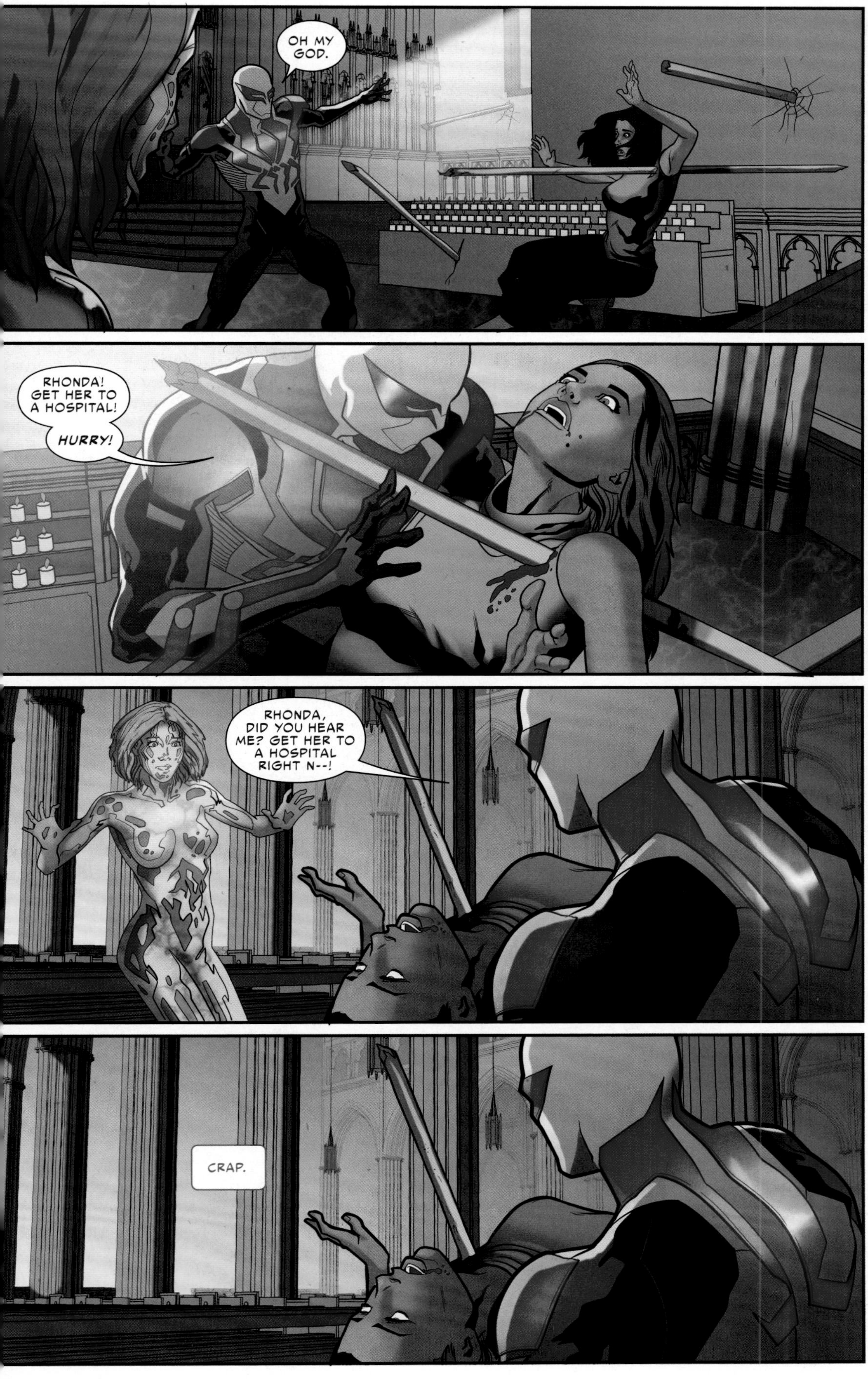
OH MY GOD.
RHONDA! GET HER TO A HOSPITAL!
HURRY!
RHONDA, DID YOU HEAR ME? GET HER TO A HOSPITAL RIGHT N--!
CRAP.

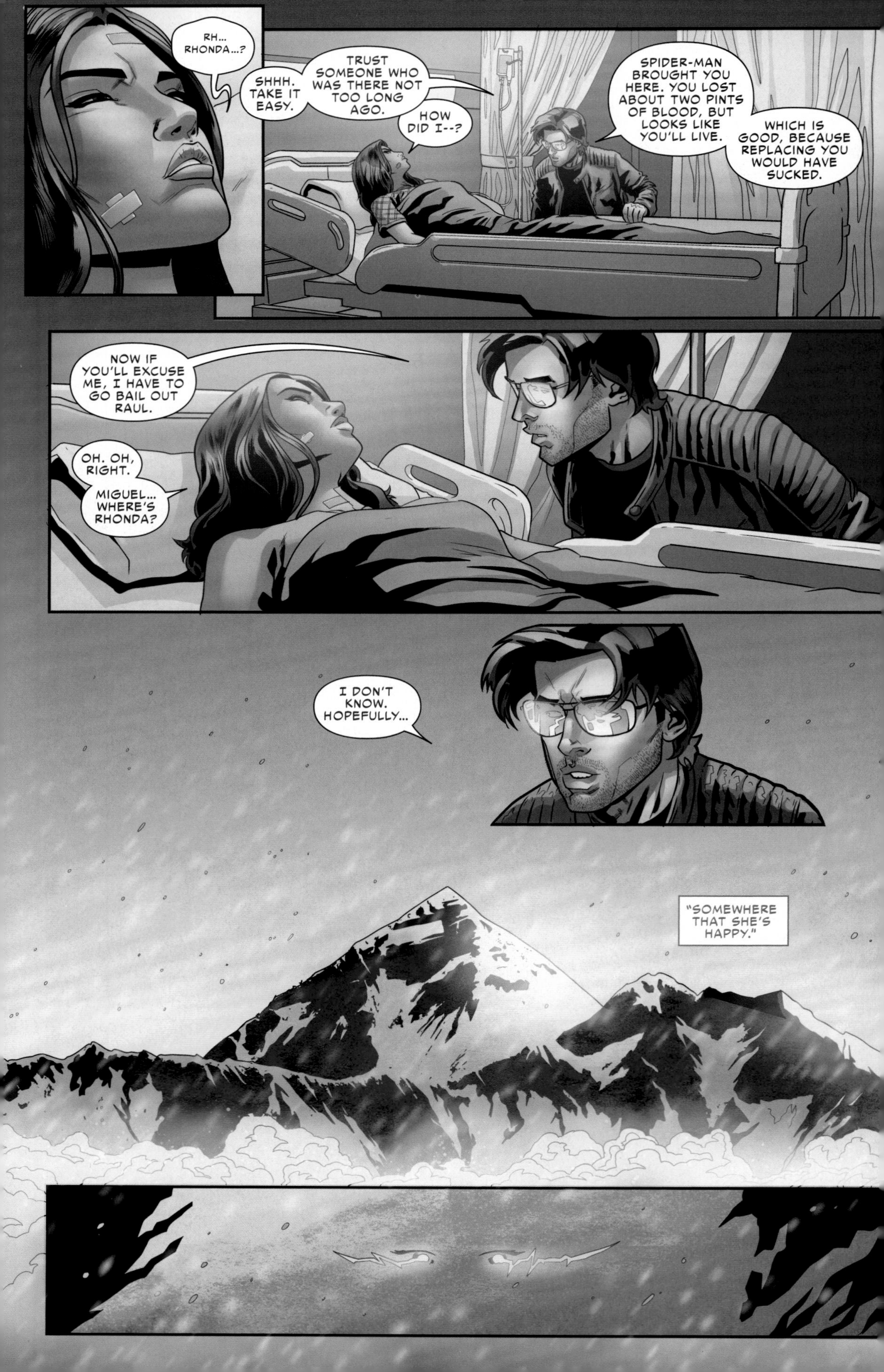
RH... RHONDA...?
SHHH. TAKE IT EASY.
TRUST SOMEONE WHO WAS THERE NOT TOO LONG AGO.
HOW DID I--?
SPIDER-MAN BROUGHT YOU HERE. YOU LOST ABOUT TWO PINTS OF BLOOD, BUT LOOKS LIKE YOU'LL LIVE.
WHICH IS GOOD, BECAUSE REPLACING YOU WOULD HAVE SUCKED.
NOW IF YOU'LL EXCUSE ME, I HAVE TO GO BAIL OUT RAUL.
OH. OH, RIGHT.
MIGUEL... WHERE'S RHONDA?
I DON'T KNOW. HOPEFULLY...
"SOMEWHERE THAT SHE'S HAPPY."

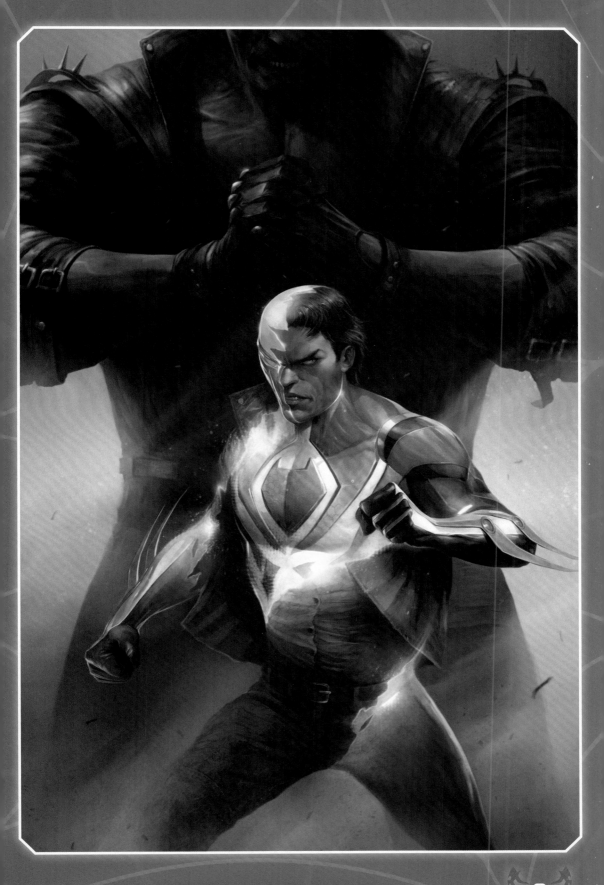

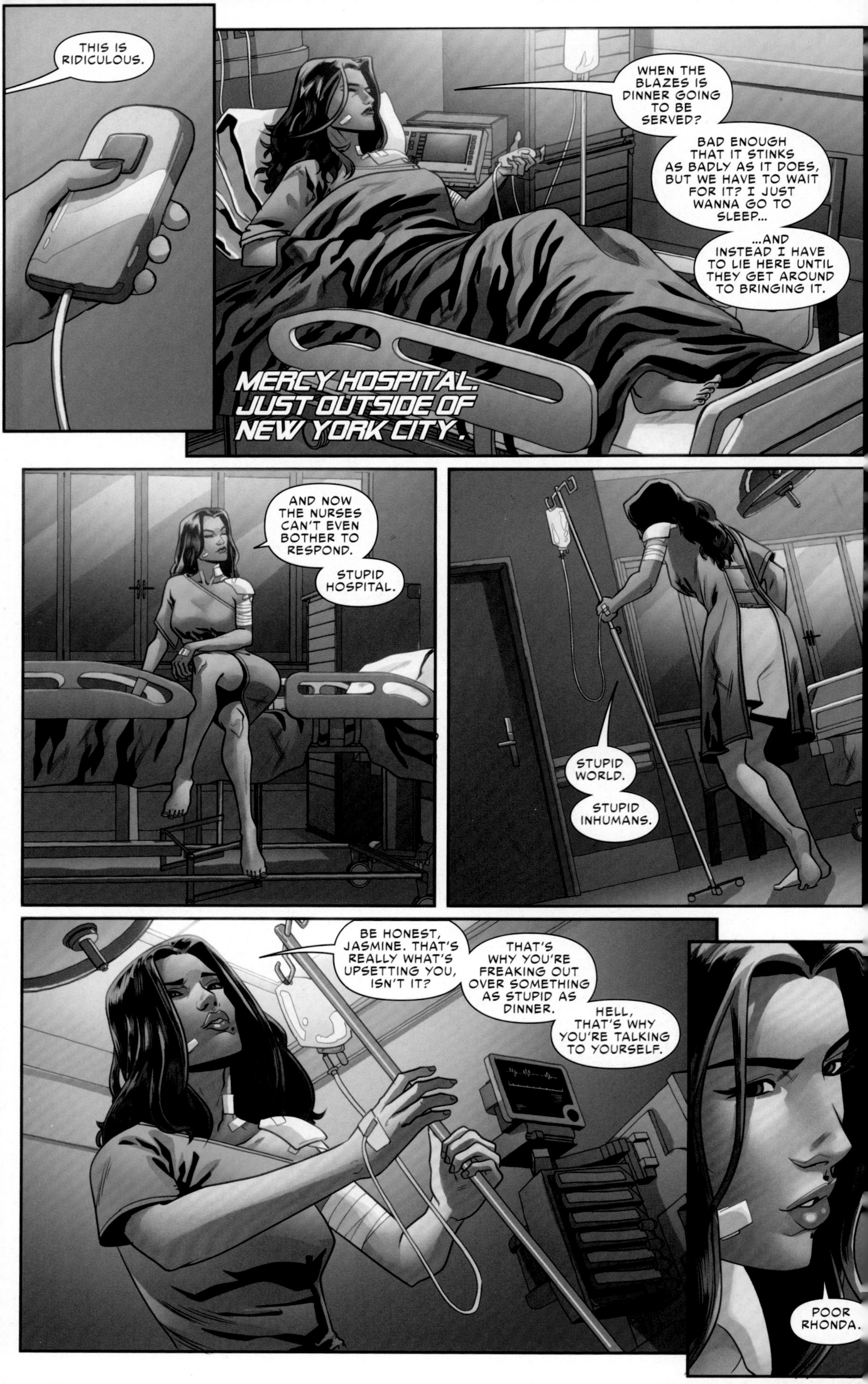
THIS IS RIDICULOUS.
WHEN THE BLAZES IS DINNER GOING TO BE SERVED?
BAD ENOUGH THAT IT STINKS AS BADLY AS IT DOES, BUT WE HAVE TO WAIT FOR IT? I JUST WANNA GO TO SLEEP...
...AND INSTEAD I HAVE TO LIE HERE UNTIL THEY GET AROUND TO BRINGING IT.
MERCY HOSPITAL. JUST OUTSIDE OF NEW YORK CITY.
AND NOW THE NURSES CAN'T EVEN BOTHER TO RESPOND.
STUPID HOSPITAL.
STUPID WORLD.
STUPID INHUMANS.
BE HONEST, JASMINE. THAT'S REALLY WHAT'S UPSETTING YOU, ISN'T IT?
THAT'S WHY YOU'RE FREAKING OUT OVER SOMETHING AS STUPID AS DINNER.
HELL, THAT'S WHY YOU'RE TALKING TO YOURSELF.
POOR RHONDA.

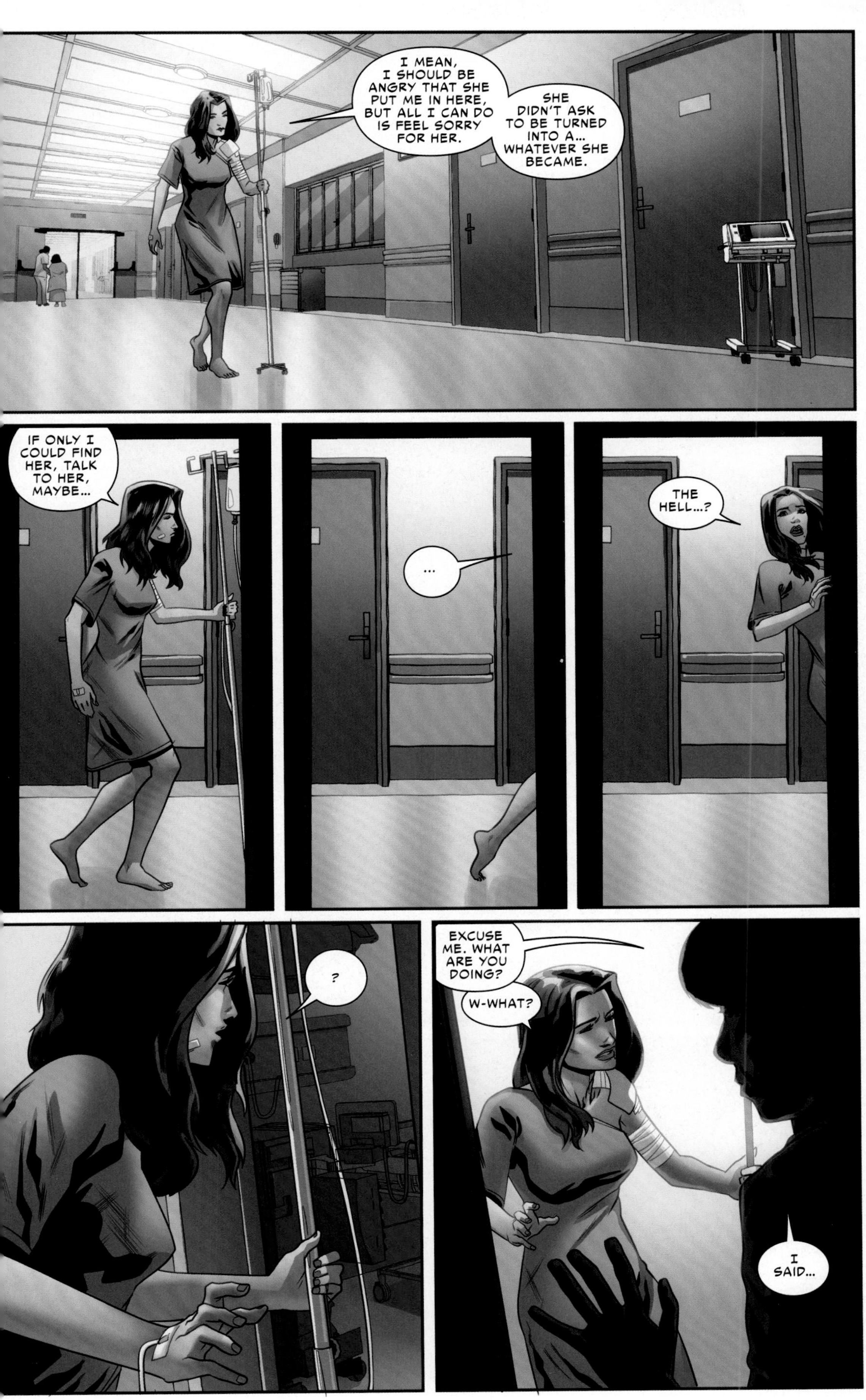
I MEAN, I SHOULD BE ANGRY THAT SHE PUT ME IN HERE, BUT ALL I CAN DO IS FEEL SORRY FOR HER.
SHE DIDN'T ASK TO BE TURNED INTO A... WHATEVER SHE BECAME.
IF ONLY I COULD FIND HER, TALK TO HER, MAYBE...
...
THE HELL...?
?
EXCUSE ME. WHAT ARE YOU DOING?
W-WHAT?
I SAID...

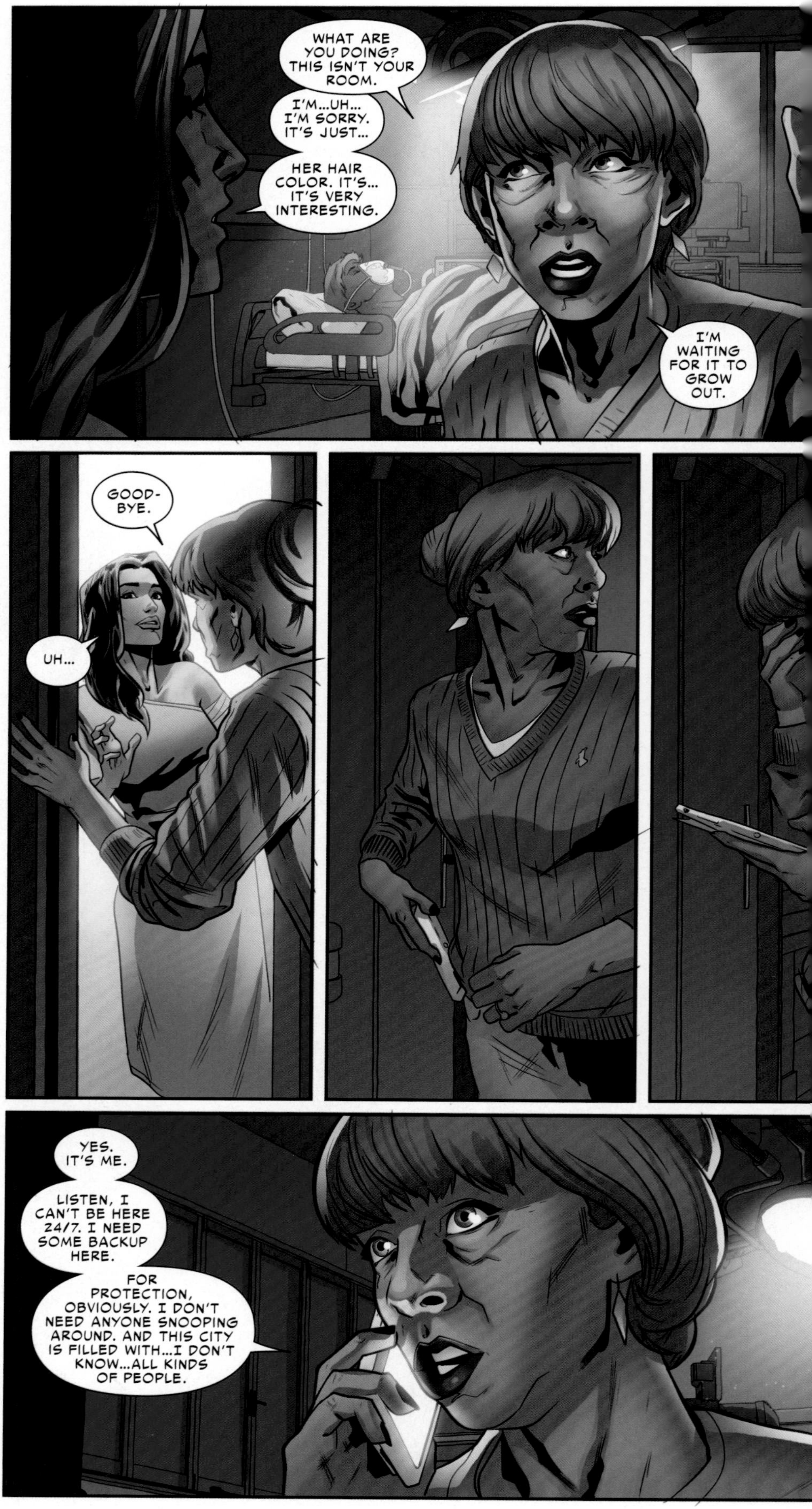
WHAT ARE YOU DOING? THIS ISN'T YOUR ROOM.
I'M...UH... I'M SORRY. IT'S JUST...
HER HAIR COLOR. IT'S... IT'S VERY INTERESTING.
I'M WAITING FOR IT TO GROW OUT.
GOOD-BYE.
UH...
YES. IT'S ME.
LISTEN, I CAN'T BE HERE 24/7. I NEED SOME BACKUP HERE.
FOR PROTECTION, OBVIOUSLY. I DON'T NEED ANYONE SNOOPING AROUND. AND THIS CITY IS FILLED WITH...I DON'T KNOW...ALL KINDS OF PEOPLE.

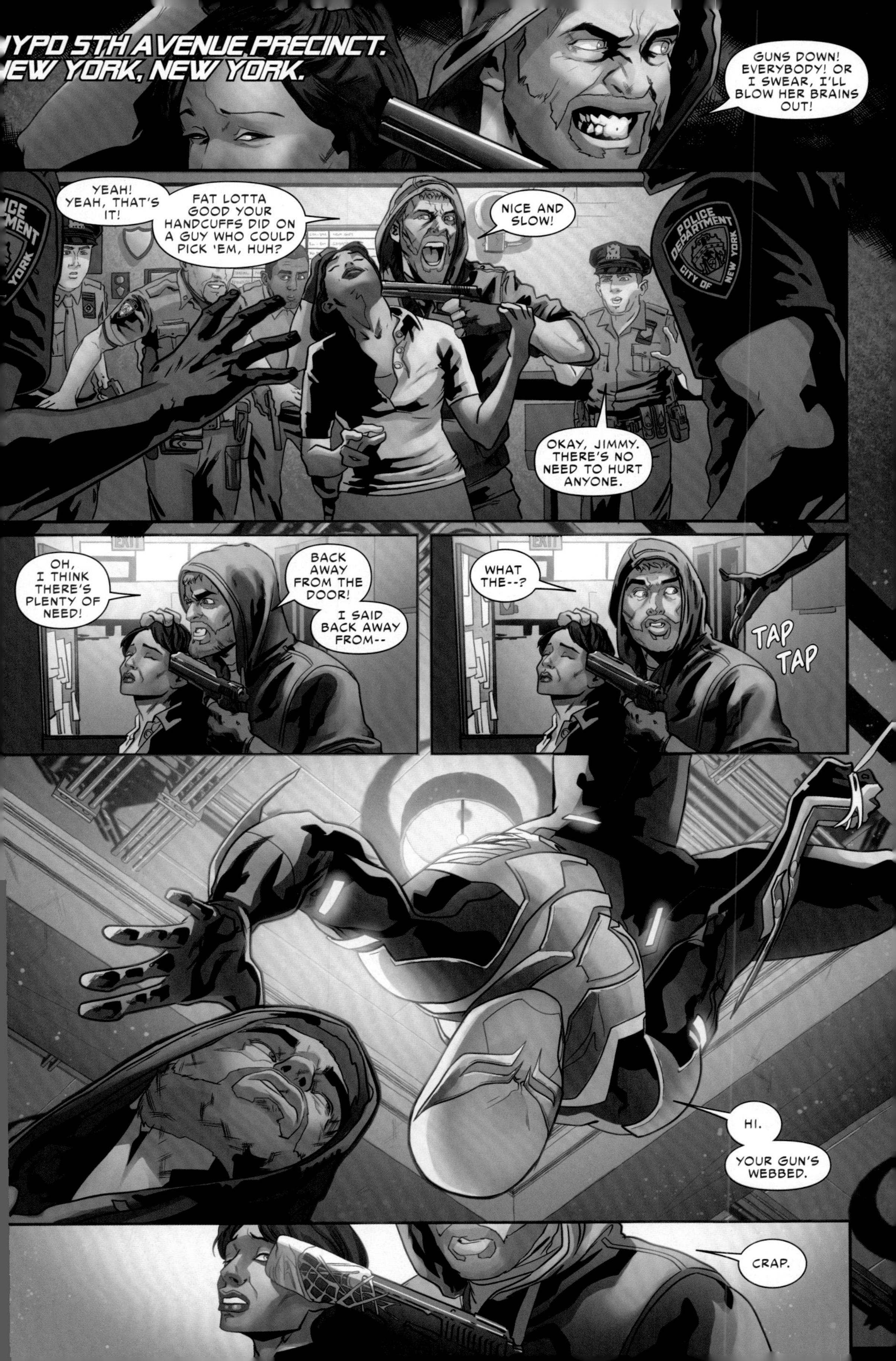
NYPD 5TH AVENUE PRECINCT.
NEW YORK, NEW YORK.
GUNS DOWN! EVERYBODY! OR I SWEAR, I'LL BLOW HER BRAINS OUT!
YEAH! YEAH, THAT'S IT!
FAT LOTTA GOOD YOUR HANDCUFFS DID ON A GUY WHO COULD PICK 'EM, HUH?
NICE AND SLOW!
OKAY, JIMMY. THERE'S NO NEED TO HURT ANYONE.
OH, I THINK THERE'S PLENTY OF NEED!
BACK AWAY FROM THE DOOR!
I SAID BACK AWAY FROM--
WHAT THE--?
TAP TAP
HI.
YOUR GUN'S WEBBED.
CRAP.

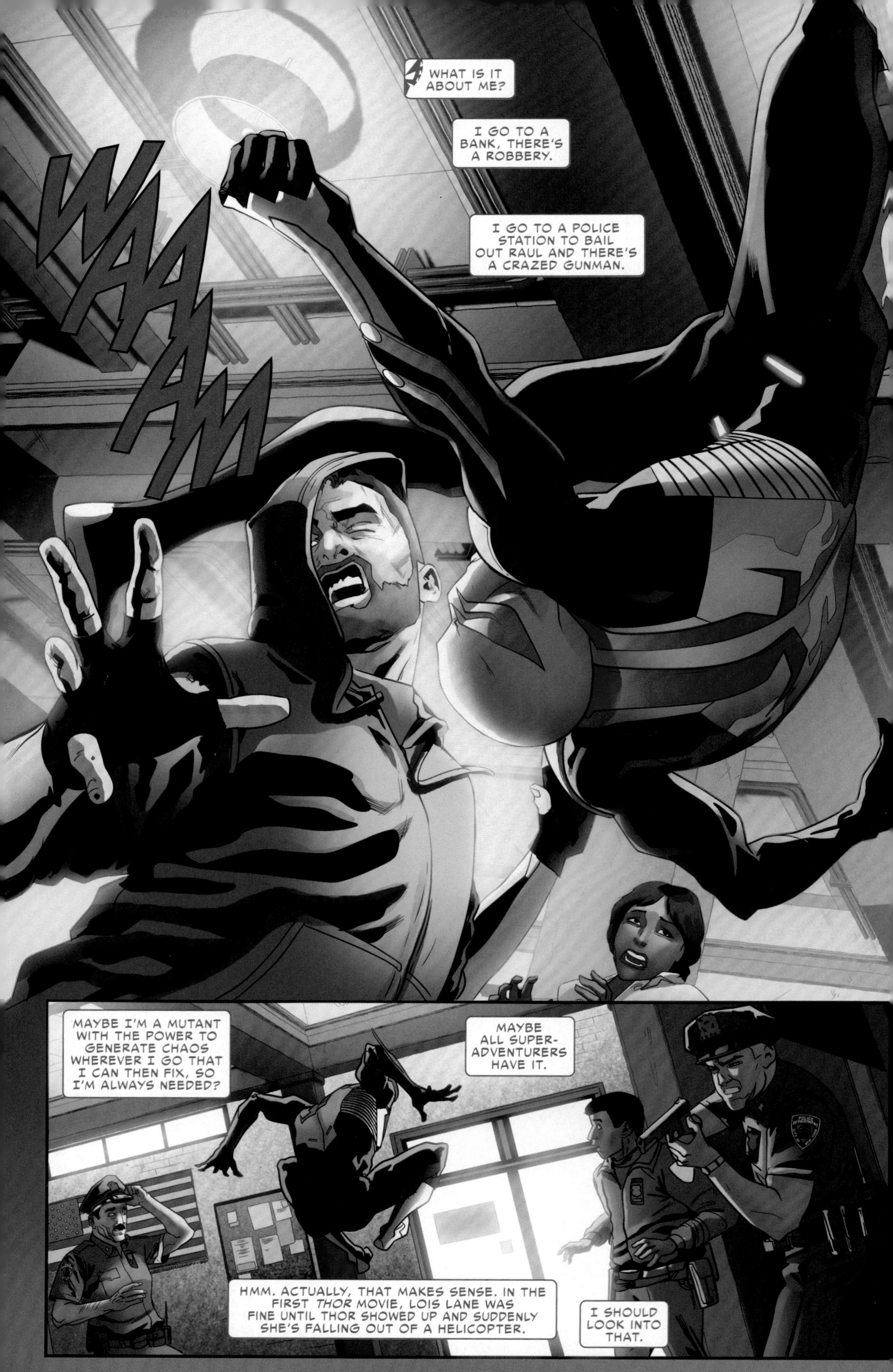
WHAT IS IT ABOUT ME?
I GO TO A BANK, THERE'S A ROBBERY.
I GO TO A POLICE STATION TO BAIL OUT RAUL AND THERE'S A CRAZED GUNMAN.
WAAAM
MAYBE I'M A MUTANT WITH THE POWER TO GENERATE CHAOS WHEREVER I GO THAT I CAN THEN FIX, SO I'M ALWAYS NEEDED?
MAYBE ALL SUPER-ADVENTURERS HAVE IT.
HMM. ACTUALLY, THAT MAKES SENSE. IN THE FIRST *THOR* MOVIE, LOIS LANE WAS FINE UNTIL THOR SHOWED UP AND SUDDENLY SHE'S FALLING OUT OF A HELICOPTER.
I SHOULD LOOK INTO THAT.

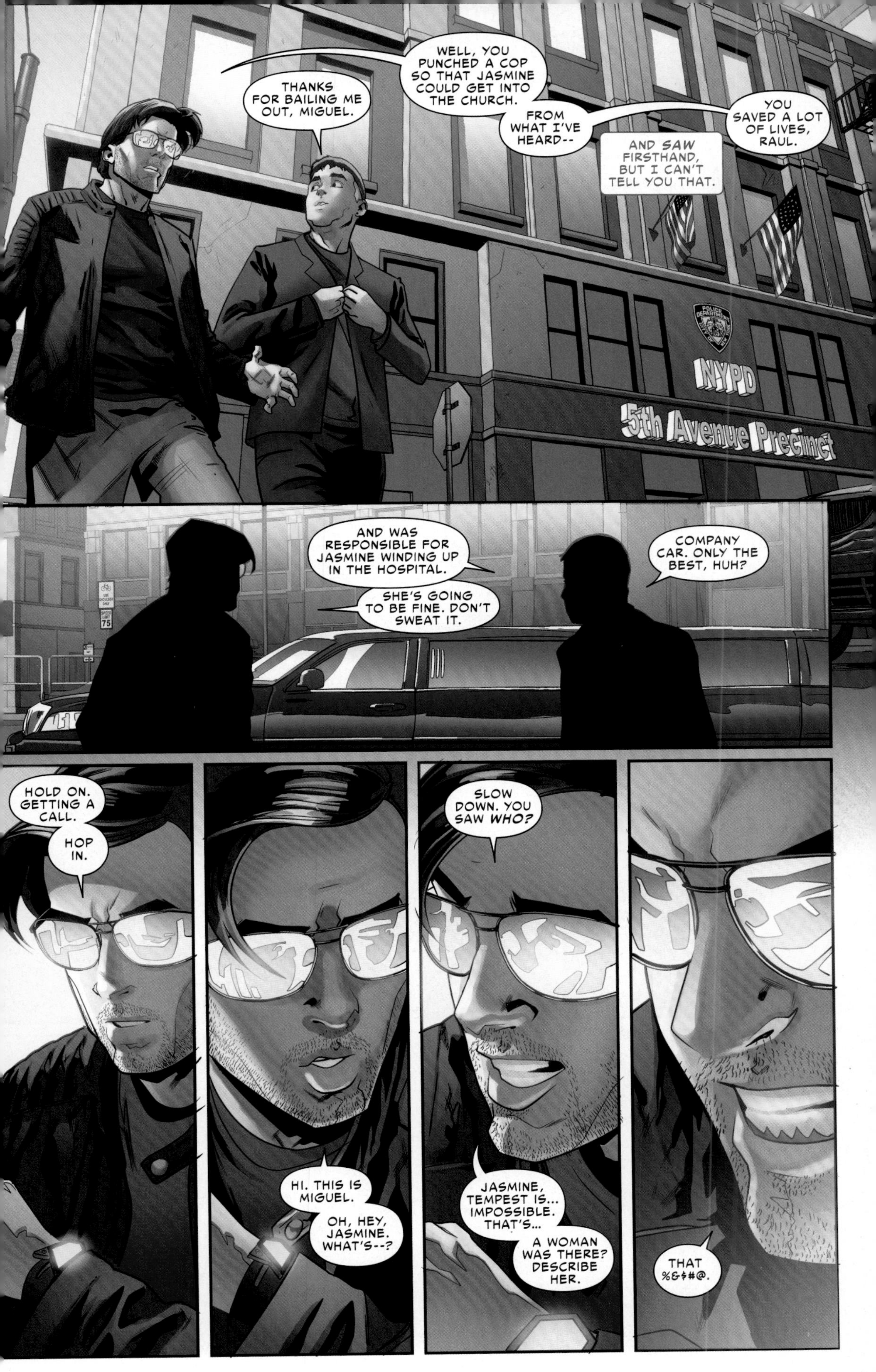
THANKS FOR BAILING ME OUT, MIGUEL.
WELL, YOU PUNCHED A COP SO THAT JASMINE COULD GET INTO THE CHURCH.
FROM WHAT I'VE HEARD--
YOU SAVED A LOT OF LIVES, RAUL.
AND SAW FIRSTHAND, BUT I CAN'T TELL YOU THAT.
NYPD
5th Avenue Precinct
AND WAS RESPONSIBLE FOR JASMINE WINDING UP IN THE HOSPITAL.
SHE'S GOING TO BE FINE. DON'T SWEAT IT.
COMPANY CAR. ONLY THE BEST, HUH?
HOLD ON. GETTING A CALL.
HOP IN.
HI. THIS IS MIGUEL.
OH, HEY, JASMINE. WHAT'S--?
SLOW DOWN. YOU SAW WHO?
JASMINE, TEMPEST IS... IMPOSSIBLE. THAT'S...
A WOMAN WAS THERE? DESCRIBE HER.
THAT %&$#@.

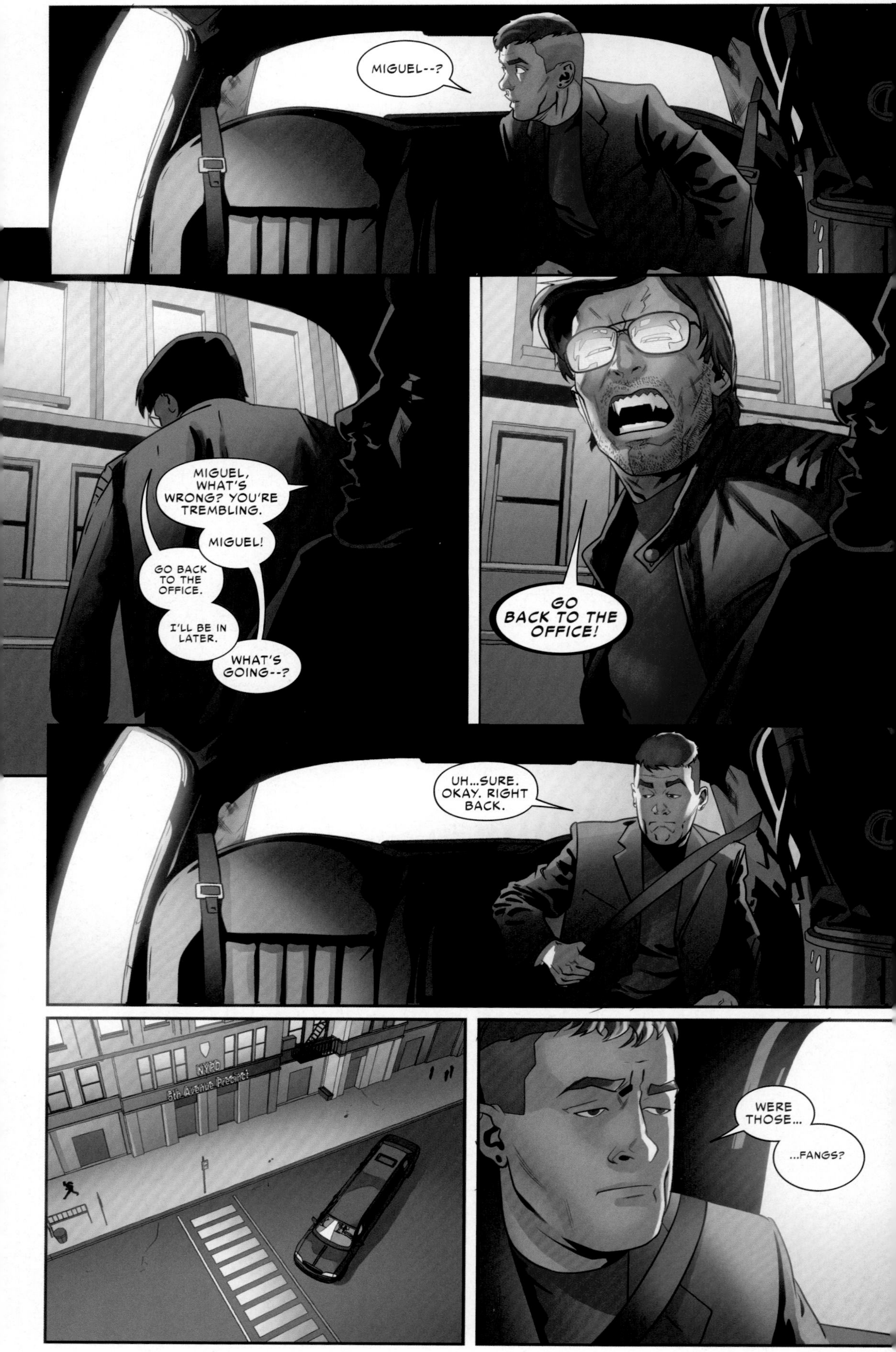
MIGUEL--?
MIGUEL, WHAT'S WRONG? YOU'RE TREMBLING.
MIGUEL!
GO BACK TO THE OFFICE.
I'LL BE IN LATER.
WHAT'S GOING--?
GO BACK TO THE OFFICE!
UH...SURE. OKAY. RIGHT BACK.
NYPD
5th Avenue Precinct
WERE THOSE...
...FANGS?

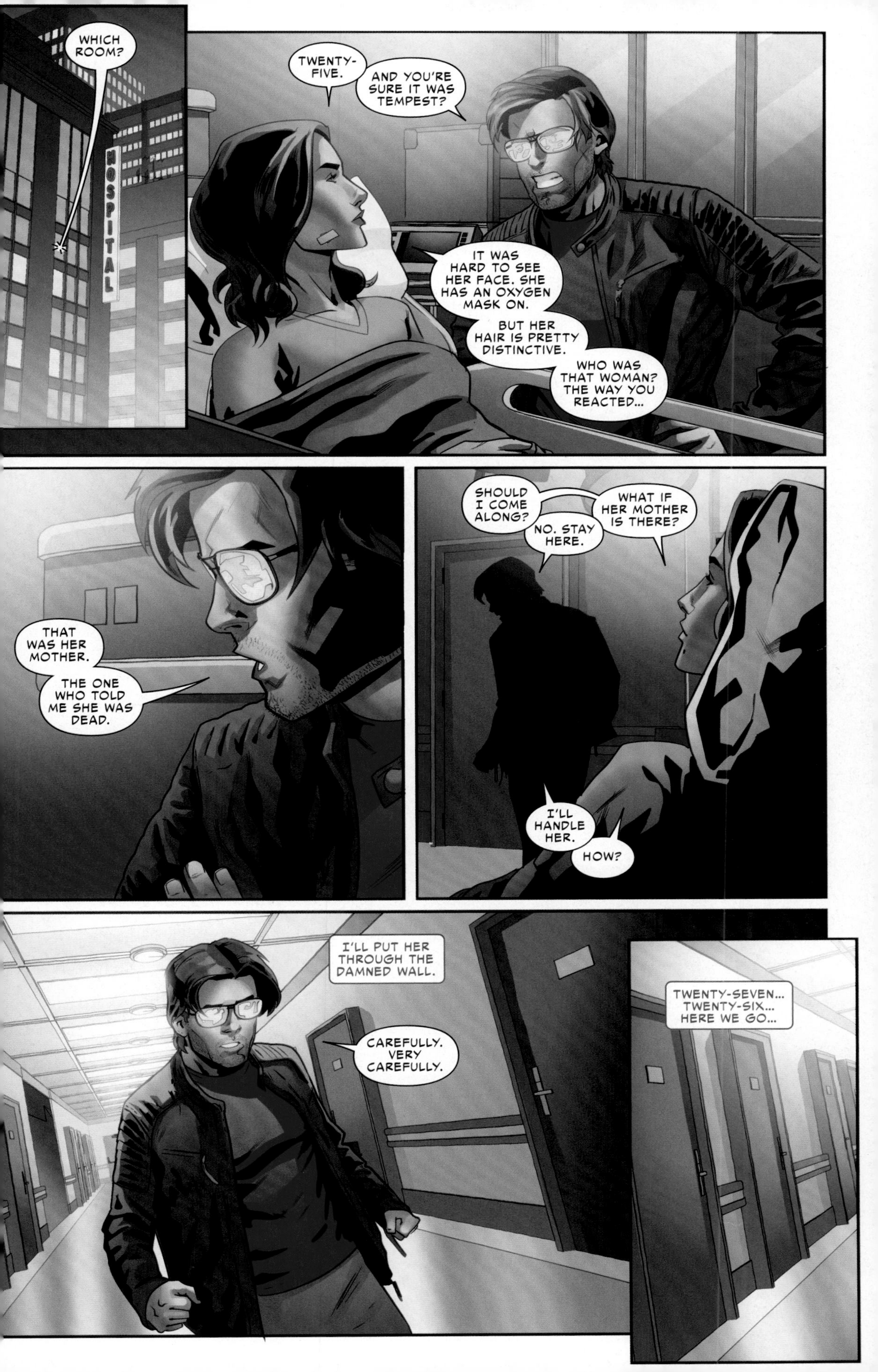
WHICH ROOM?
TWENTY-FIVE.
AND YOU'RE SURE IT WAS TEMPEST?
IT WAS HARD TO SEE HER FACE. SHE HAS AN OXYGEN MASK ON.
BUT HER HAIR IS PRETTY DISTINCTIVE.
WHO WAS THAT WOMAN? THE WAY YOU REACTED...
THAT WAS HER MOTHER.
THE ONE WHO TOLD ME SHE WAS DEAD.
SHOULD I COME ALONG?
NO. STAY HERE.
WHAT IF HER MOTHER IS THERE?
I'LL HANDLE HER.
HOW?
I'LL PUT HER THROUGH THE DAMNED WALL.
CAREFULLY. VERY CAREFULLY.
TWENTY-SEVEN... TWENTY-SIX... HERE WE GO...

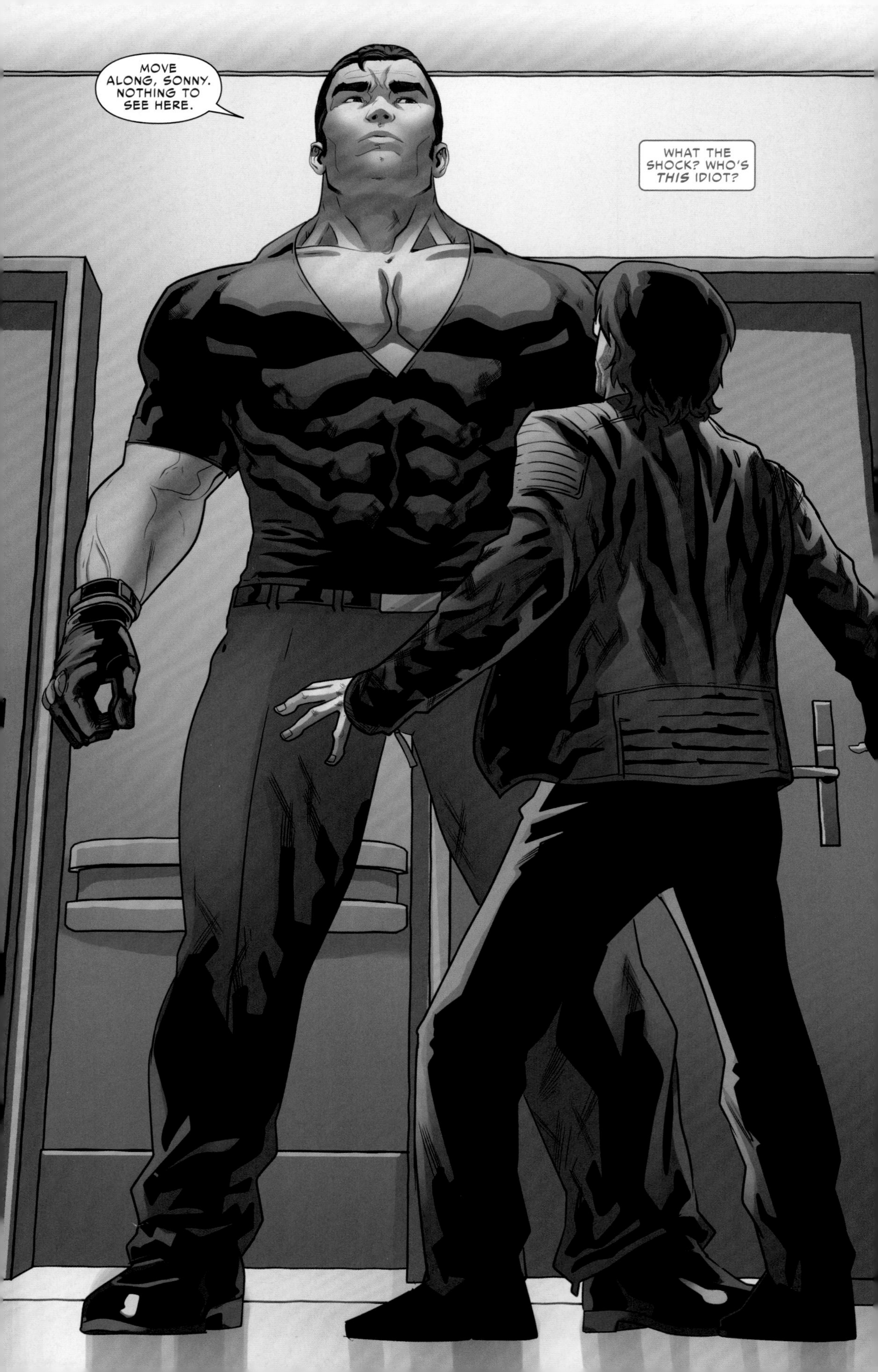
MOVE ALONG, SONNY. NOTHING TO SEE HERE.
WHAT THE SHOCK? WHO'S *THIS* IDIOT?

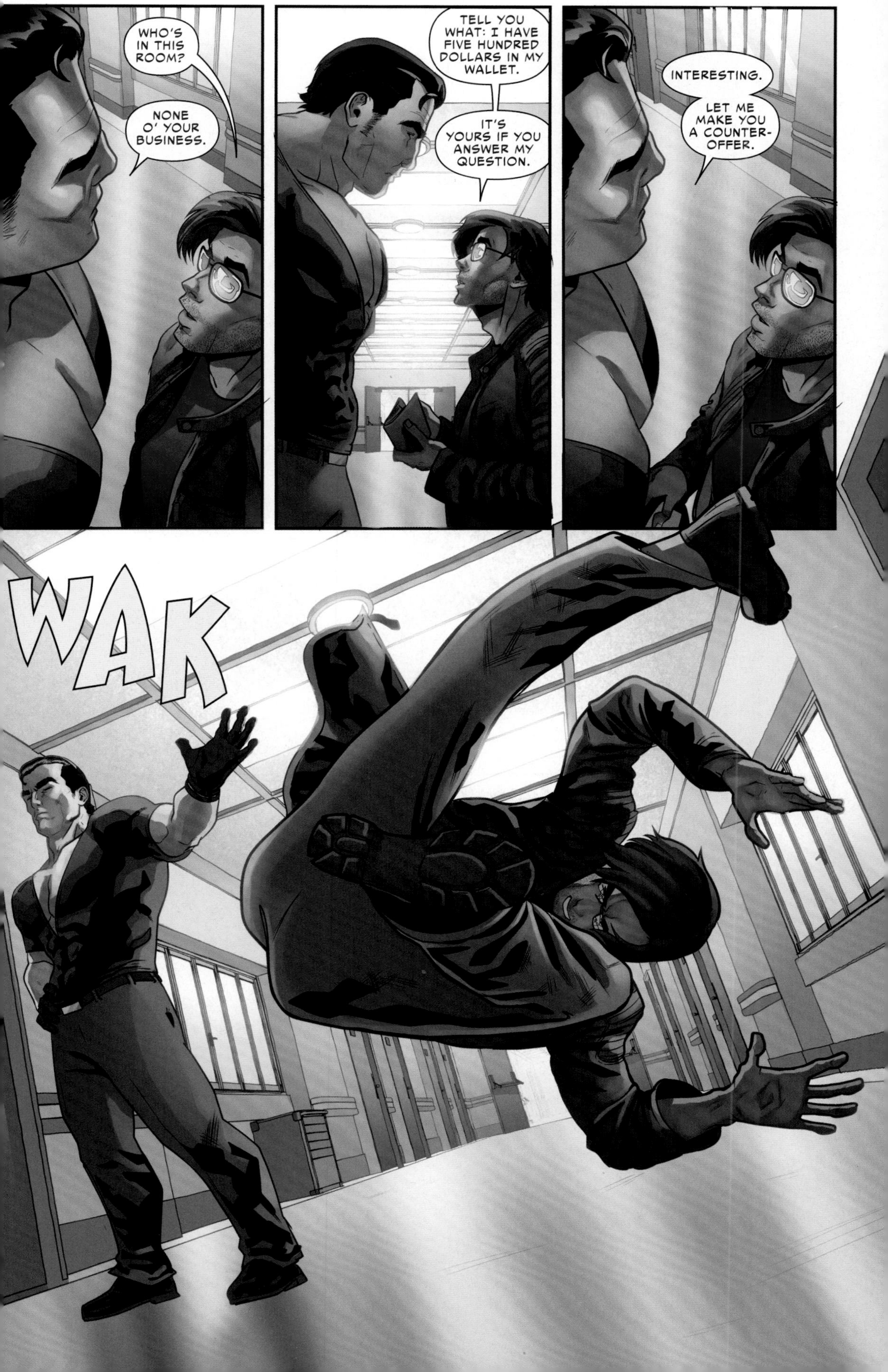
WHO'S IN THIS ROOM?
NONE O' YOUR BUSINESS.
TELL YOU WHAT: I HAVE FIVE HUNDRED DOLLARS IN MY WALLET.
IT'S YOURS IF YOU ANSWER MY QUESTION.
INTERESTING.
LET ME MAKE YOU A COUNTER-OFFER.
WAK

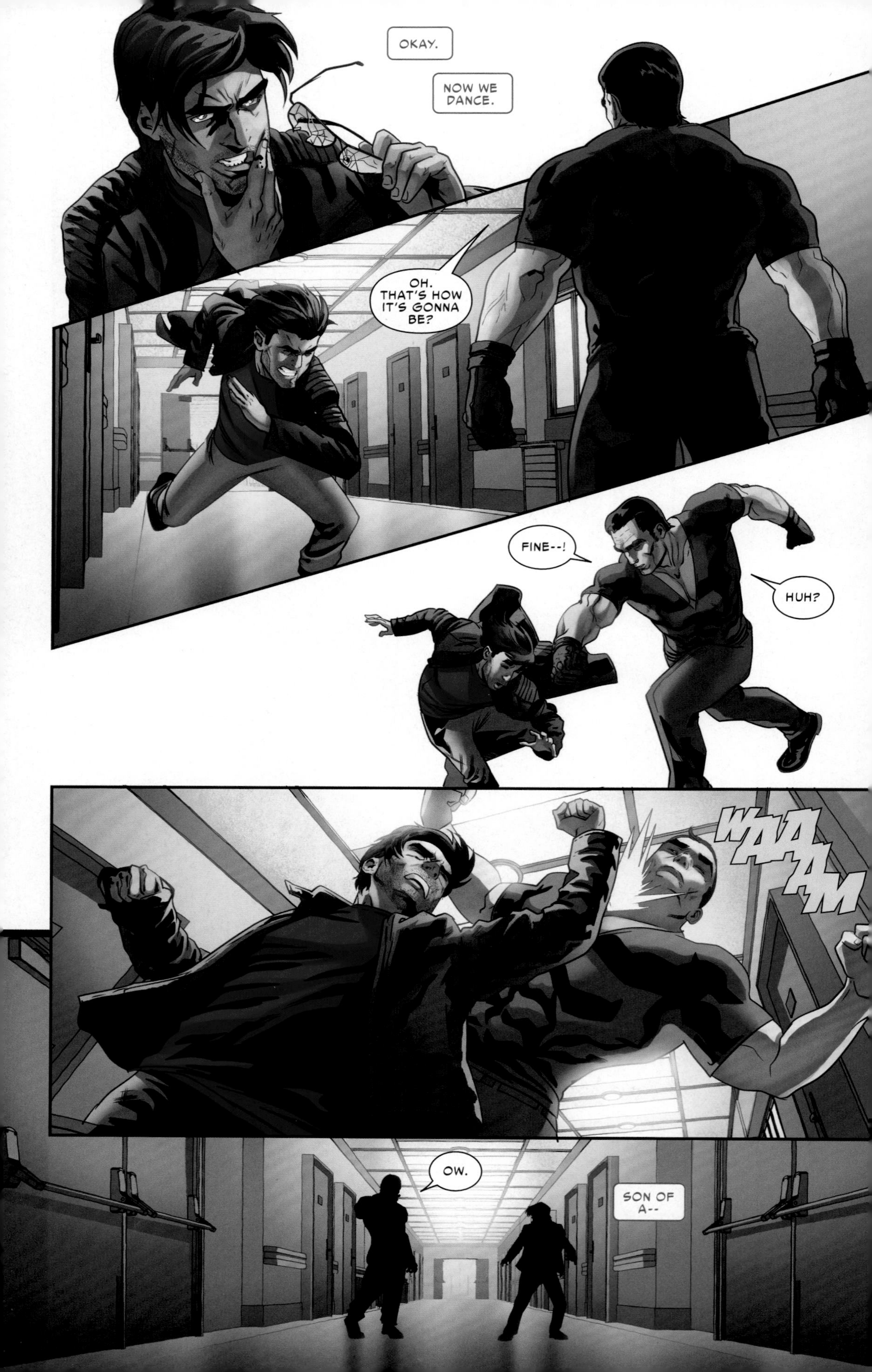
OKAY.
NOW WE DANCE.
OH. THAT'S HOW IT'S GONNA BE?
FINE--!
HUH?
WAAAM
OW.
SON OF A--

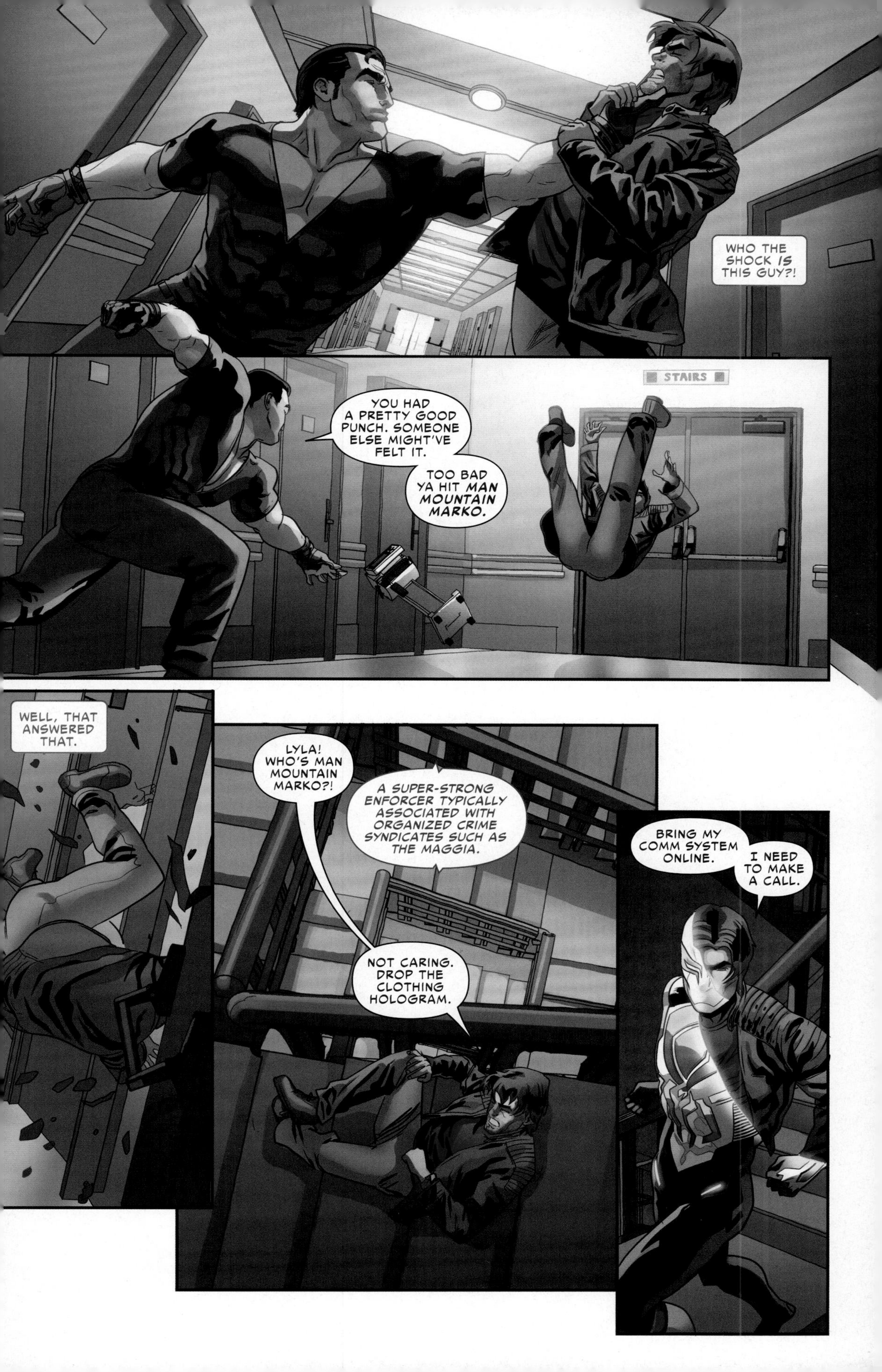
WHO THE SHOCK *IS* THIS GUY?!
STAIRS
YOU HAD A PRETTY GOOD PUNCH. SOMEONE ELSE MIGHT'VE FELT IT.
TOO BAD YA HIT *MAN MOUNTAIN MARKO.*
WELL, THAT ANSWERED THAT.
LYLA! WHO'S MAN MOUNTAIN MARKO?!
A SUPER-STRONG ENFORCER TYPICALLY ASSOCIATED WITH ORGANIZED CRIME SYNDICATES SUCH AS THE MAGGIA.
NOT CARING. DROP THE CLOTHING HOLOGRAM.
BRING MY COMM SYSTEM ONLINE.
I NEED TO MAKE A CALL.

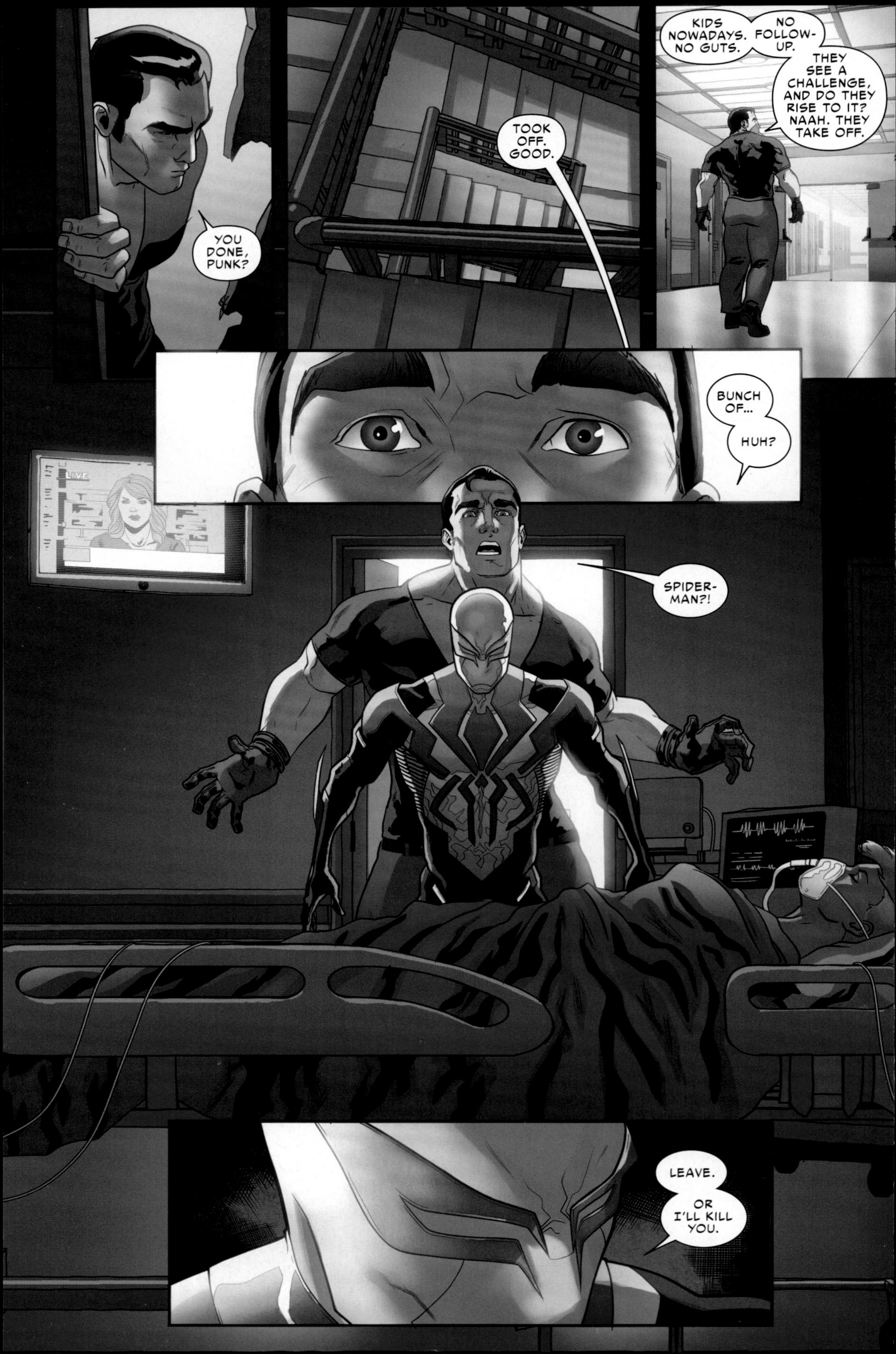
YOU DONE, PUNK?
TOOK OFF. GOOD.
KIDS NOWADAYS. NO GUTS.
NO FOLLOW-UP.
THEY SEE A CHALLENGE, AND DO THEY RISE TO IT? NAAH. THEY TAKE OFF.
BUNCH OF...
HUH?
LIVE
SPIDER-MAN?!
LEAVE.
OR I'LL KILL YOU.

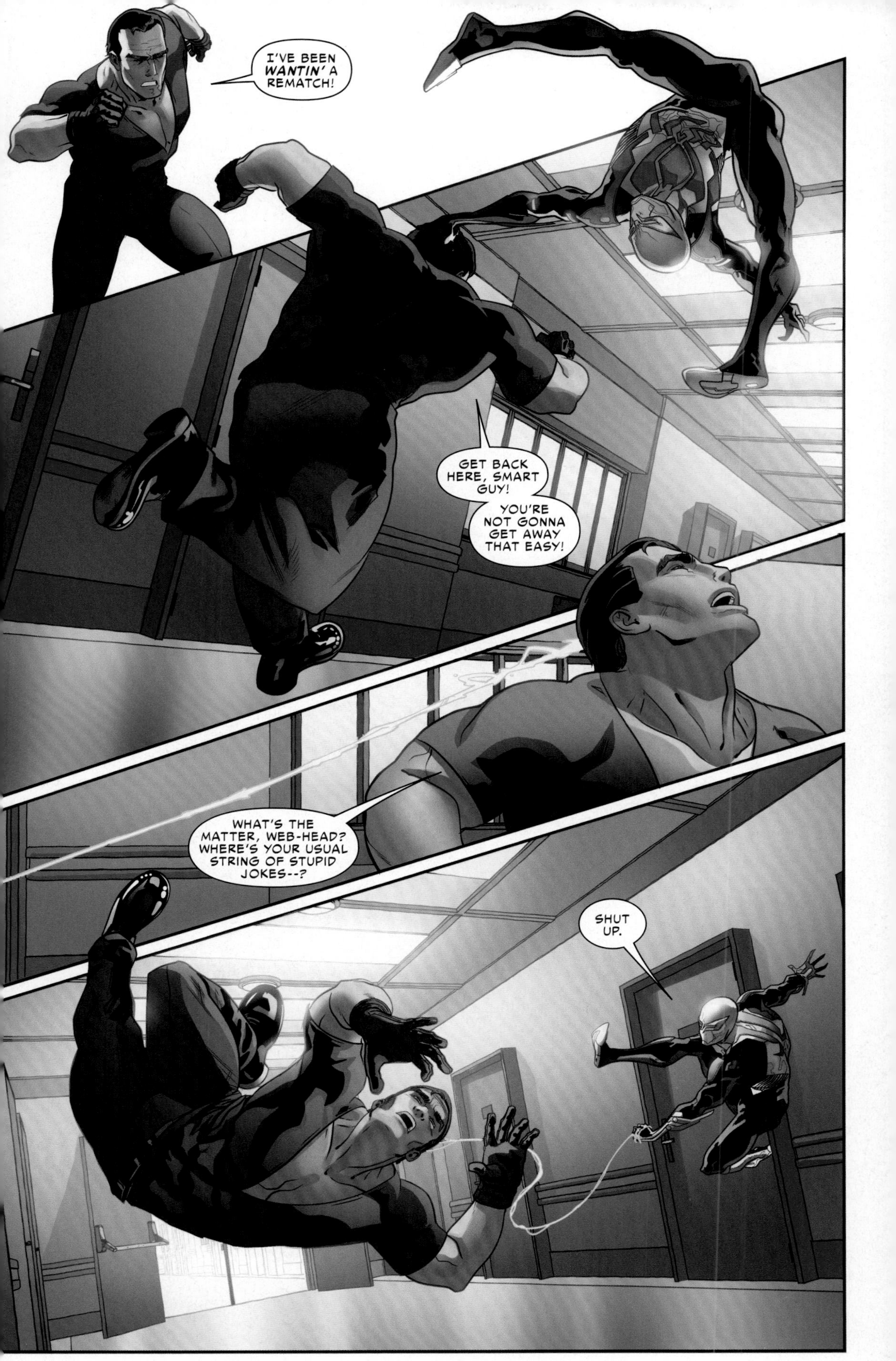
I'VE BEEN WANTIN' A REMATCH!
GET BACK HERE, SMART GUY!
YOU'RE NOT GONNA GET AWAY THAT EASY!
WHAT'S THE MATTER, WEB-HEAD? WHERE'S YOUR USUAL STRING OF STUPID JOKES--?
SHUT UP.

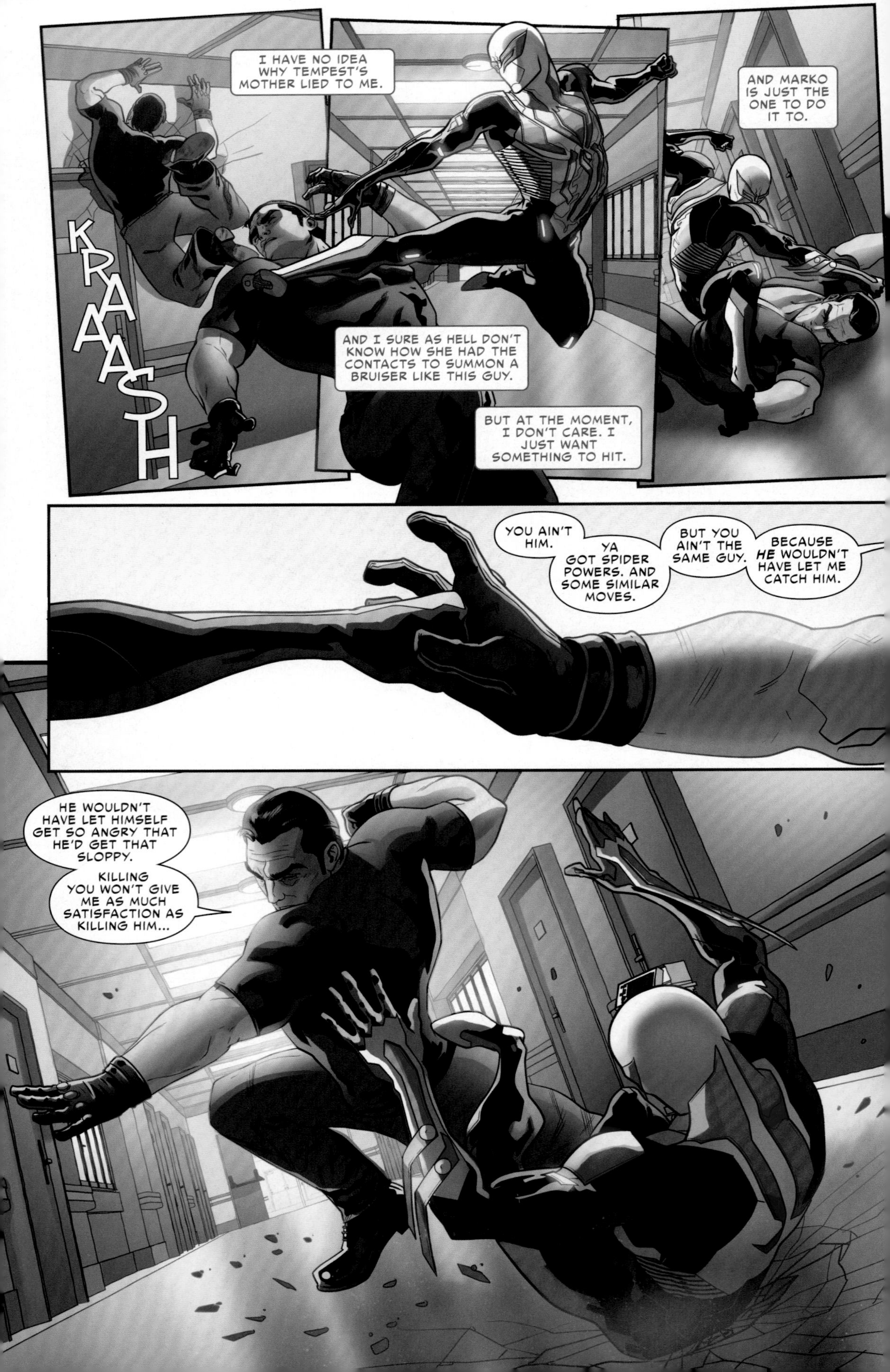
I HAVE NO IDEA WHY TEMPEST'S MOTHER LIED TO ME.
KRAAASH
AND I SURE AS HELL DON'T KNOW HOW SHE HAD THE CONTACTS TO SUMMON A BRUISER LIKE THIS GUY.
BUT AT THE MOMENT, I DON'T CARE. I JUST WANT SOMETHING TO HIT.
AND MARKO IS JUST THE ONE TO DO IT TO.
YOU AIN'T HIM.
YA GOT SPIDER POWERS. AND SOME SIMILAR MOVES.
BUT YOU AIN'T THE SAME GUY.
BECAUSE HE WOULDN'T HAVE LET ME CATCH HIM.
HE WOULDN'T HAVE LET HIMSELF GET SO ANGRY THAT HE'D GET THAT SLOPPY.
KILLING YOU WON'T GIVE ME AS MUCH SATISFACTION AS KILLING HIM...

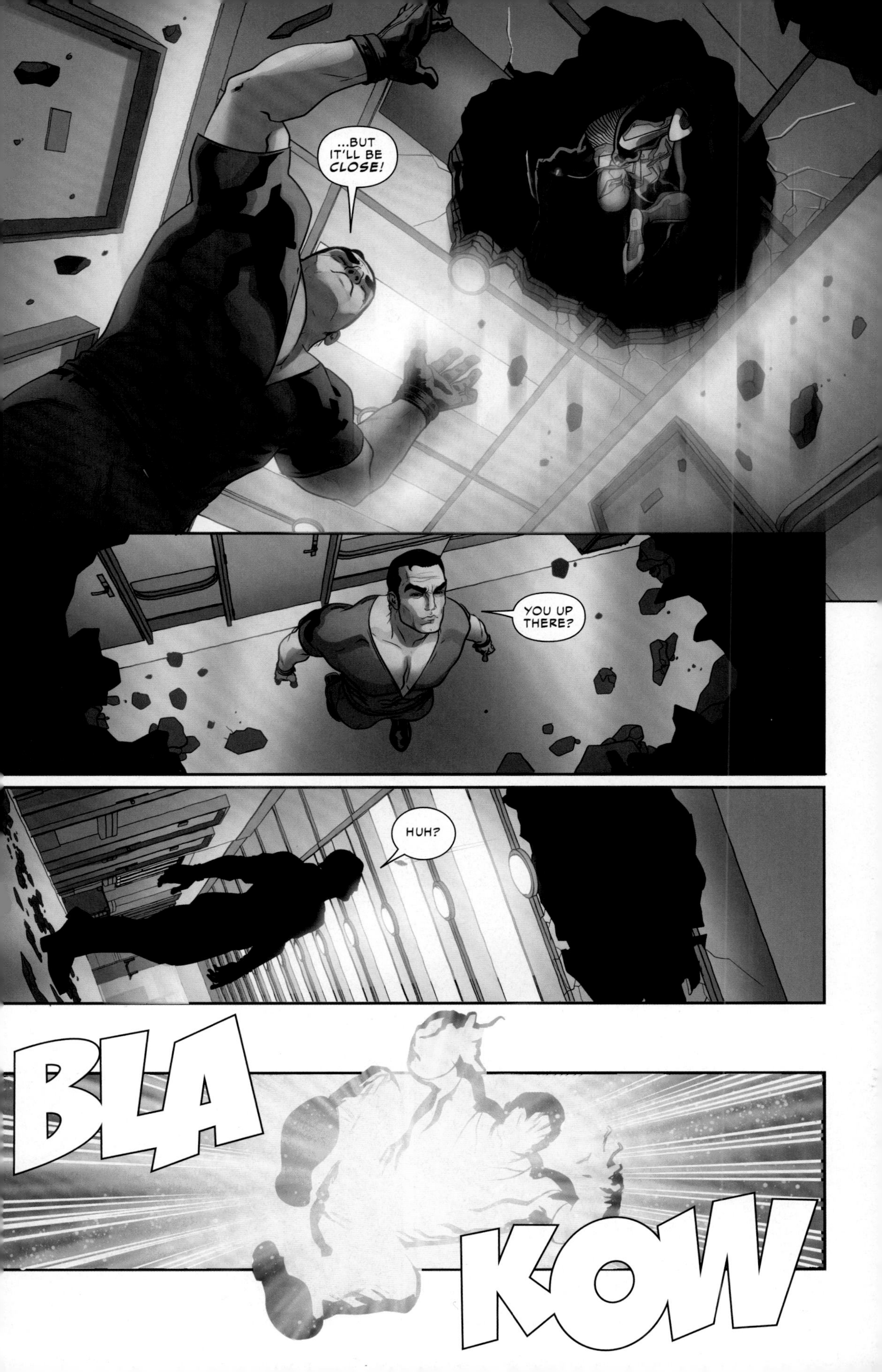
...BUT IT'LL BE CLOSE!
YOU UP THERE?
HUH?
BLA
KOW

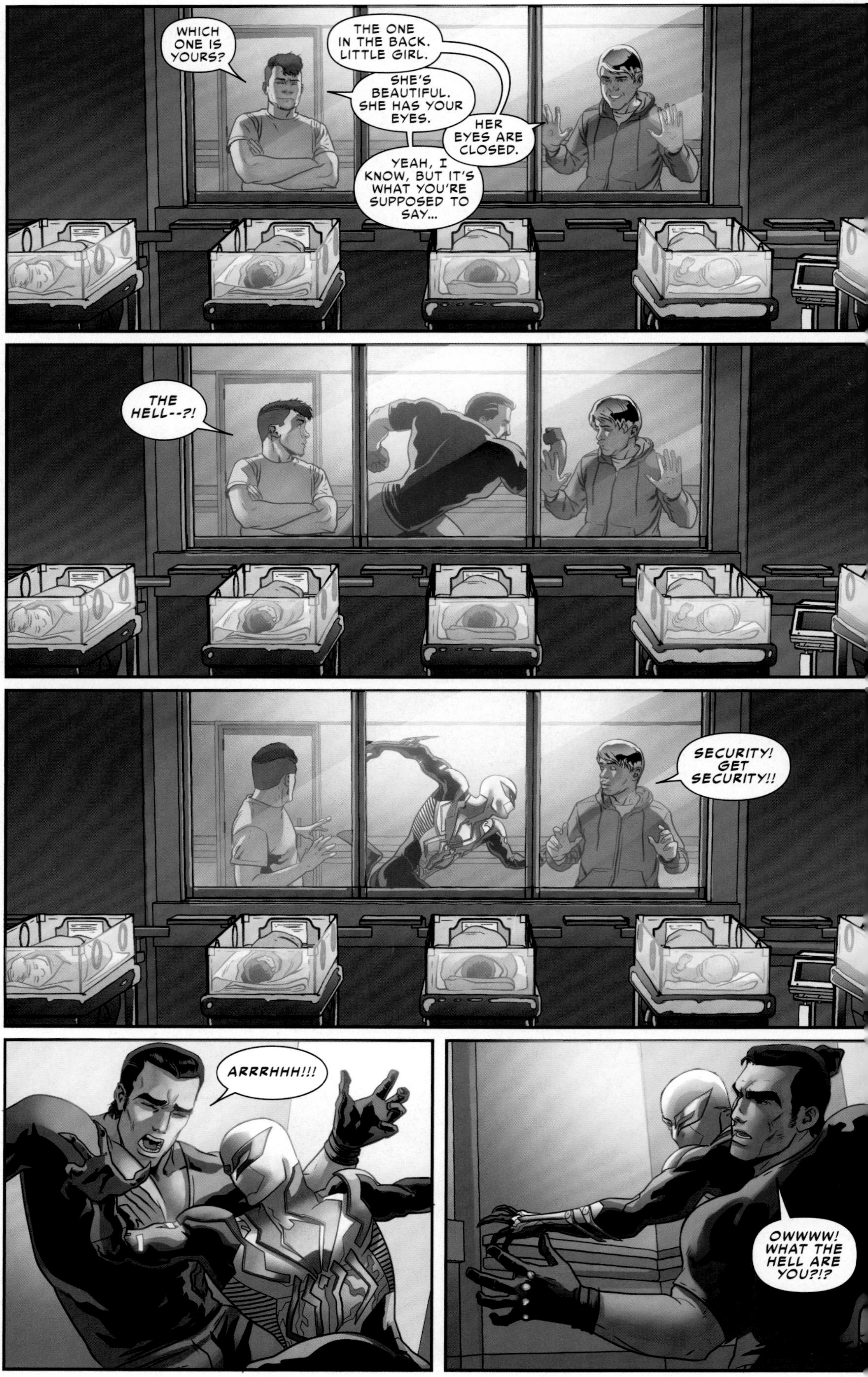

WHICH ONE IS YOURS?
THE ONE IN THE BACK. LITTLE GIRL.
SHE'S BEAUTIFUL. SHE HAS YOUR EYES.
HER EYES ARE CLOSED.
YEAH, I KNOW, BUT IT'S WHAT YOU'RE SUPPOSED TO SAY...
THE HELL--?!
SECURITY! GET SECURITY!!
ARRRHHH!!!
OWWWW! WHAT THE HELL ARE YOU?!?

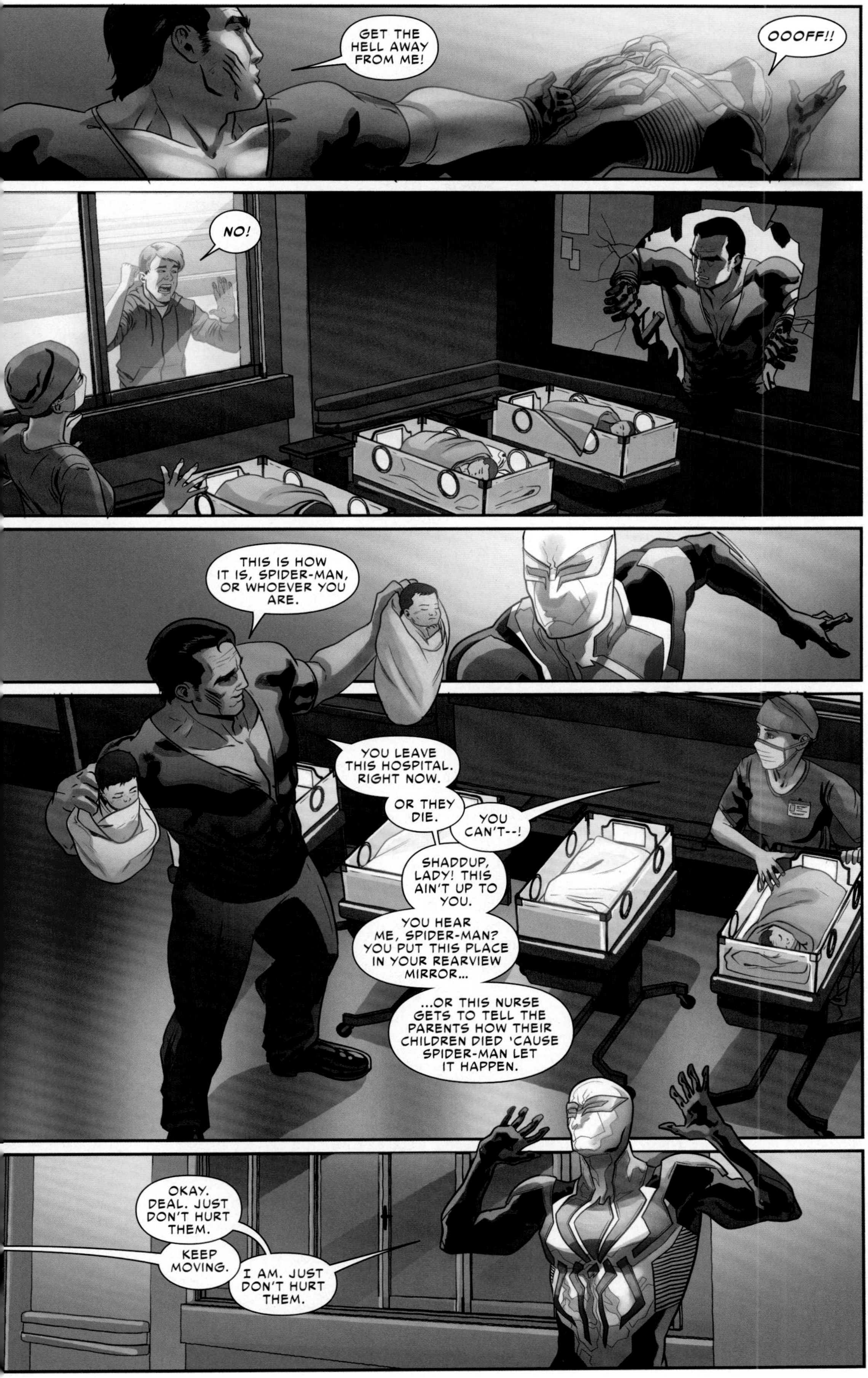
GET THE HELL AWAY FROM ME!
OOOFF!!
NO!
THIS IS HOW IT IS, SPIDER-MAN, OR WHOEVER YOU ARE.
YOU LEAVE THIS HOSPITAL. RIGHT NOW.
OR THEY DIE.
YOU CAN'T--!
SHADDUP, LADY! THIS AIN'T UP TO YOU.
YOU HEAR ME, SPIDER-MAN? YOU PUT THIS PLACE IN YOUR REARVIEW MIRROR...
...OR THIS NURSE GETS TO TELL THE PARENTS HOW THEIR CHILDREN DIED 'CAUSE SPIDER-MAN LET IT HAPPEN.
OKAY. DEAL. JUST DON'T HURT THEM.
KEEP MOVING.
I AM. JUST DON'T HURT THEM.

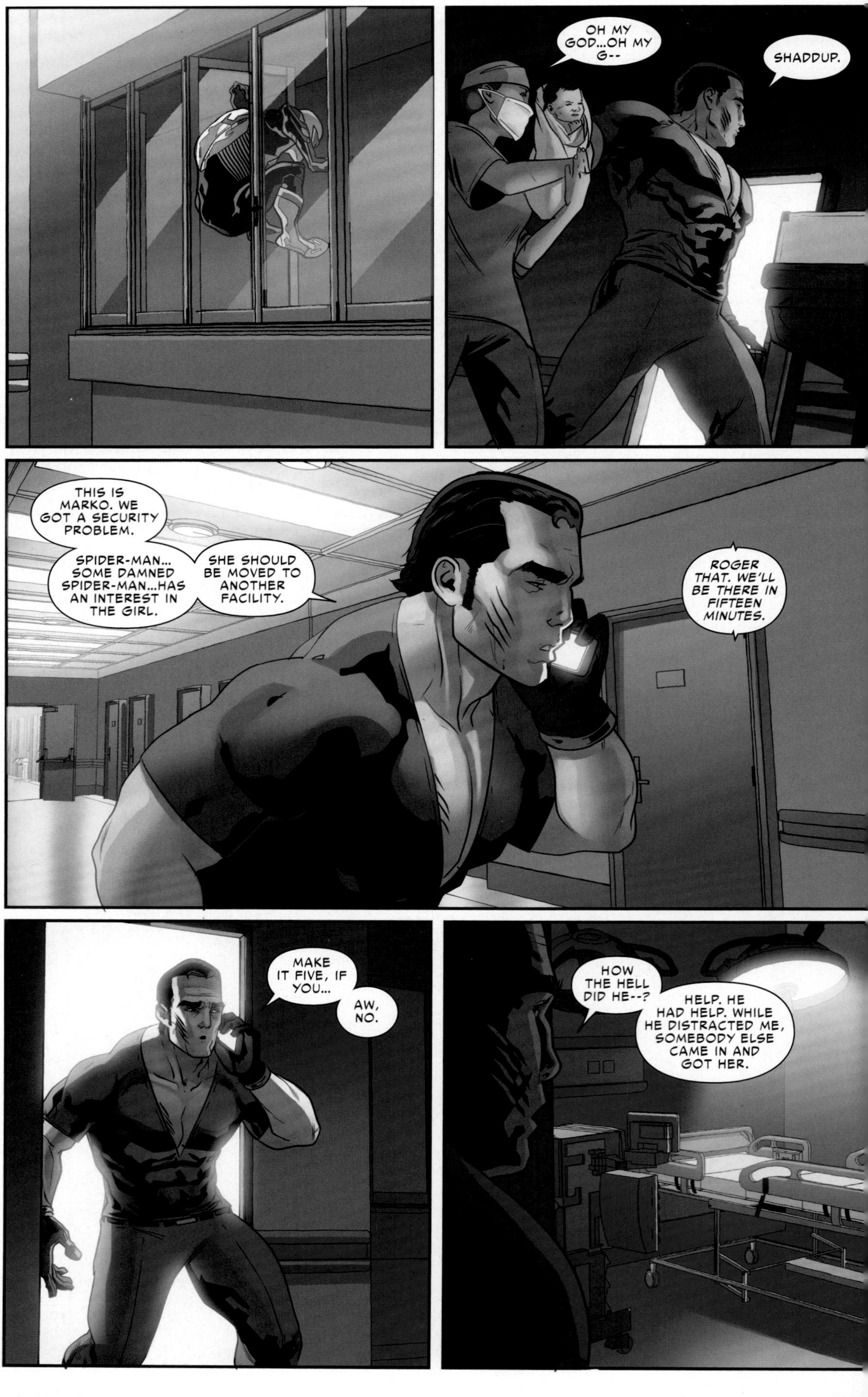
OH MY GOD...OH MY G--
SHADDUP.
THIS IS MARKO. WE GOT A SECURITY PROBLEM.
SPIDER-MAN... SOME DAMNED SPIDER-MAN...HAS AN INTEREST IN THE GIRL.
SHE SHOULD BE MOVED TO ANOTHER FACILITY.
ROGER THAT. WE'LL BE THERE IN FIFTEEN MINUTES.
MAKE IT FIVE, IF YOU...
AW, NO.
HOW THE HELL DID HE--?
HELP. HE HAD HELP. WHILE HE DISTRACTED ME, SOMEBODY ELSE CAME IN AND GOT HER.

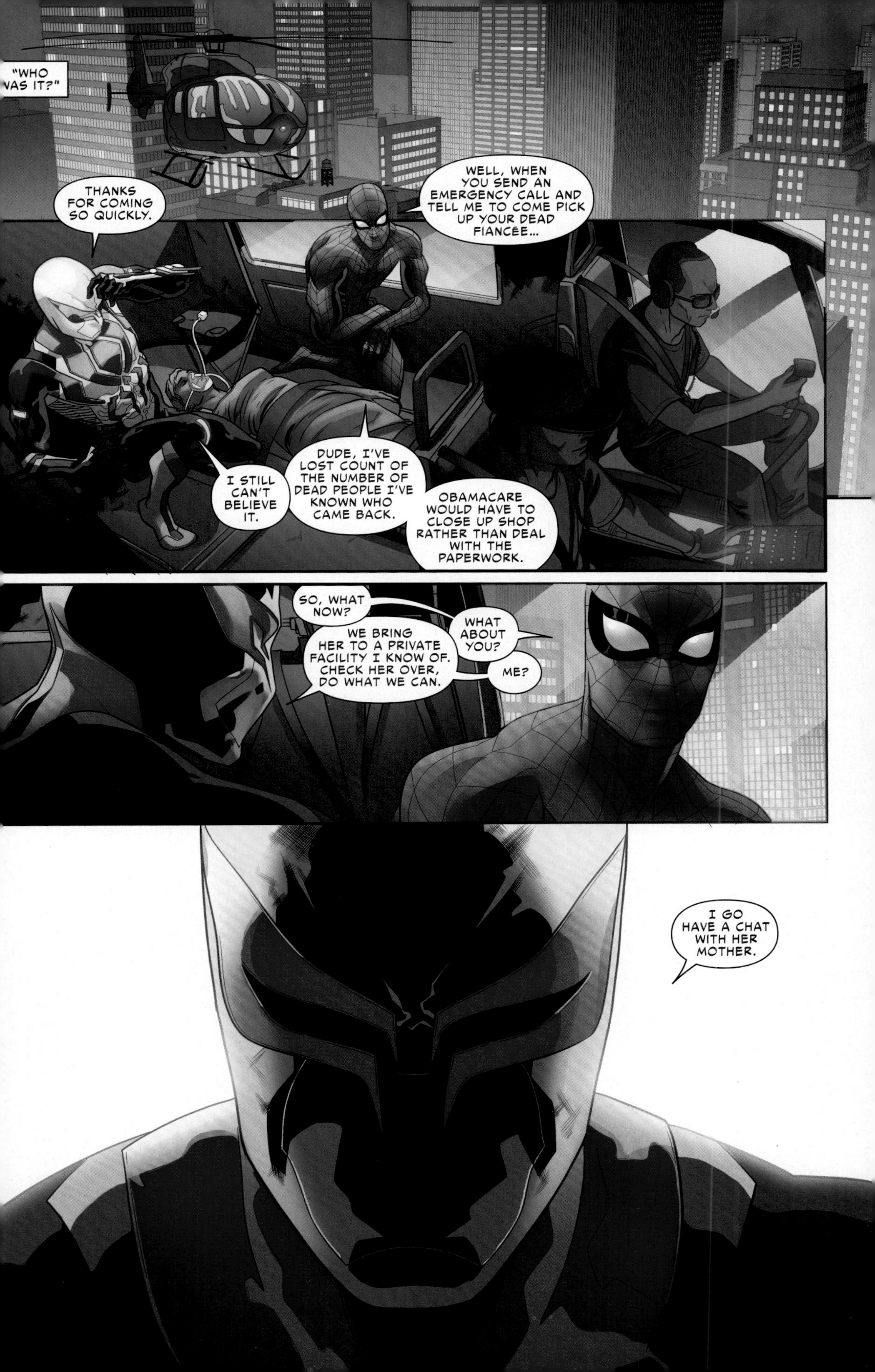
"WHO WAS IT?"
THANKS FOR COMING SO QUICKLY.
WELL, WHEN YOU SEND AN EMERGENCY CALL AND TELL ME TO COME PICK UP YOUR DEAD FIANCÉE...
I STILL CAN'T BELIEVE IT.
DUDE, I'VE LOST COUNT OF THE NUMBER OF DEAD PEOPLE I'VE KNOWN WHO CAME BACK.
OBAMACARE WOULD HAVE TO CLOSE UP SHOP RATHER THAN DEAL WITH THE PAPERWORK.
SO, WHAT NOW?
WE BRING HER TO A PRIVATE FACILITY I KNOW OF. CHECK HER OVER, DO WHAT WE CAN.
WHAT ABOUT YOU?
ME?
I GO HAVE A CHAT WITH HER MOTHER.

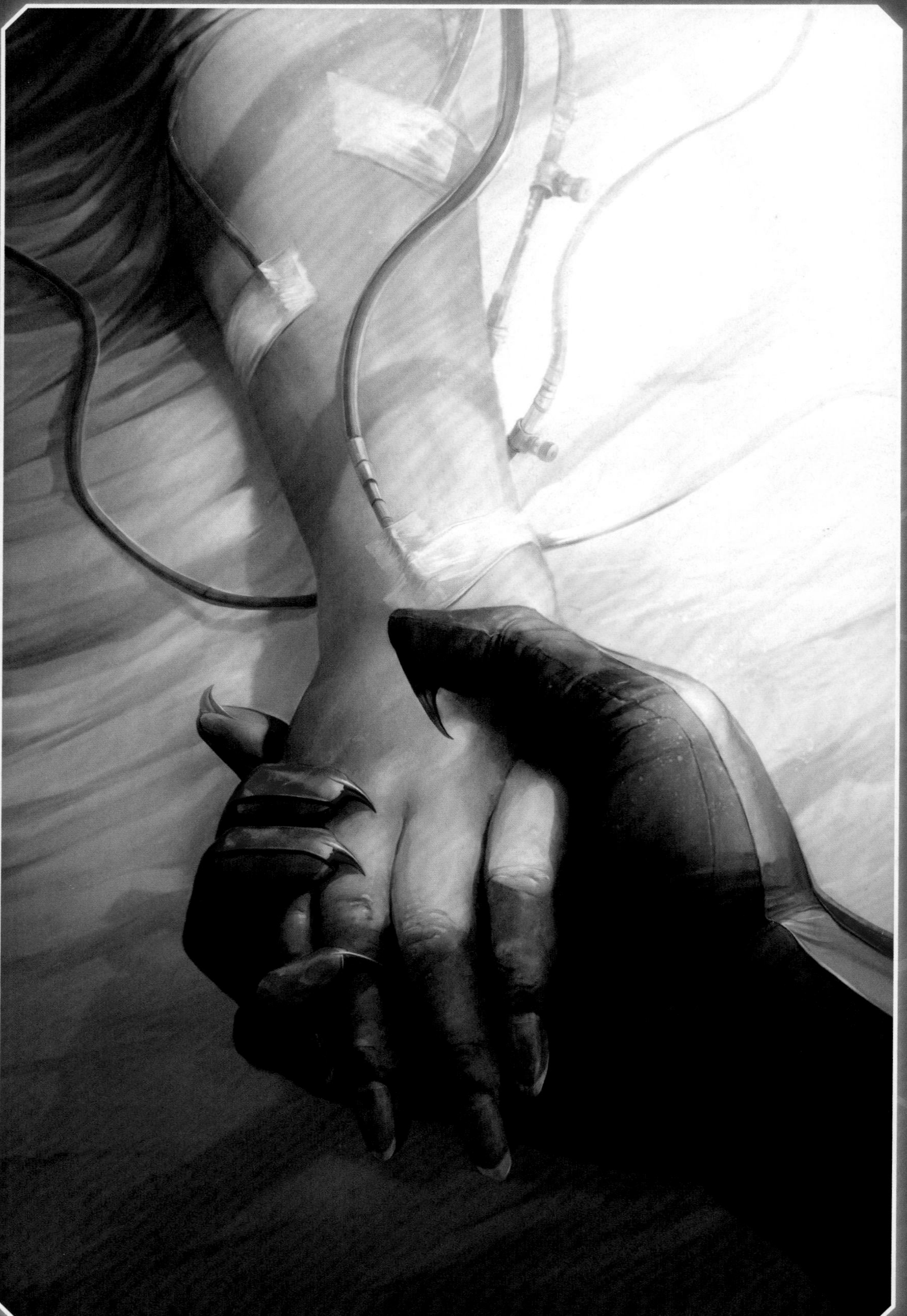

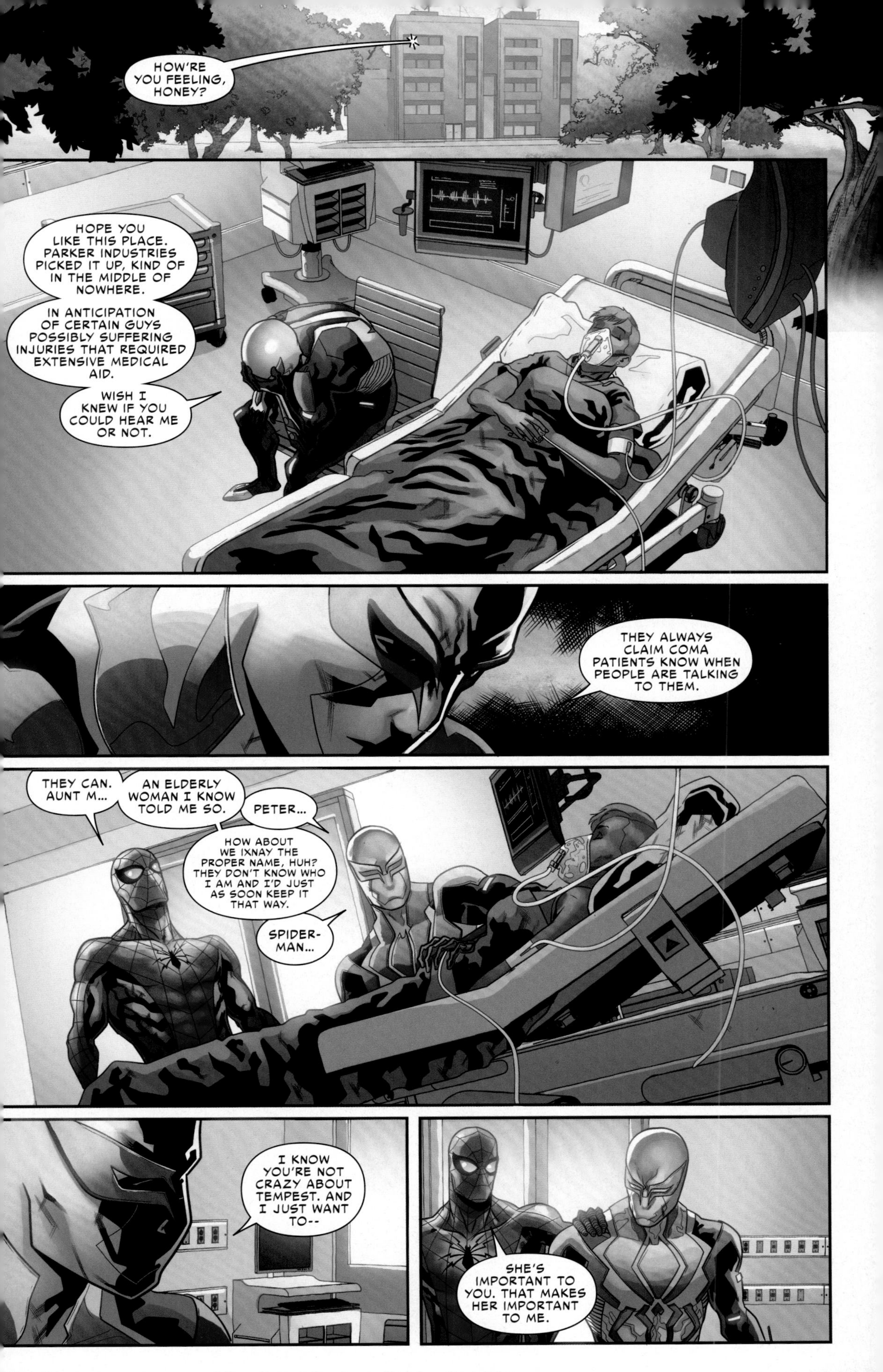

HOW'RE YOU FEELING, HONEY?
HOPE YOU LIKE THIS PLACE. PARKER INDUSTRIES PICKED IT UP, KIND OF IN THE MIDDLE OF NOWHERE.
IN ANTICIPATION OF CERTAIN GUYS POSSIBLY SUFFERING INJURIES THAT REQUIRED EXTENSIVE MEDICAL AID.
WISH I KNEW IF YOU COULD HEAR ME OR NOT.
THEY ALWAYS CLAIM COMA PATIENTS KNOW WHEN PEOPLE ARE TALKING TO THEM.
THEY CAN. AUNT M...
AN ELDERLY WOMAN I KNOW TOLD ME SO.
PETER...
HOW ABOUT WE IXNAY THE PROPER NAME, HUH? THEY DON'T KNOW WHO I AM AND I'D JUST AS SOON KEEP IT THAT WAY.
SPIDER-MAN...
I KNOW YOU'RE NOT CRAZY ABOUT TEMPEST. AND I JUST WANT TO--
SHE'S IMPORTANT TO YOU. THAT MAKES HER IMPORTANT TO ME.

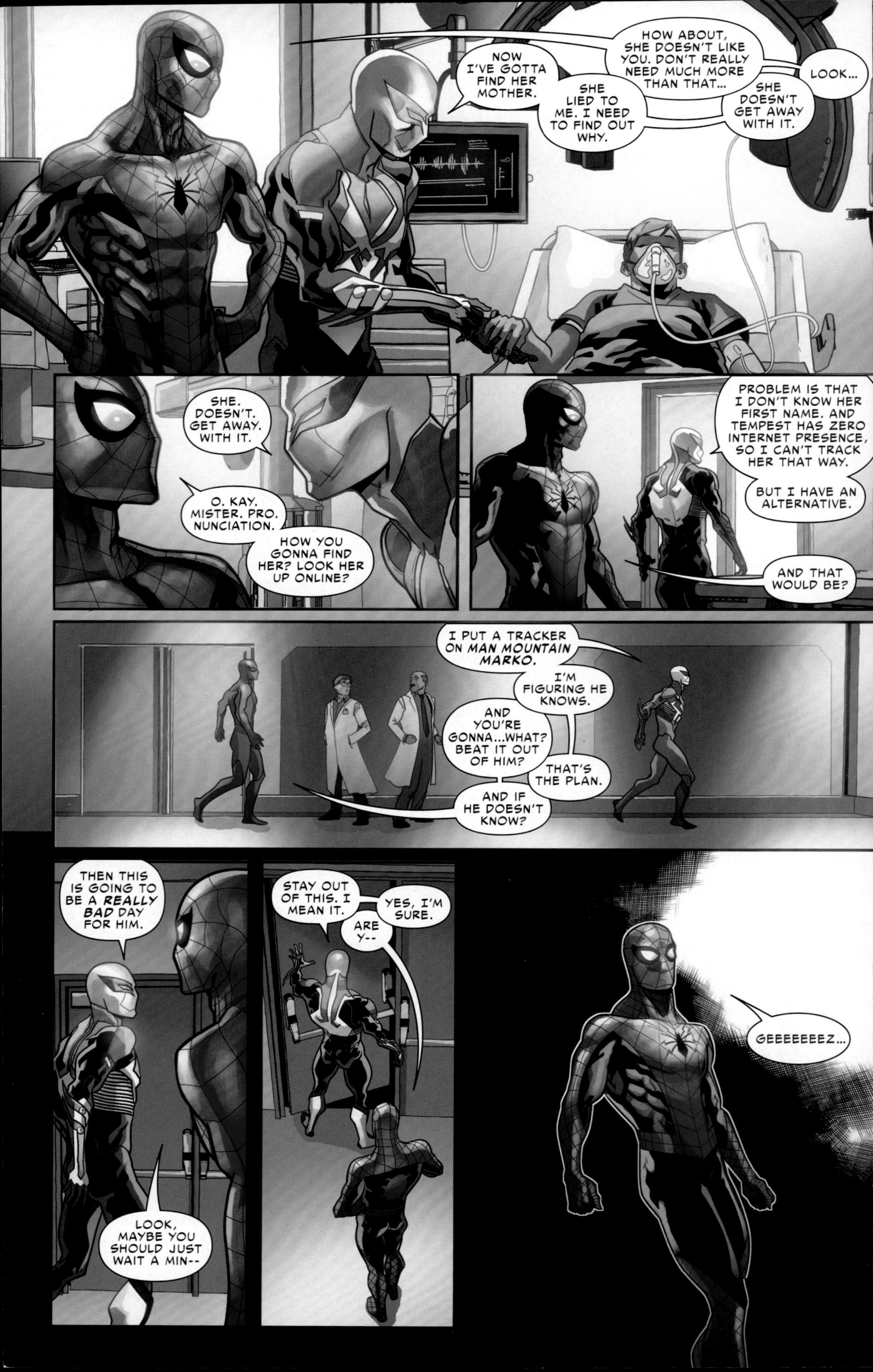
NOW I'VE GOTTA FIND HER MOTHER.
HOW ABOUT, SHE DOESN'T LIKE YOU. DON'T REALLY NEED MUCH MORE THAN THAT...
LOOK...
SHE LIED TO ME. I NEED TO FIND OUT WHY.
SHE DOESN'T GET AWAY WITH IT.
SHE. DOESN'T. GET AWAY. WITH IT.
O. KAY. MISTER. PRO. NUNCIATION.
HOW YOU GONNA FIND HER? LOOK HER UP ONLINE?
PROBLEM IS THAT I DON'T KNOW HER FIRST NAME. AND TEMPEST HAS ZERO INTERNET PRESENCE, SO I CAN'T TRACK HER THAT WAY.
BUT I HAVE AN ALTERNATIVE.
AND THAT WOULD BE?
I PUT A TRACKER ON *MAN MOUNTAIN MARKO.*
I'M FIGURING HE KNOWS.
AND YOU'RE GONNA...WHAT? BEAT IT OUT OF HIM?
THAT'S THE PLAN.
AND IF HE DOESN'T KNOW?
THEN THIS IS GOING TO BE A ***REALLY BAD*** DAY FOR HIM.
LOOK, MAYBE YOU SHOULD JUST WAIT A MIN--
STAY OUT OF THIS. I MEAN IT.
ARE Y--
YES, I'M SURE.
GEEEEEEEZ...

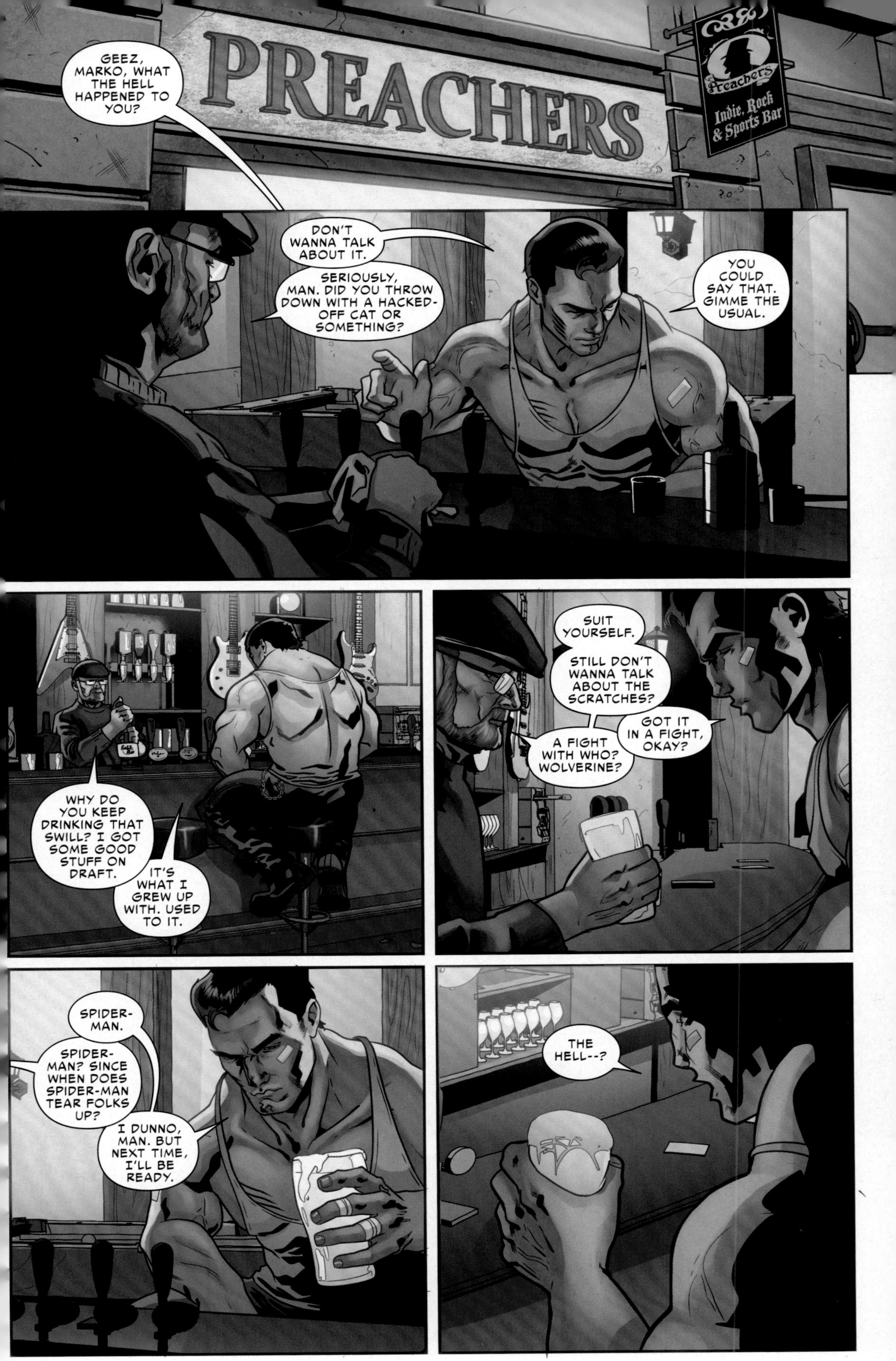
PREACHERS
Preachers
Indie, Rock & Sports Bar
GEEZ, MARKO, WHAT THE HELL HAPPENED TO YOU?
DON'T WANNA TALK ABOUT IT.
SERIOUSLY, MAN. DID YOU THROW DOWN WITH A HACKED-OFF CAT OR SOMETHING?
YOU COULD SAY THAT. GIMME THE USUAL.
WHY DO YOU KEEP DRINKING THAT SWILL? I GOT SOME GOOD STUFF ON DRAFT.
IT'S WHAT I GREW UP WITH. USED TO IT.
SUIT YOURSELF.
STILL DON'T WANNA TALK ABOUT THE SCRATCHES?
GOT IT IN A FIGHT, OKAY?
A FIGHT WITH WHO? WOLVERINE?
SPIDER-MAN.
SPIDER-MAN? SINCE WHEN DOES SPIDER-MAN TEAR FOLKS UP?
I DUNNO, MAN. BUT NEXT TIME, I'LL BE READY.
THE HELL--?

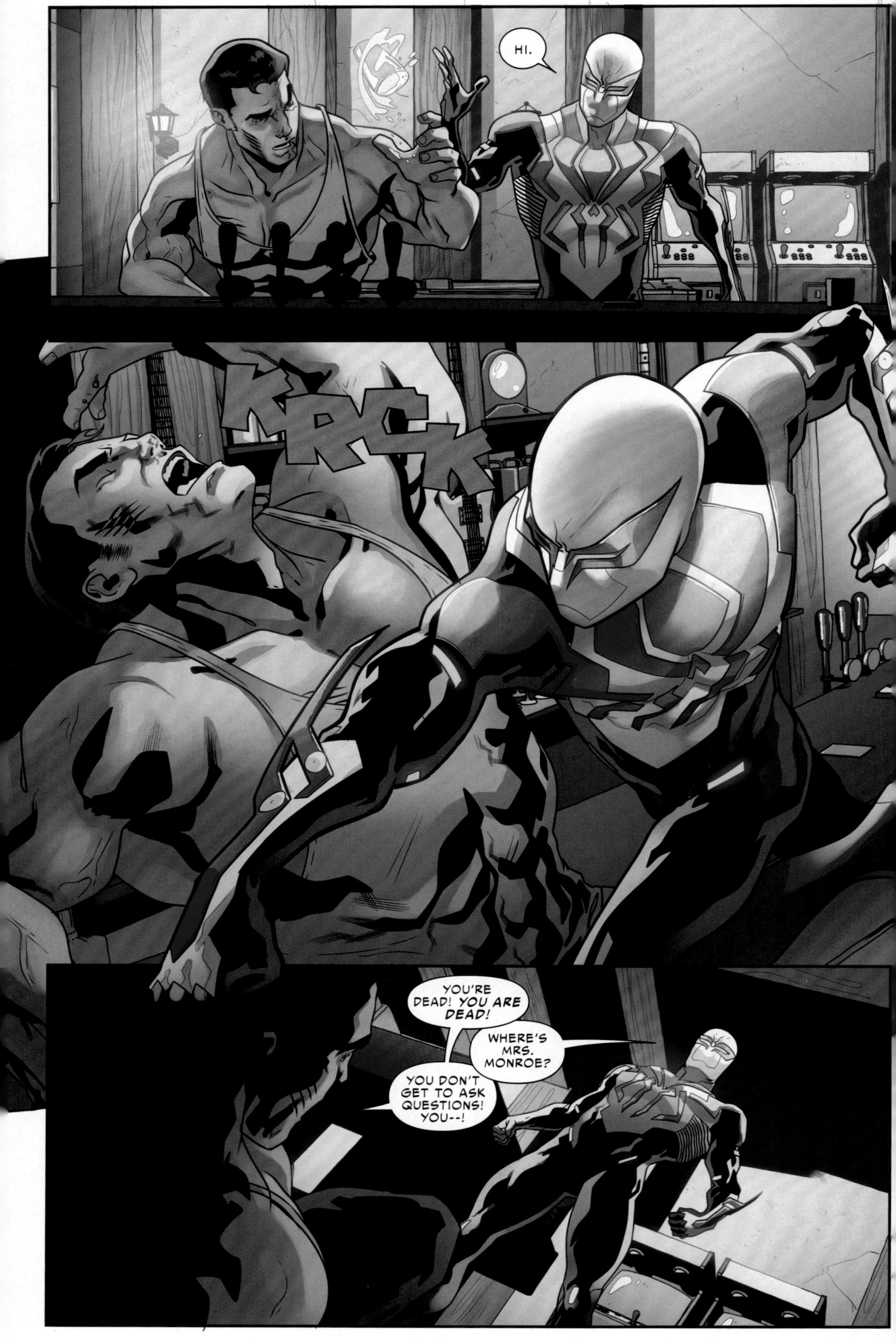
HI.
KRCK
YOU'RE DEAD! YOU ARE DEAD!
WHERE'S MRS. MONROE?
YOU DON'T GET TO ASK QUESTIONS! YOU--!

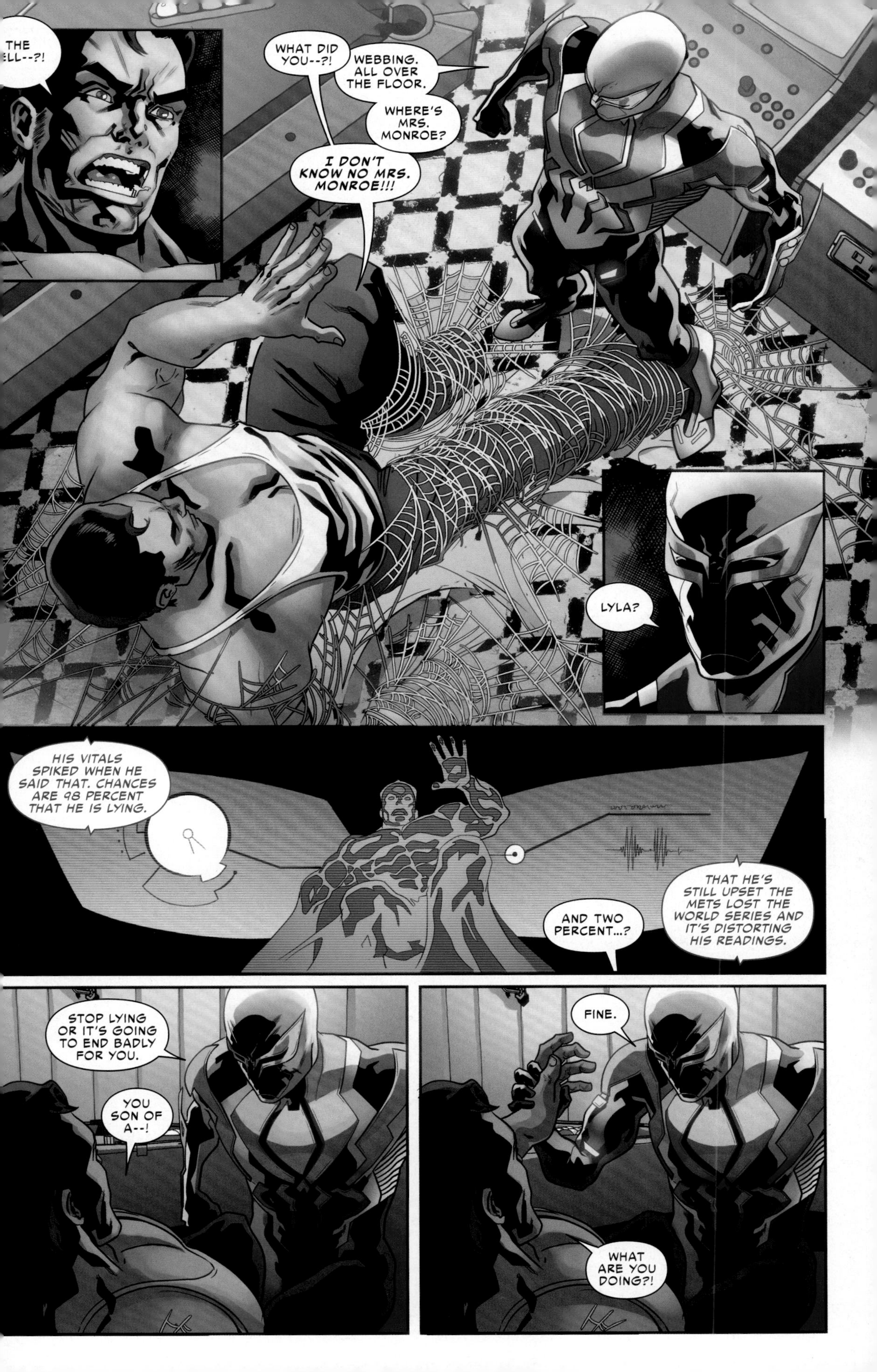
THE
...ELL--?!
WHAT DID YOU--?!
WEBBING. ALL OVER THE FLOOR.
WHERE'S MRS. MONROE?
I DON'T KNOW NO MRS. MONROE!!!
LYLA?
HIS VITALS SPIKED WHEN HE SAID THAT. CHANCES ARE 98 PERCENT THAT HE IS LYING.
AND TWO PERCENT...?
THAT HE'S STILL UPSET THE METS LOST THE WORLD SERIES AND IT'S DISTORTING HIS READINGS.
STOP LYING OR IT'S GOING TO END BADLY FOR YOU.
YOU SON OF A--!
FINE.
WHAT ARE YOU DOING?!

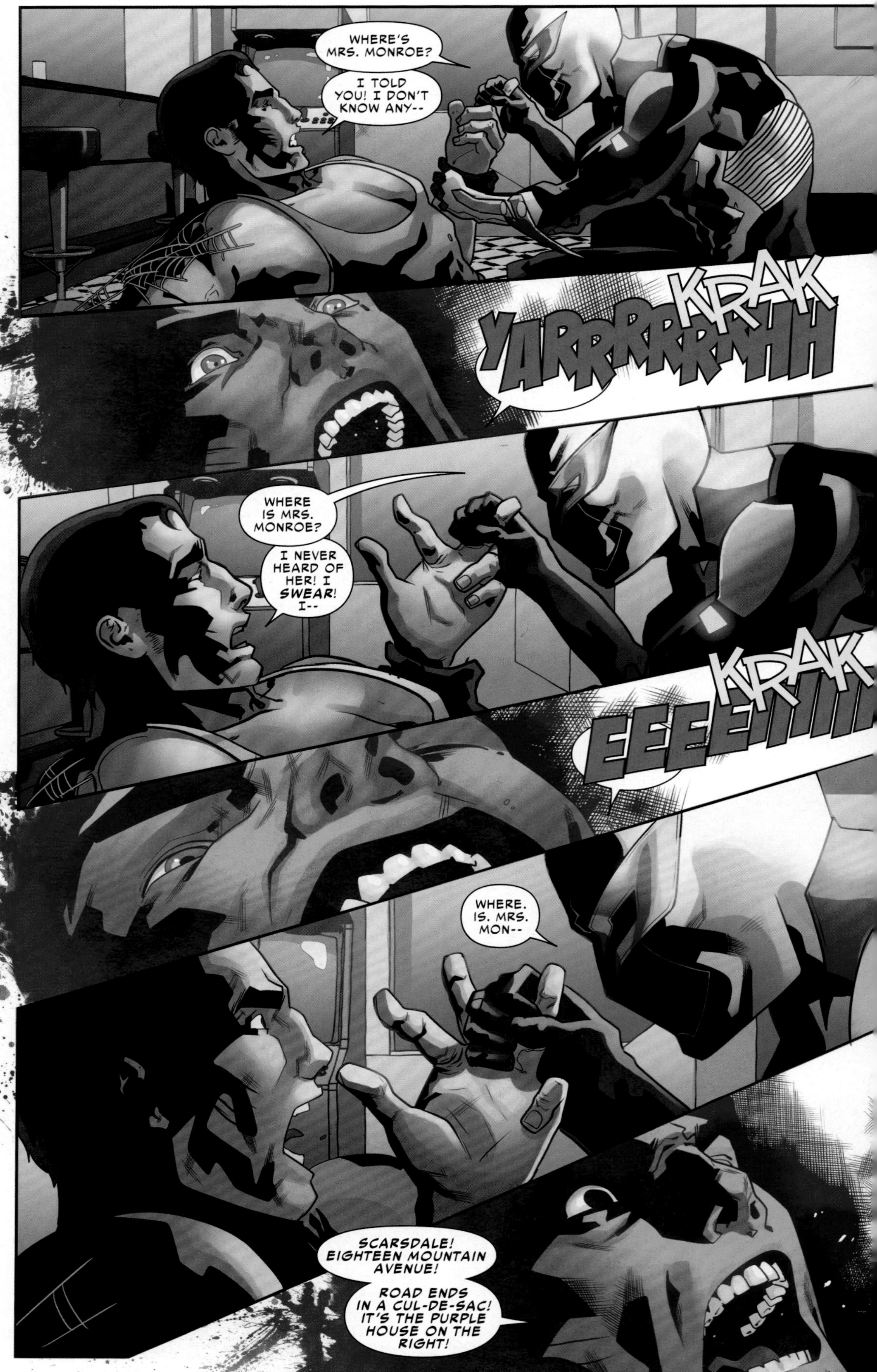
WHERE'S MRS. MONROE?
I TOLD YOU! I DON'T KNOW ANY--
KRAK
YARRRRRRRHH
WHERE IS MRS. MONROE?
I NEVER HEARD OF HER! I SWEAR! I--
KRAK
EEEEIIIIII
WHERE. IS. MRS. MON--
SCARSDALE! EIGHTEEN MOUNTAIN AVENUE!
ROAD ENDS IN A CUL-DE-SAC! IT'S THE PURPLE HOUSE ON THE RIGHT!

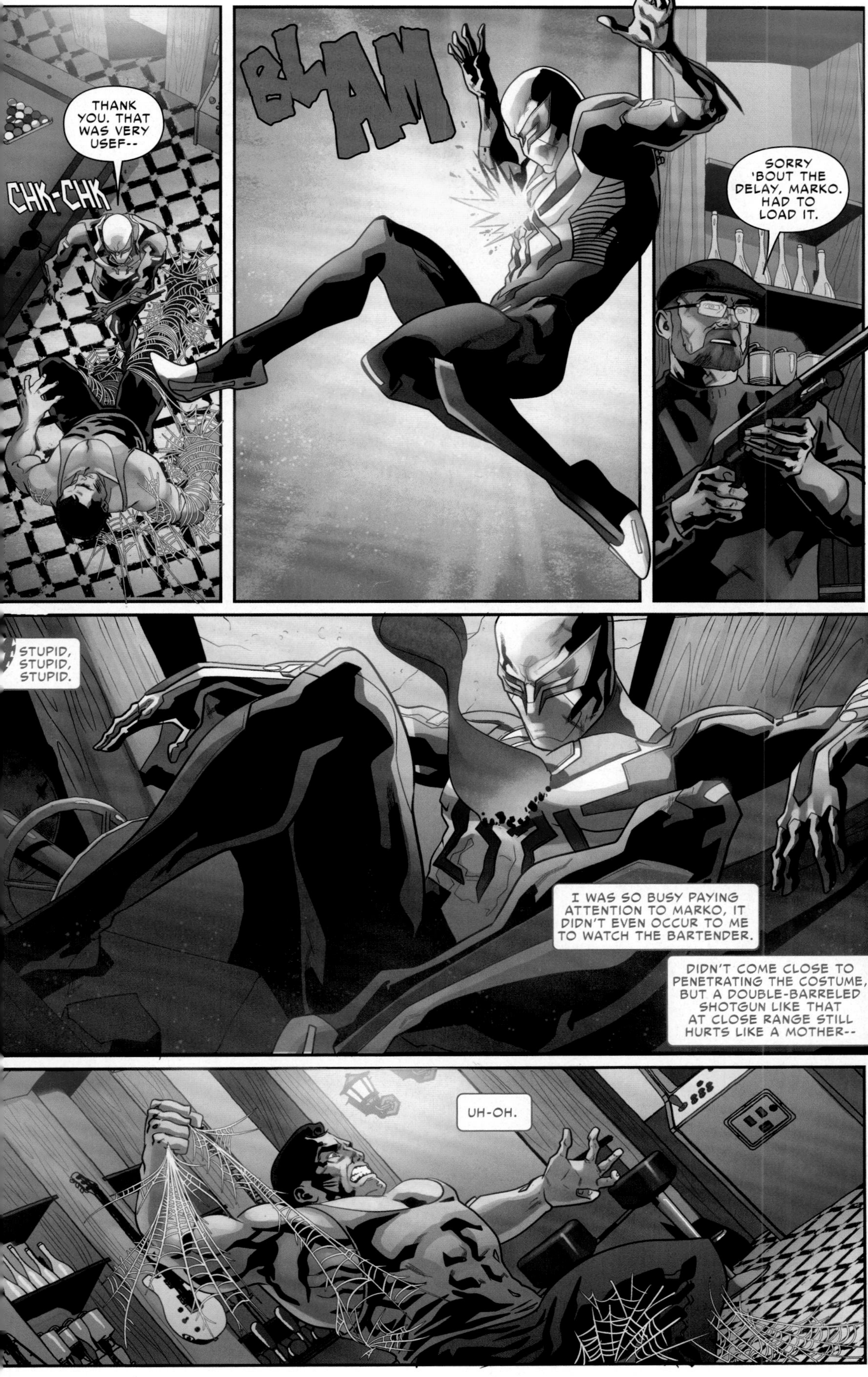
THANK YOU. THAT WAS VERY USEF--
CHK-CHK
BLAM
SORRY 'BOUT THE DELAY, MARKO. HAD TO LOAD IT.
STUPID, STUPID, STUPID.
I WAS SO BUSY PAYING ATTENTION TO MARKO, IT DIDN'T EVEN OCCUR TO ME TO WATCH THE BARTENDER.
DIDN'T COME CLOSE TO PENETRATING THE COSTUME, BUT A DOUBLE-BARRELED SHOTGUN LIKE THAT AT CLOSE RANGE STILL HURTS LIKE A MOTHER--
UH-OH.

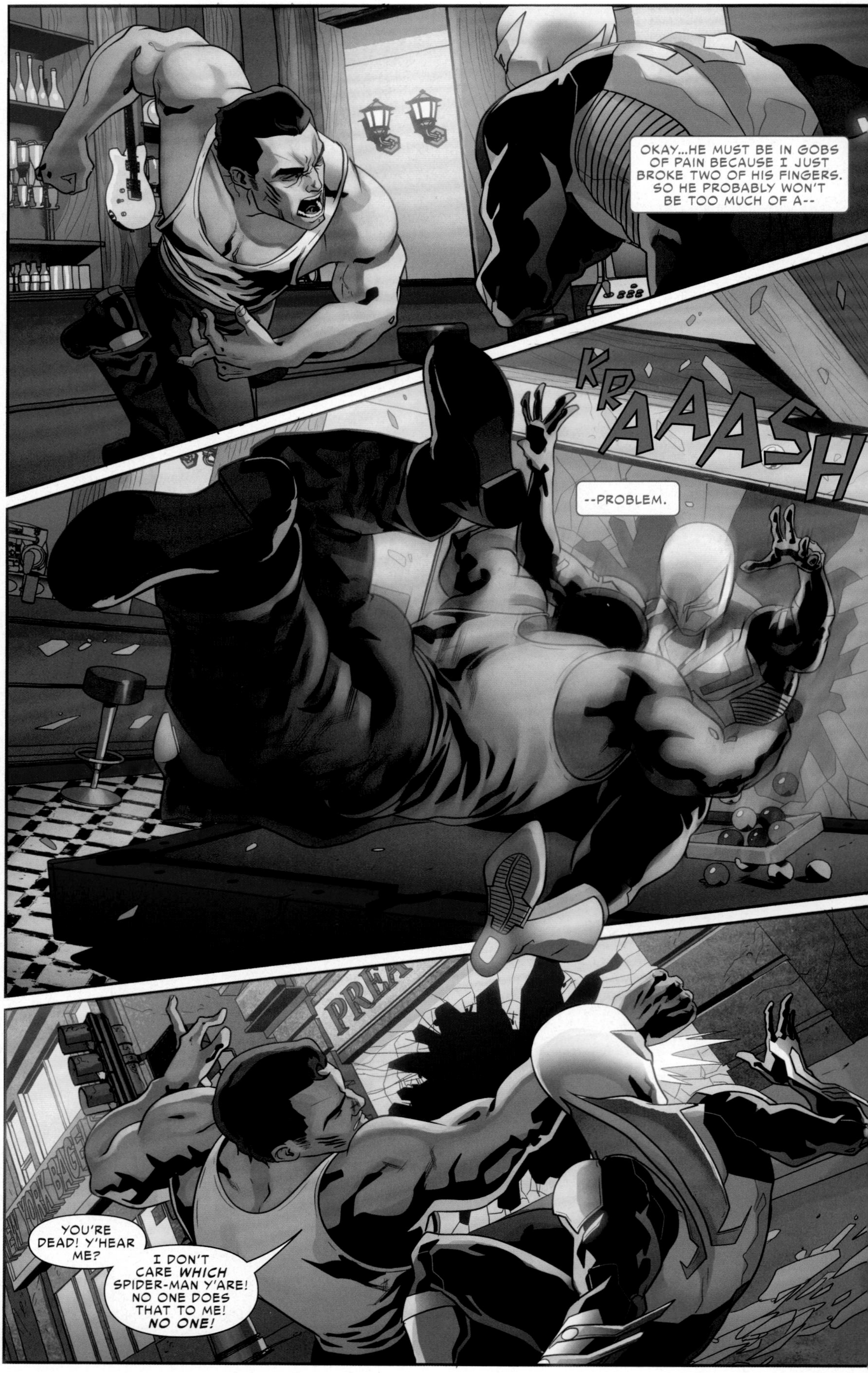

OKAY...HE MUST BE IN GOBS OF PAIN BECAUSE I JUST BROKE TWO OF HIS FINGERS. SO HE PROBABLY WON'T BE TOO MUCH OF A--
KRAAAASH
--PROBLEM.
PREA
NEW YORK BAGEL
YOU'RE DEAD! Y'HEAR ME?
I DON'T CARE WHICH SPIDER-MAN Y'ARE! NO ONE DOES THAT TO ME! NO ONE!

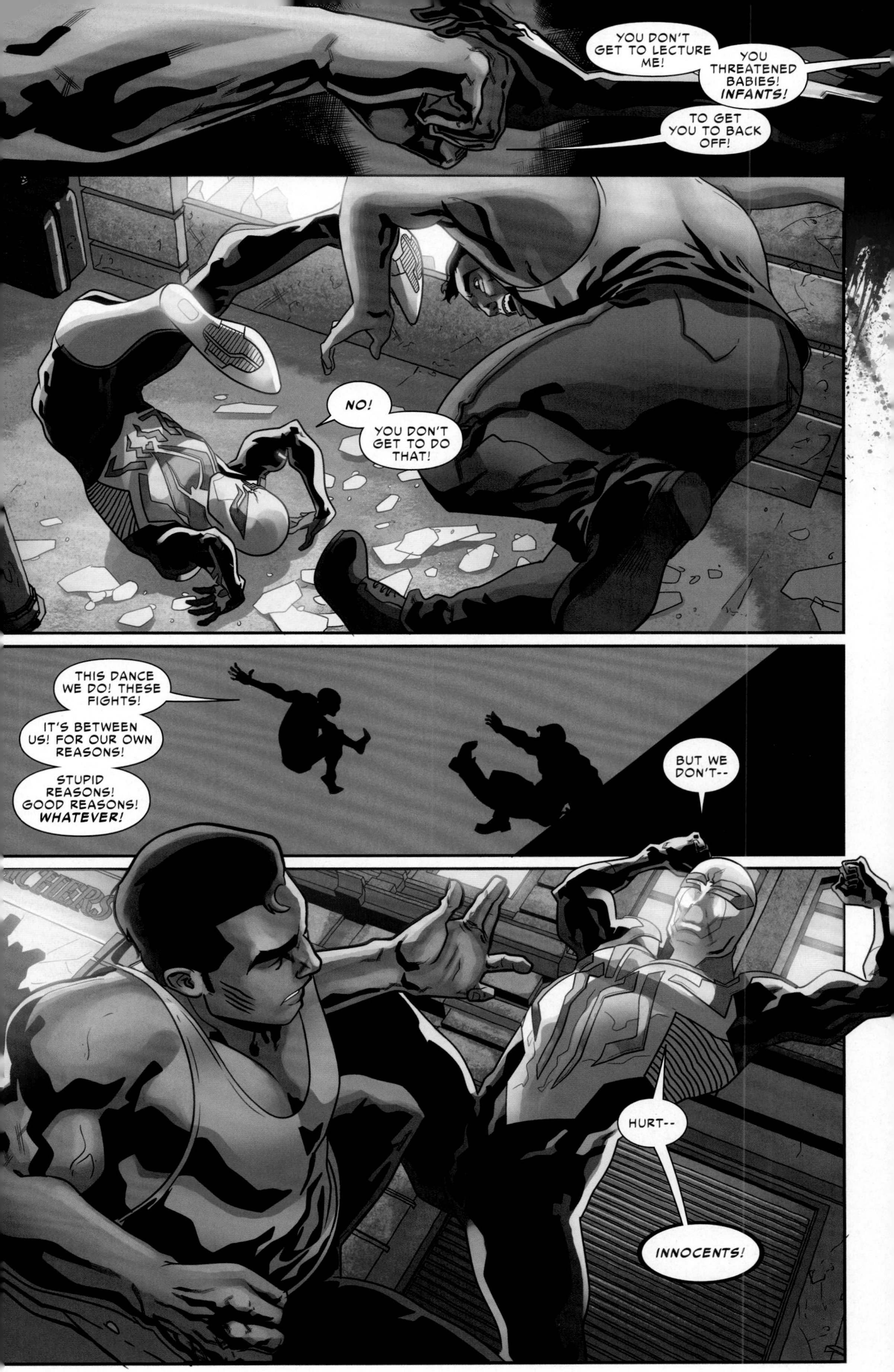

YOU DON'T GET TO LECTURE ME!
YOU THREATENED BABIES! INFANTS!
TO GET YOU TO BACK OFF!
NO!
YOU DON'T GET TO DO THAT!
THIS DANCE WE DO! THESE FIGHTS!
IT'S BETWEEN US! FOR OUR OWN REASONS!
STUPID REASONS! GOOD REASONS! WHATEVER!
BUT WE DON'T--
HURT--
INNOCENTS!

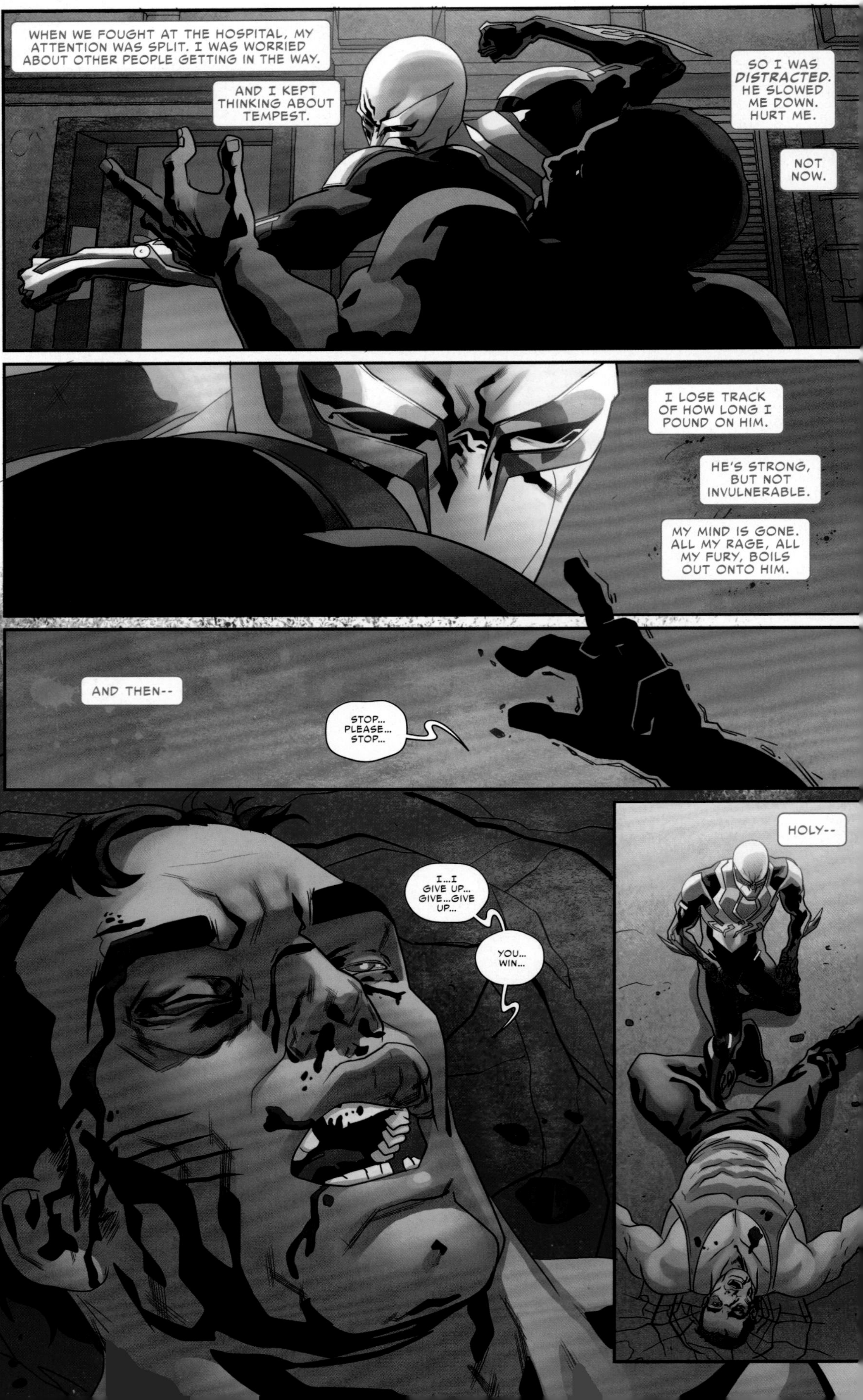
WHEN WE FOUGHT AT THE HOSPITAL, MY ATTENTION WAS SPLIT. I WAS WORRIED ABOUT OTHER PEOPLE GETTING IN THE WAY.
AND I KEPT THINKING ABOUT TEMPEST.
SO I WAS DISTRACTED. HE SLOWED ME DOWN. HURT ME.
NOT NOW.
I LOSE TRACK OF HOW LONG I POUND ON HIM.
HE'S STRONG, BUT NOT INVULNERABLE.
MY MIND IS GONE. ALL MY RAGE, ALL MY FURY, BOILS OUT ONTO HIM.
AND THEN--
STOP... PLEASE... STOP...
I...I GIVE UP... GIVE...GIVE UP...
YOU... WIN...
HOLY--

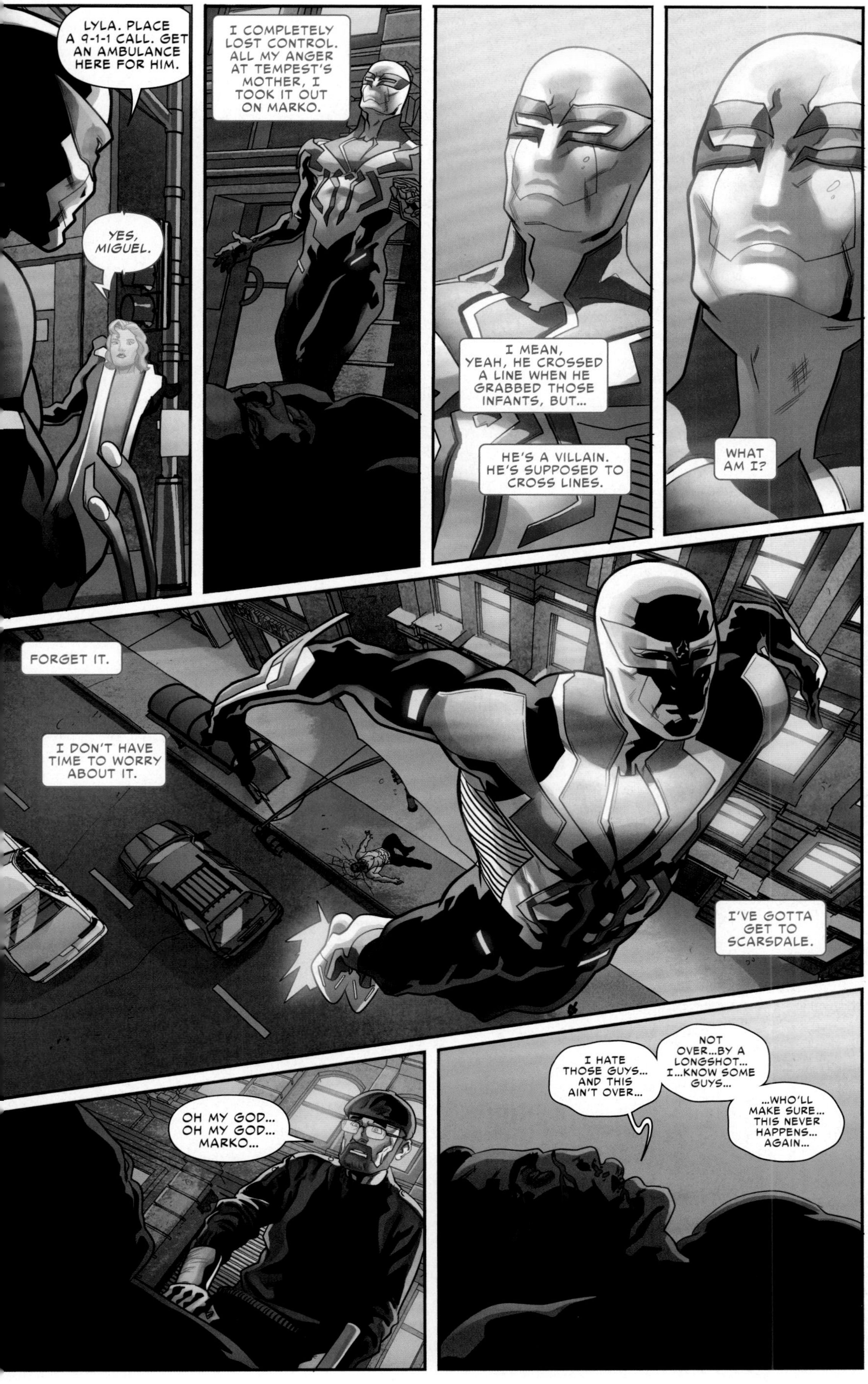
LYLA. PLACE A 9-1-1 CALL. GET AN AMBULANCE HERE FOR HIM.
YES, MIGUEL.
I COMPLETELY LOST CONTROL. ALL MY ANGER AT TEMPEST'S MOTHER, I TOOK IT OUT ON MARKO.
I MEAN, YEAH, HE CROSSED A LINE WHEN HE GRABBED THOSE INFANTS, BUT...
HE'S A VILLAIN. HE'S SUPPOSED TO CROSS LINES.
WHAT AM I?
FORGET IT.
I DON'T HAVE TIME TO WORRY ABOUT IT.
I'VE GOTTA GET TO SCARSDALE.
OH MY GOD... OH MY GOD... MARKO...
I HATE THOSE GUYS... AND THIS AIN'T OVER...
NOT OVER...BY A LONGSHOT... I...KNOW SOME GUYS...
...WHO'LL MAKE SURE... THIS NEVER HAPPENS... AGAIN...

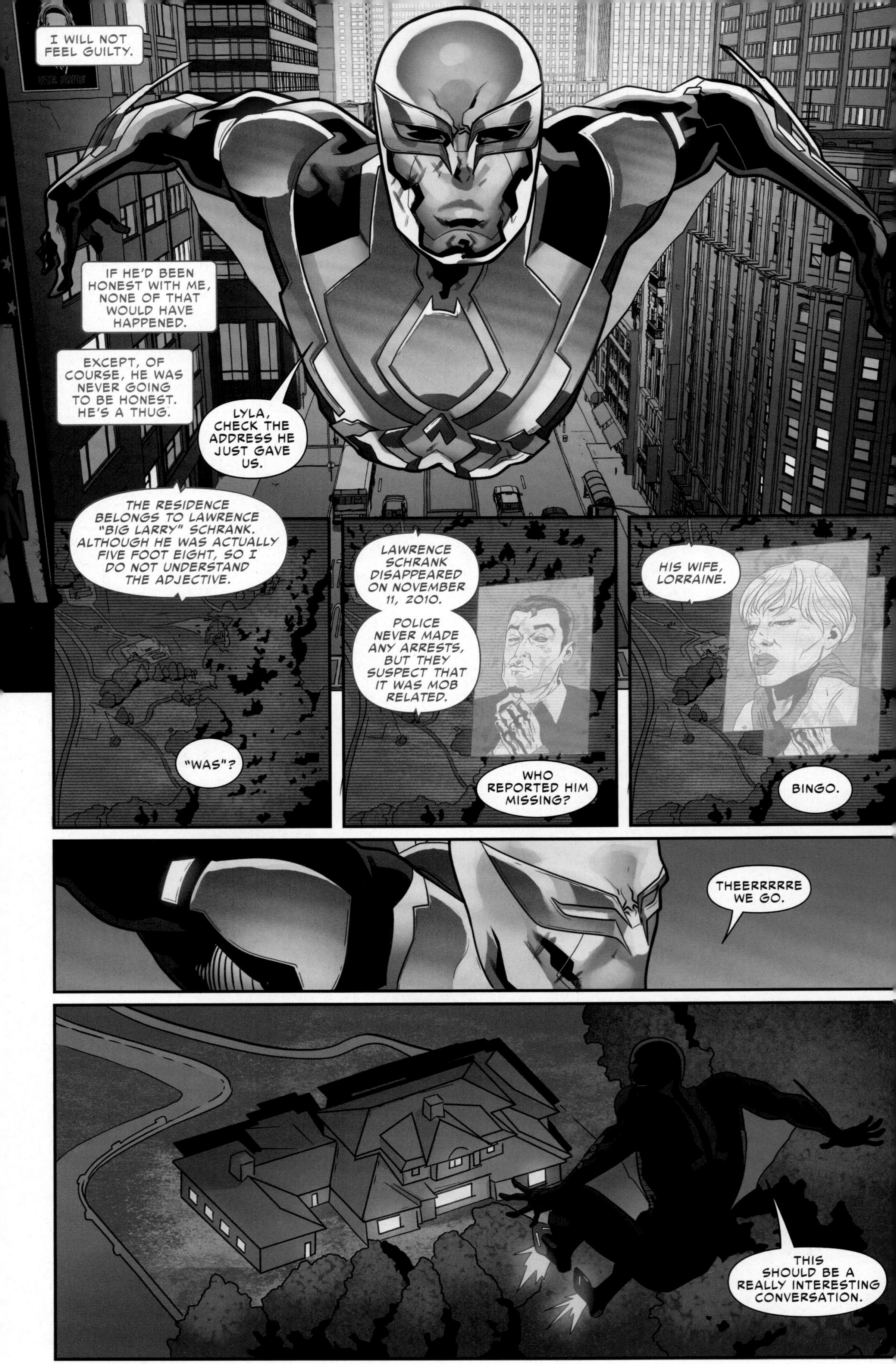
I WILL NOT FEEL GUILTY.
IF HE'D BEEN HONEST WITH ME, NONE OF THAT WOULD HAVE HAPPENED.
EXCEPT, OF COURSE, HE WAS NEVER GOING TO BE HONEST. HE'S A THUG.
LYLA, CHECK THE ADDRESS HE JUST GAVE US.
THE RESIDENCE BELONGS TO LAWRENCE "BIG LARRY" SCHRANK. ALTHOUGH HE WAS ACTUALLY FIVE FOOT EIGHT, SO I DO NOT UNDERSTAND THE ADJECTIVE.
"WAS"?
LAWRENCE SCHRANK DISAPPEARED ON NOVEMBER 11, 2010.
POLICE NEVER MADE ANY ARRESTS, BUT THEY SUSPECT THAT IT WAS MOB RELATED.
WHO REPORTED HIM MISSING?
HIS WIFE, LORRAINE.
BINGO.
THEERRRRRE WE GO.
THIS SHOULD BE A REALLY INTERESTING CONVERSATION.

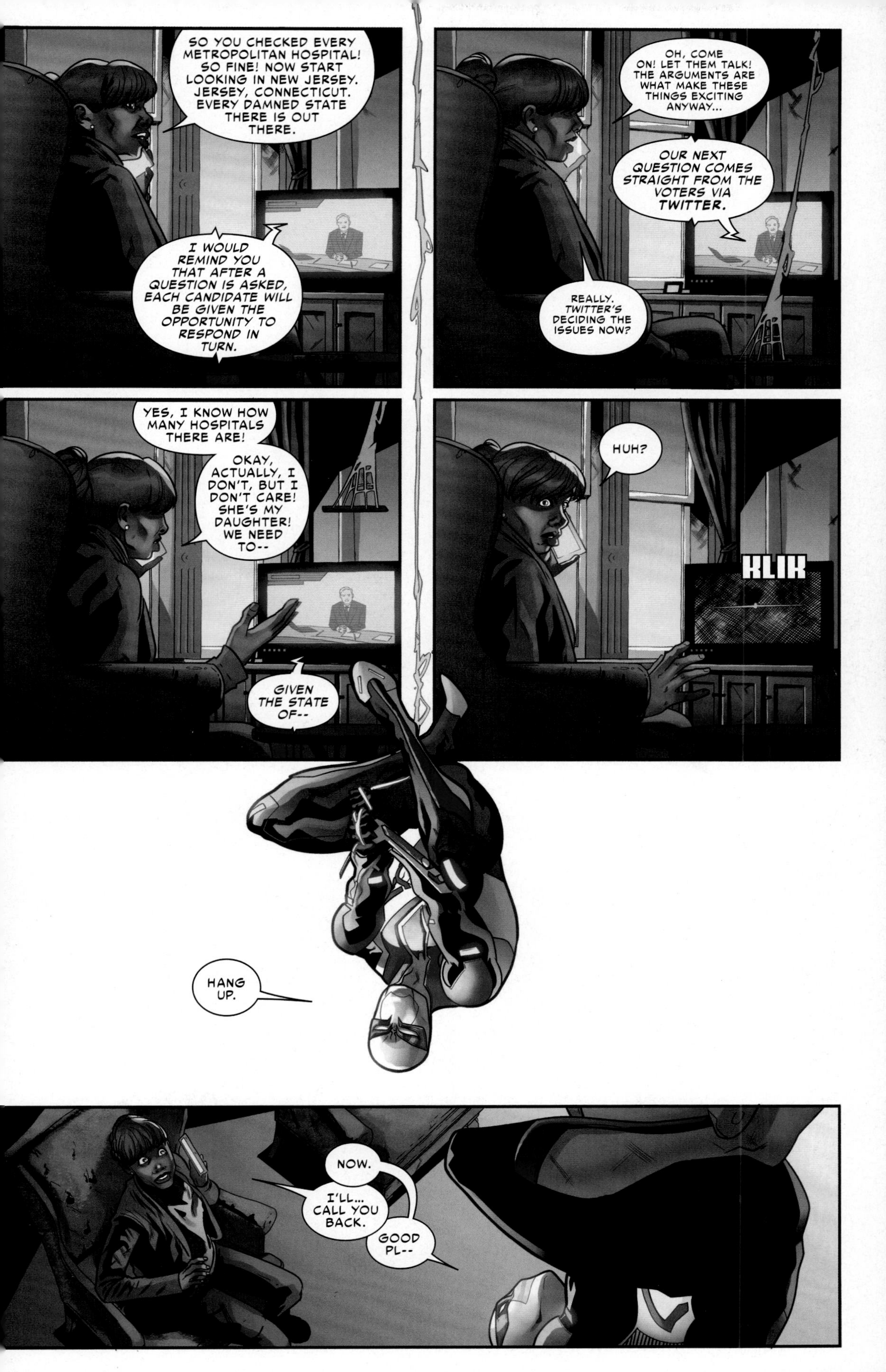
SO YOU CHECKED EVERY METROPOLITAN HOSPITAL! SO FINE! NOW START LOOKING IN NEW JERSEY. JERSEY, CONNECTICUT. EVERY DAMNED STATE THERE IS OUT THERE.
I WOULD REMIND YOU THAT AFTER A QUESTION IS ASKED, EACH CANDIDATE WILL BE GIVEN THE OPPORTUNITY TO RESPOND IN TURN.
OH, COME ON! LET THEM TALK! THE ARGUMENTS ARE WHAT MAKE THESE THINGS EXCITING ANYWAY...
OUR NEXT QUESTION COMES STRAIGHT FROM THE VOTERS VIA TWITTER.
REALLY. TWITTER'S DECIDING THE ISSUES NOW?
YES, I KNOW HOW MANY HOSPITALS THERE ARE!
OKAY, ACTUALLY, I DON'T, BUT I DON'T CARE! SHE'S MY DAUGHTER! WE NEED TO--
GIVEN THE STATE OF--
HUH?
KLIK
HANG UP.
NOW.
I'LL... CALL YOU BACK.
GOOD PL--

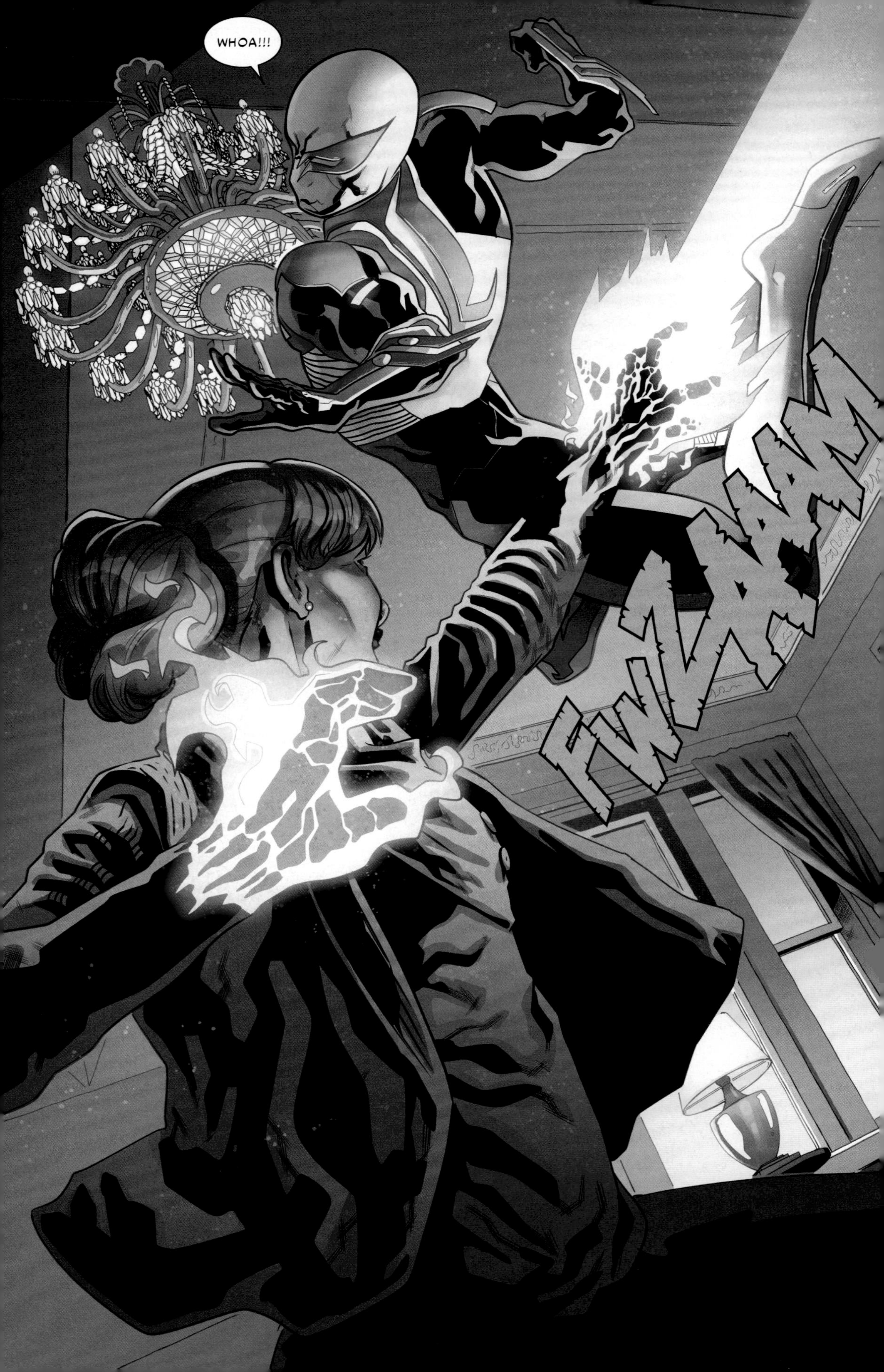
WHOA!!!
FWZAAM

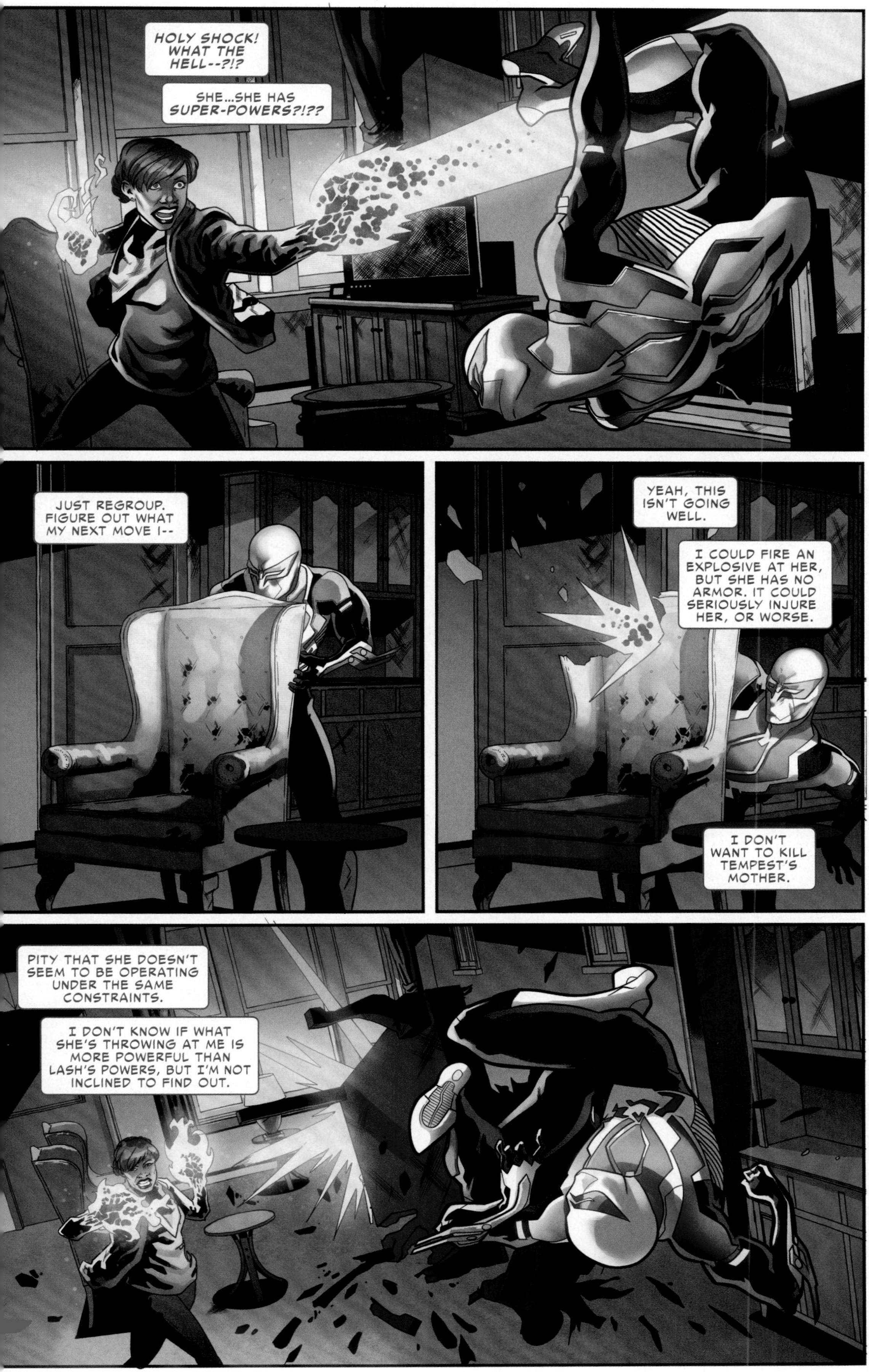
HOLY SHOCK! WHAT THE HELL--?!?
SHE...SHE HAS SUPER-POWERS?!??
JUST REGROUP. FIGURE OUT WHAT MY NEXT MOVE I--
YEAH, THIS ISN'T GOING WELL.
I COULD FIRE AN EXPLOSIVE AT HER, BUT SHE HAS NO ARMOR. IT COULD SERIOUSLY INJURE HER, OR WORSE.
I DON'T WANT TO KILL TEMPEST'S MOTHER.
PITY THAT SHE DOESN'T SEEM TO BE OPERATING UNDER THE SAME CONSTRAINTS.
I DON'T KNOW IF WHAT SHE'S THROWING AT ME IS MORE POWERFUL THAN LASH'S POWERS, BUT I'M NOT INCLINED TO FIND OUT.

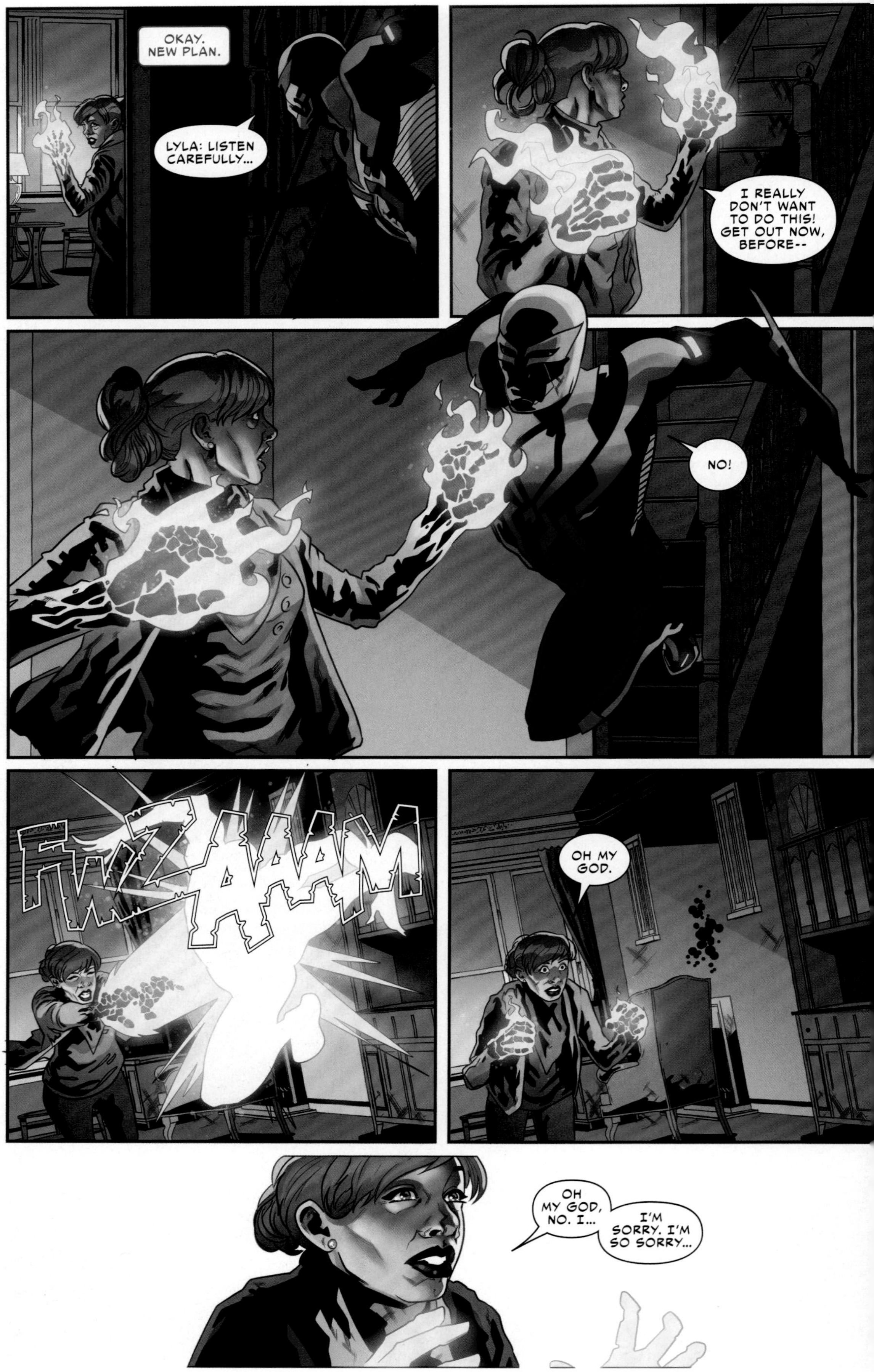
OKAY. NEW PLAN.
LYLA: LISTEN CAREFULLY...
I REALLY DON'T WANT TO DO THIS! GET OUT NOW, BEFORE--
NO!
FWZAAAM
OH MY GOD.
OH MY GOD, NO. I...
I'M SORRY. I'M SO SORRY...

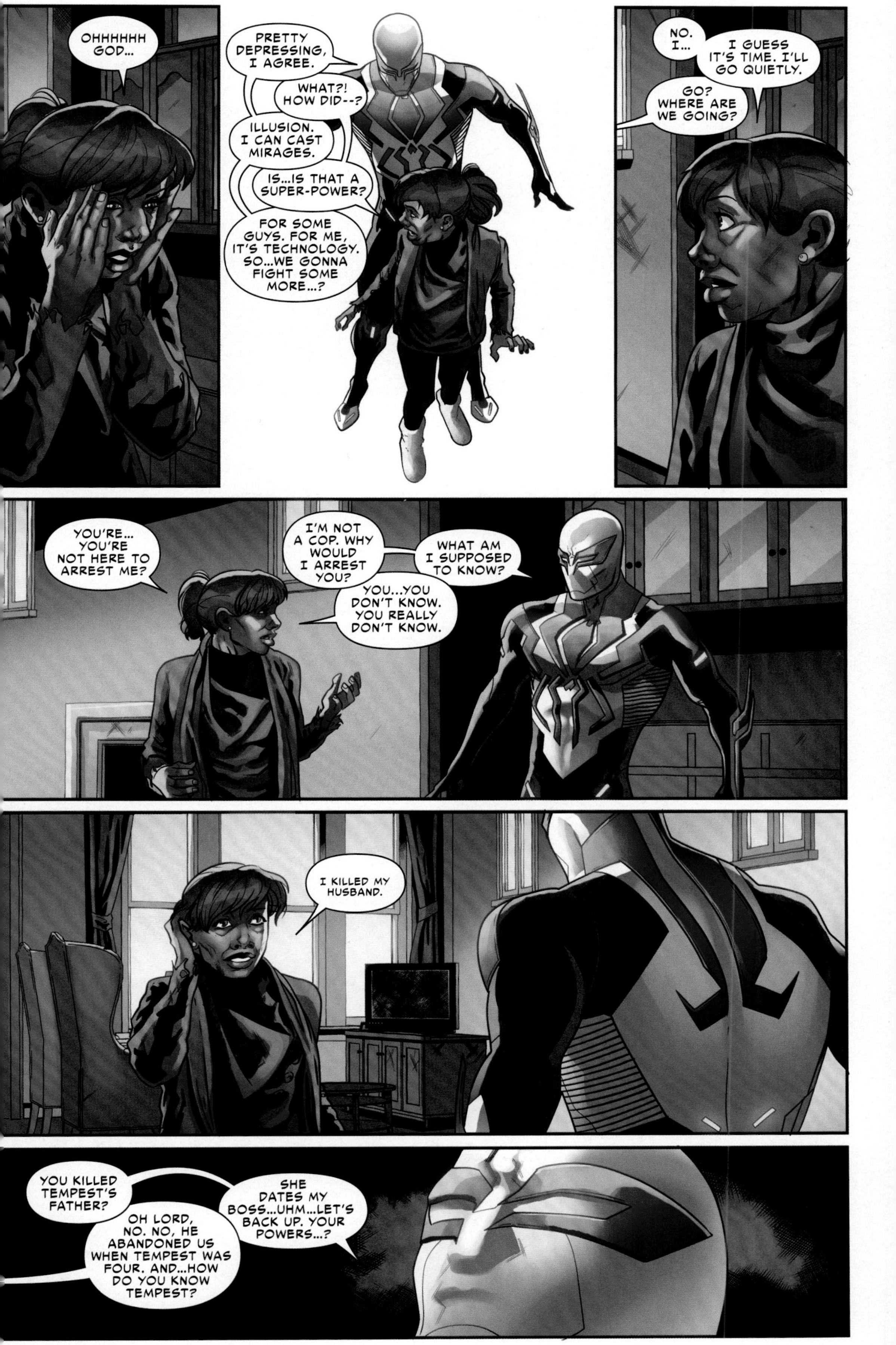
OHHHHHH GOD...
PRETTY DEPRESSING, I AGREE.
WHAT?! HOW DID--?
ILLUSION. I CAN CAST MIRAGES.
IS...IS THAT A SUPER-POWER?
FOR SOME GUYS. FOR ME, IT'S TECHNOLOGY. SO...WE GONNA FIGHT SOME MORE...?
NO. I...
I GUESS IT'S TIME. I'LL GO QUIETLY.
GO? WHERE ARE WE GOING?
YOU'RE... YOU'RE NOT HERE TO ARREST ME?
I'M NOT A COP. WHY WOULD I ARREST YOU?
WHAT AM I SUPPOSED TO KNOW?
YOU...YOU DON'T KNOW. YOU REALLY DON'T KNOW.
I KILLED MY HUSBAND.
YOU KILLED TEMPEST'S FATHER?
OH LORD, NO. NO, HE ABANDONED US WHEN TEMPEST WAS FOUR. AND...HOW DO YOU KNOW TEMPEST?
SHE DATES MY BOSS...UHM...LET'S BACK UP. YOUR POWERS...?

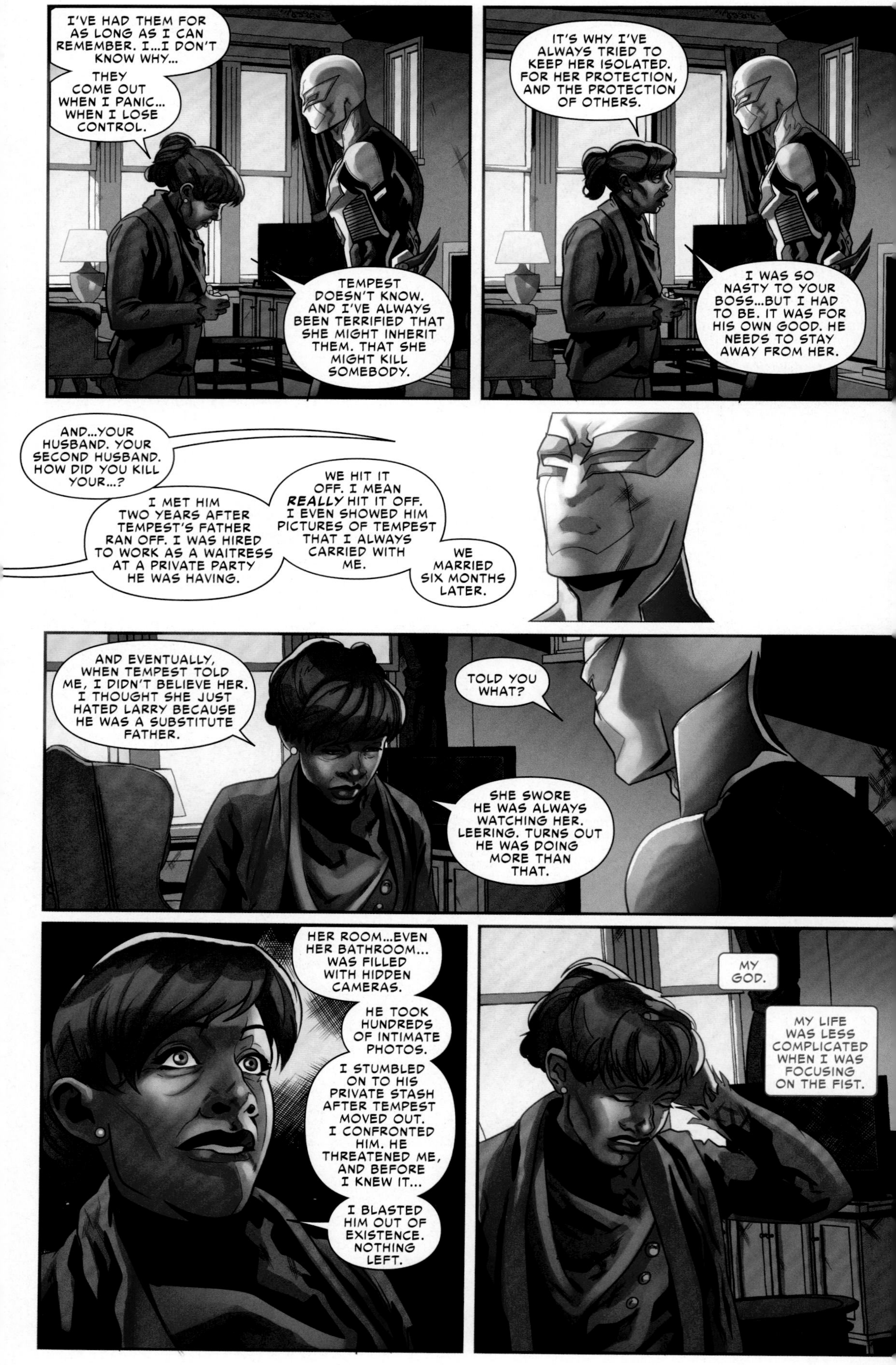

I'VE HAD THEM FOR AS LONG AS I CAN REMEMBER. I...I DON'T KNOW WHY...
THEY COME OUT WHEN I PANIC... WHEN I LOSE CONTROL.
TEMPEST DOESN'T KNOW. AND I'VE ALWAYS BEEN TERRIFIED THAT SHE MIGHT INHERIT THEM. THAT SHE MIGHT KILL SOMEBODY.
IT'S WHY I'VE ALWAYS TRIED TO KEEP HER ISOLATED. FOR HER PROTECTION, AND THE PROTECTION OF OTHERS.
I WAS SO NASTY TO YOUR BOSS...BUT I HAD TO BE. IT WAS FOR HIS OWN GOOD. HE NEEDS TO STAY AWAY FROM HER.
AND...YOUR HUSBAND. YOUR SECOND HUSBAND. HOW DID YOU KILL YOUR...?
I MET HIM TWO YEARS AFTER TEMPEST'S FATHER RAN OFF. I WAS HIRED TO WORK AS A WAITRESS AT A PRIVATE PARTY HE WAS HAVING.
WE HIT IT OFF. I MEAN ***REALLY*** HIT IT OFF. I EVEN SHOWED HIM PICTURES OF TEMPEST THAT I ALWAYS CARRIED WITH ME.
WE MARRIED SIX MONTHS LATER.
AND EVENTUALLY, WHEN TEMPEST TOLD ME, I DIDN'T BELIEVE HER. I THOUGHT SHE JUST HATED LARRY BECAUSE HE WAS A SUBSTITUTE FATHER.
TOLD YOU WHAT?
SHE SWORE HE WAS ALWAYS WATCHING HER. LEERING. TURNS OUT HE WAS DOING MORE THAN THAT.
HER ROOM...EVEN HER BATHROOM... WAS FILLED WITH HIDDEN CAMERAS.
HE TOOK HUNDREDS OF INTIMATE PHOTOS.
I STUMBLED ON TO HIS PRIVATE STASH AFTER TEMPEST MOVED OUT. I CONFRONTED HIM. HE THREATENED ME, AND BEFORE I KNEW IT...
I BLASTED HIM OUT OF EXISTENCE. NOTHING LEFT.
MY GOD.
MY LIFE WAS LESS COMPLICATED WHEN I WAS FOCUSING ON THE FIST.

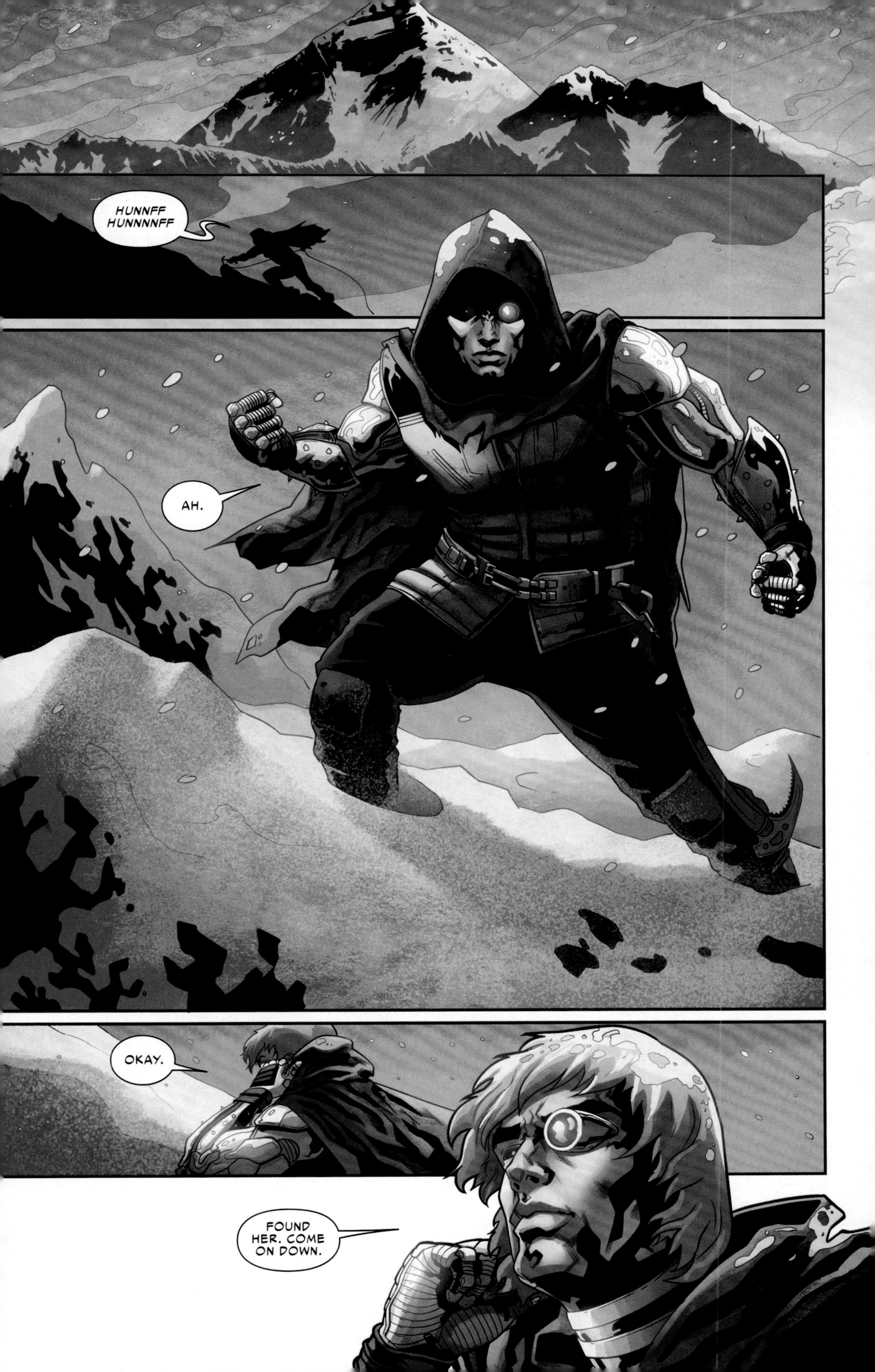
HUNNFF HUNNNNFF
AH.
OKAY.
FOUND HER. COME ON DOWN.

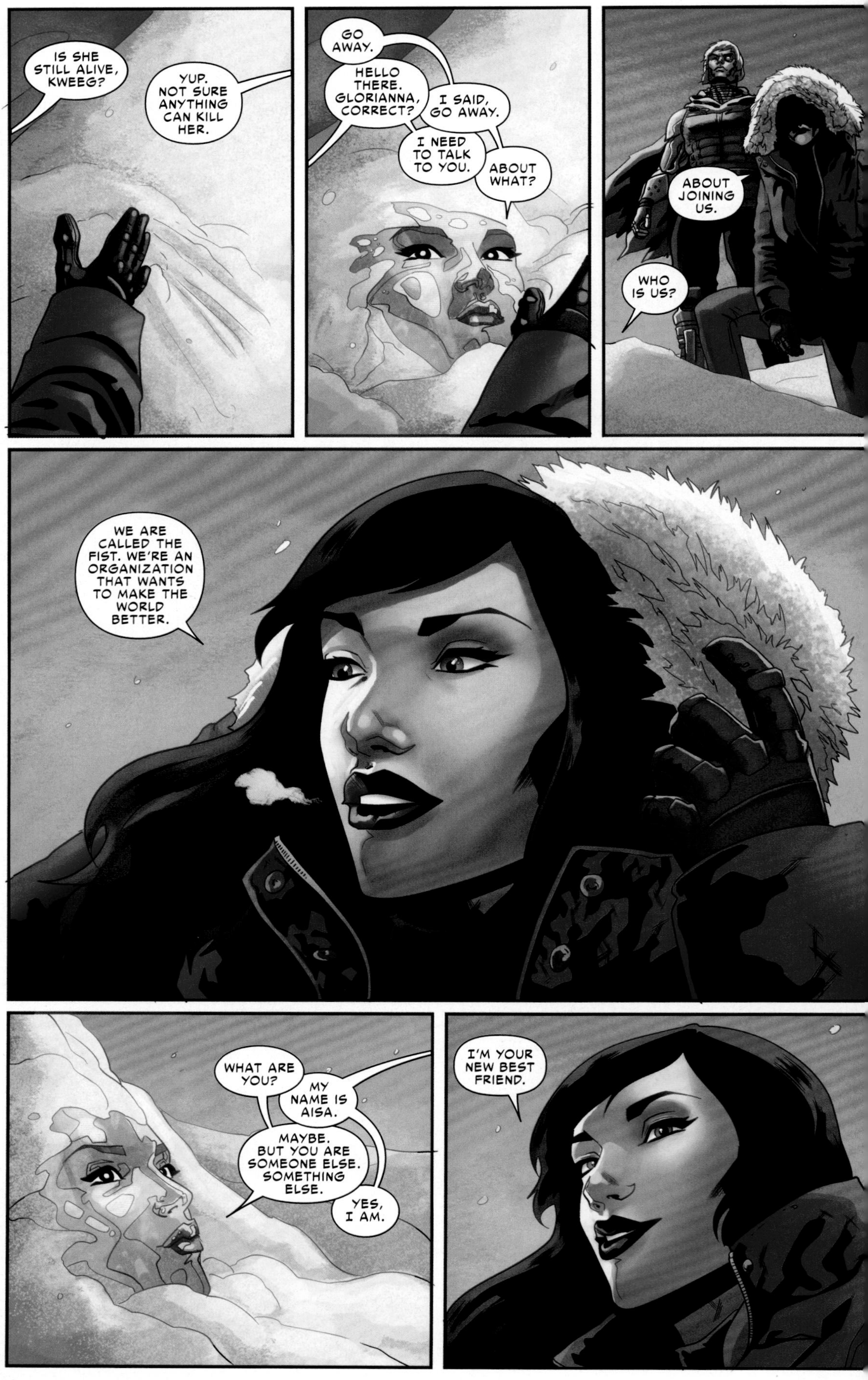
IS SHE STILL ALIVE, KWEEG?
YUP. NOT SURE ANYTHING CAN KILL HER.
GO AWAY.
HELLO THERE. GLORIANNA, CORRECT?
I SAID, GO AWAY.
I NEED TO TALK TO YOU.
ABOUT WHAT?
ABOUT JOINING US.
WHO IS US?
WE ARE CALLED THE FIST. WE'RE AN ORGANIZATION THAT WANTS TO MAKE THE WORLD BETTER.
WHAT ARE YOU?
MY NAME IS AISA.
MAYBE. BUT YOU ARE SOMEONE ELSE. SOMETHING ELSE.
YES, I AM.
I'M YOUR NEW BEST FRIEND.

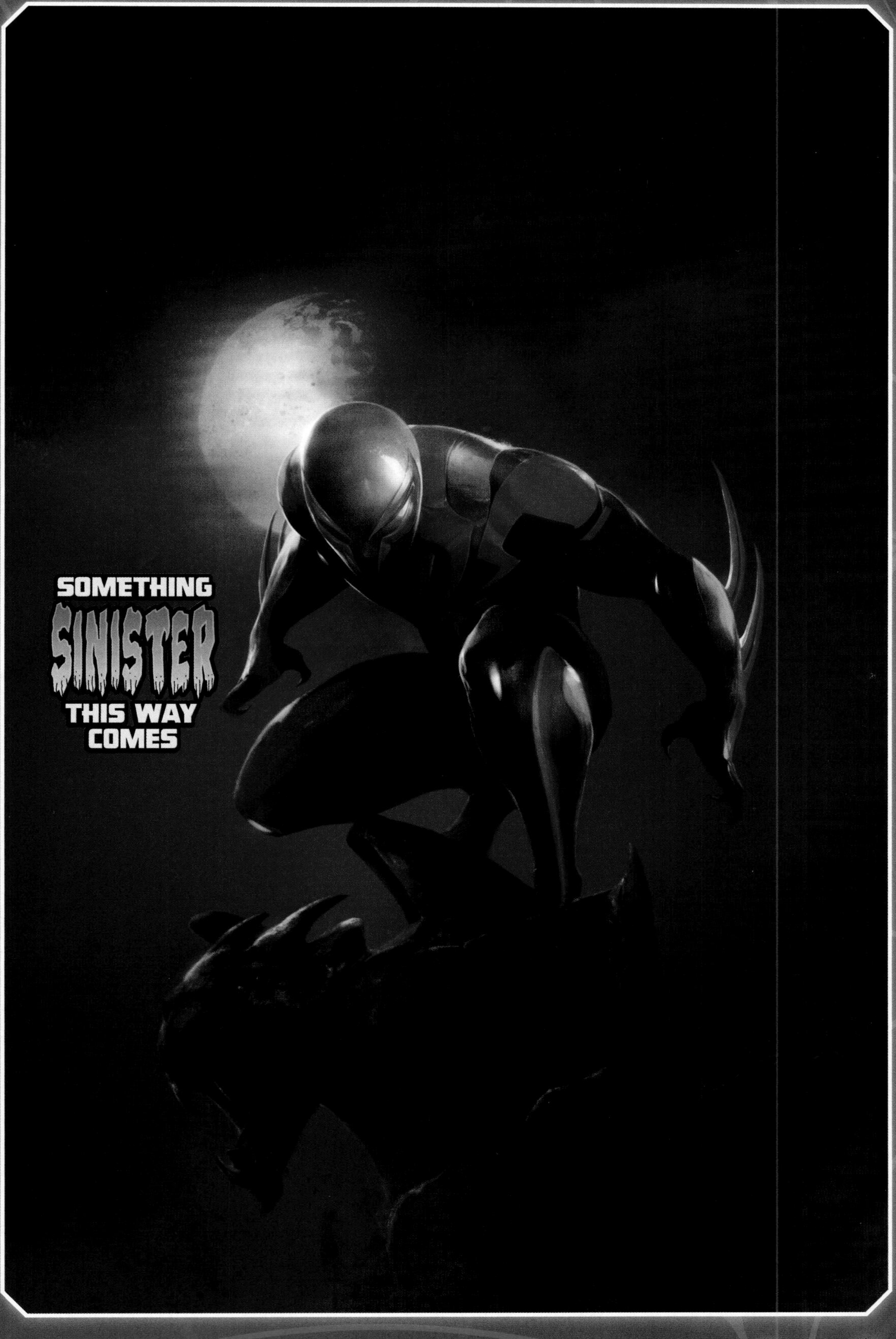
SOMETHING
SINISTER
THIS WAY
COMES

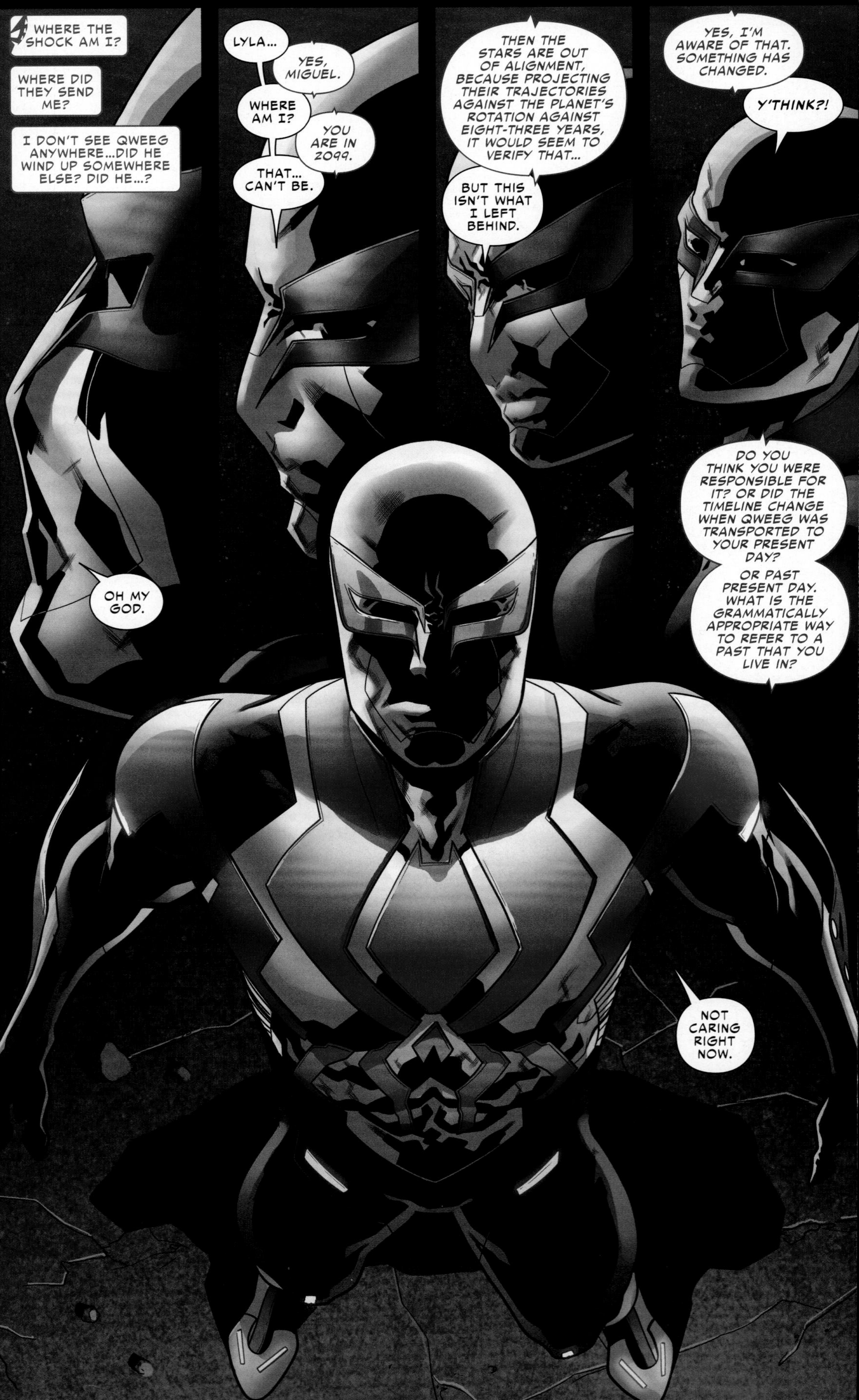
WHERE THE SHOCK AM I?
WHERE DID THEY SEND ME?
I DON'T SEE QWEEG ANYWHERE...DID HE WIND UP SOMEWHERE ELSE? DID HE...?
LYLA...
YES, MIGUEL.
WHERE AM I?
YOU ARE IN 2099.
THAT... CAN'T BE.
THEN THE STARS ARE OUT OF ALIGNMENT, BECAUSE PROJECTING THEIR TRAJECTORIES AGAINST THE PLANET'S ROTATION AGAINST EIGHT-THREE YEARS, IT WOULD SEEM TO VERIFY THAT...
BUT THIS ISN'T WHAT I LEFT BEHIND.
YES, I'M AWARE OF THAT. SOMETHING HAS CHANGED.
Y'THINK?!
OH MY GOD.
DO YOU THINK YOU WERE RESPONSIBLE FOR IT? OR DID THE TIMELINE CHANGE WHEN QWEEG WAS TRANSPORTED TO YOUR PRESENT DAY?
OR PAST PRESENT DAY. WHAT IS THE GRAMMATICALLY APPROPRIATE WAY TO REFER TO A PAST THAT YOU LIVE IN?
NOT CARING RIGHT NOW.

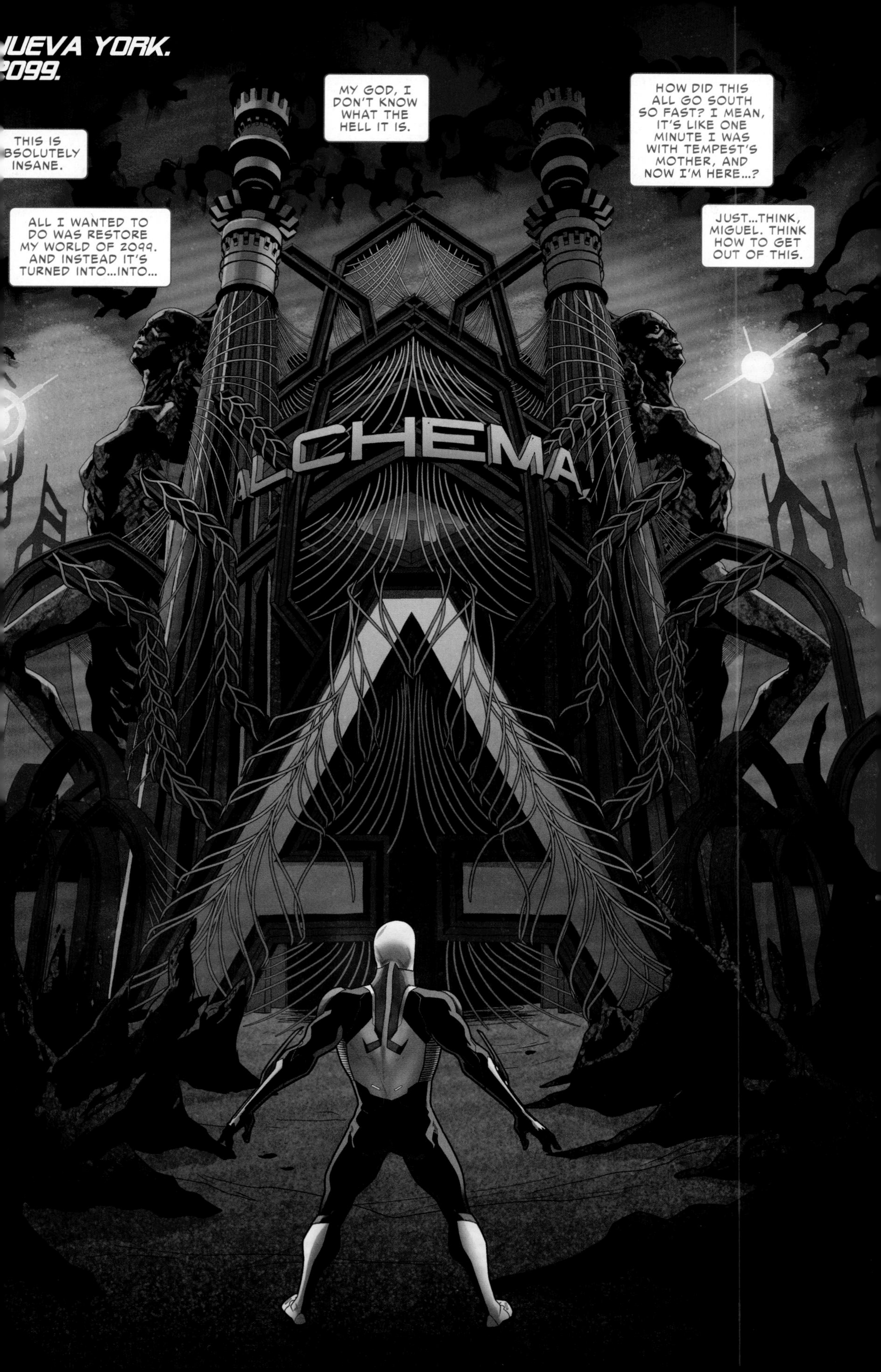

UEVA YORK.
2099.
THIS IS
BSOLUTELY
INSANE.
ALL I WANTED TO
DO WAS RESTORE
MY WORLD OF 2099.
AND INSTEAD IT'S
TURNED INTO...INTO...
MY GOD, I
DON'T KNOW
WHAT THE
HELL IT IS.
HOW DID THIS
ALL GO SOUTH
SO FAST? I MEAN,
IT'S LIKE ONE
MINUTE I WAS
WITH TEMPEST'S
MOTHER, AND
NOW I'M HERE...?
JUST...THINK,
MIGUEL. THINK
HOW TO GET
OUT OF THIS.
LCHEMA

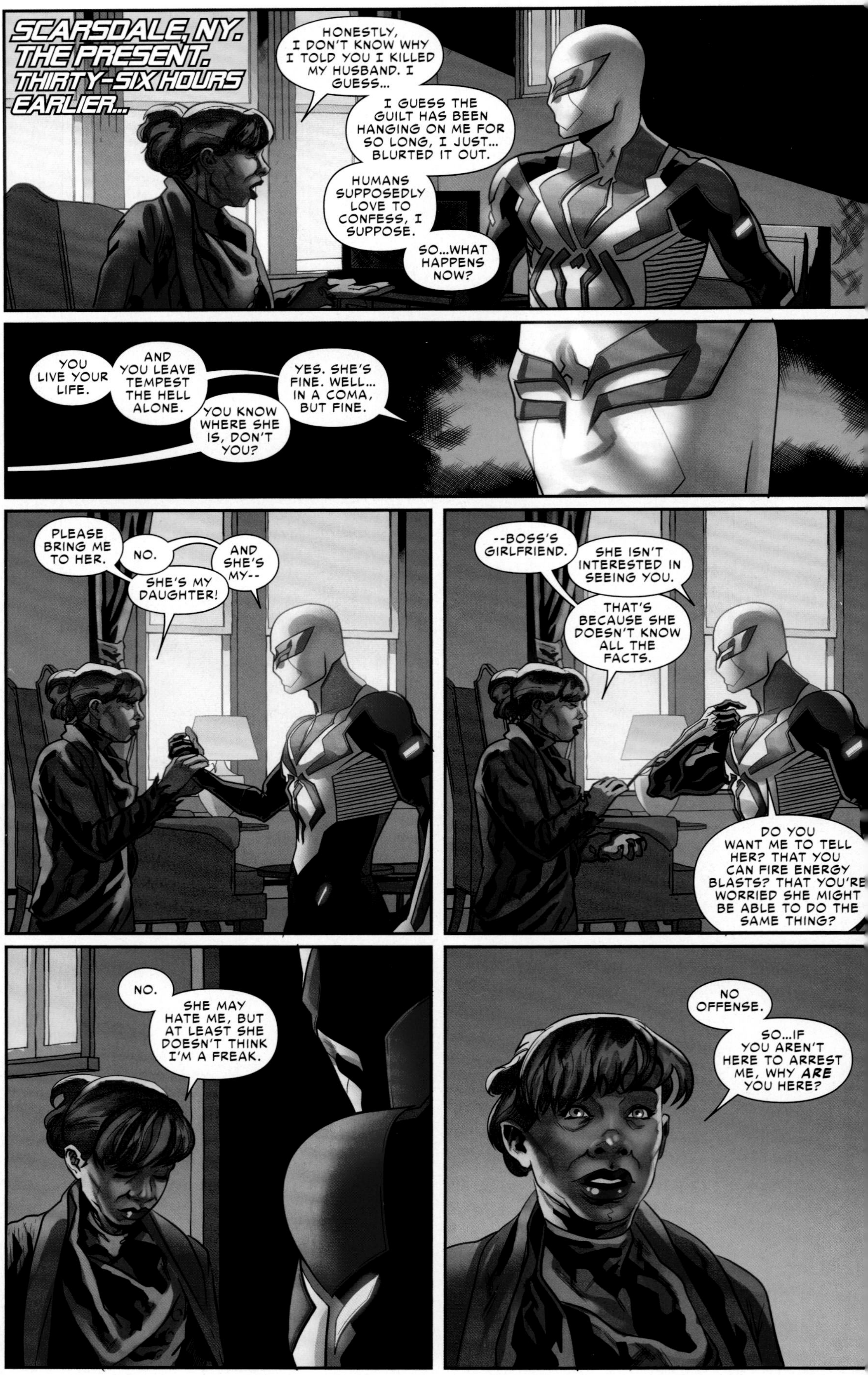
SCARSDALE, NY. THE PRESENT. THIRTY-SIX HOURS EARLIER...
HONESTLY, I DON'T KNOW WHY I TOLD YOU I KILLED MY HUSBAND. I GUESS...
I GUESS THE GUILT HAS BEEN HANGING ON ME FOR SO LONG, I JUST... BLURTED IT OUT.
HUMANS SUPPOSEDLY LOVE TO CONFESS, I SUPPOSE.
SO...WHAT HAPPENS NOW?
YOU LIVE YOUR LIFE.
AND YOU LEAVE TEMPEST THE HELL ALONE.
YOU KNOW WHERE SHE IS, DON'T YOU?
YES. SHE'S FINE. WELL... IN A COMA, BUT FINE.
PLEASE BRING ME TO HER.
NO.
SHE'S MY DAUGHTER!
AND SHE'S MY--
--BOSS'S GIRLFRIEND.
SHE ISN'T INTERESTED IN SEEING YOU.
THAT'S BECAUSE SHE DOESN'T KNOW ALL THE FACTS.
DO YOU WANT ME TO TELL HER? THAT YOU CAN FIRE ENERGY BLASTS? THAT YOU'RE WORRIED SHE MIGHT BE ABLE TO DO THE SAME THING?
NO.
SHE MAY HATE ME, BUT AT LEAST SHE DOESN'T THINK I'M A FREAK.
NO OFFENSE.
SO...IF YOU AREN'T HERE TO ARREST ME, WHY ARE YOU HERE?

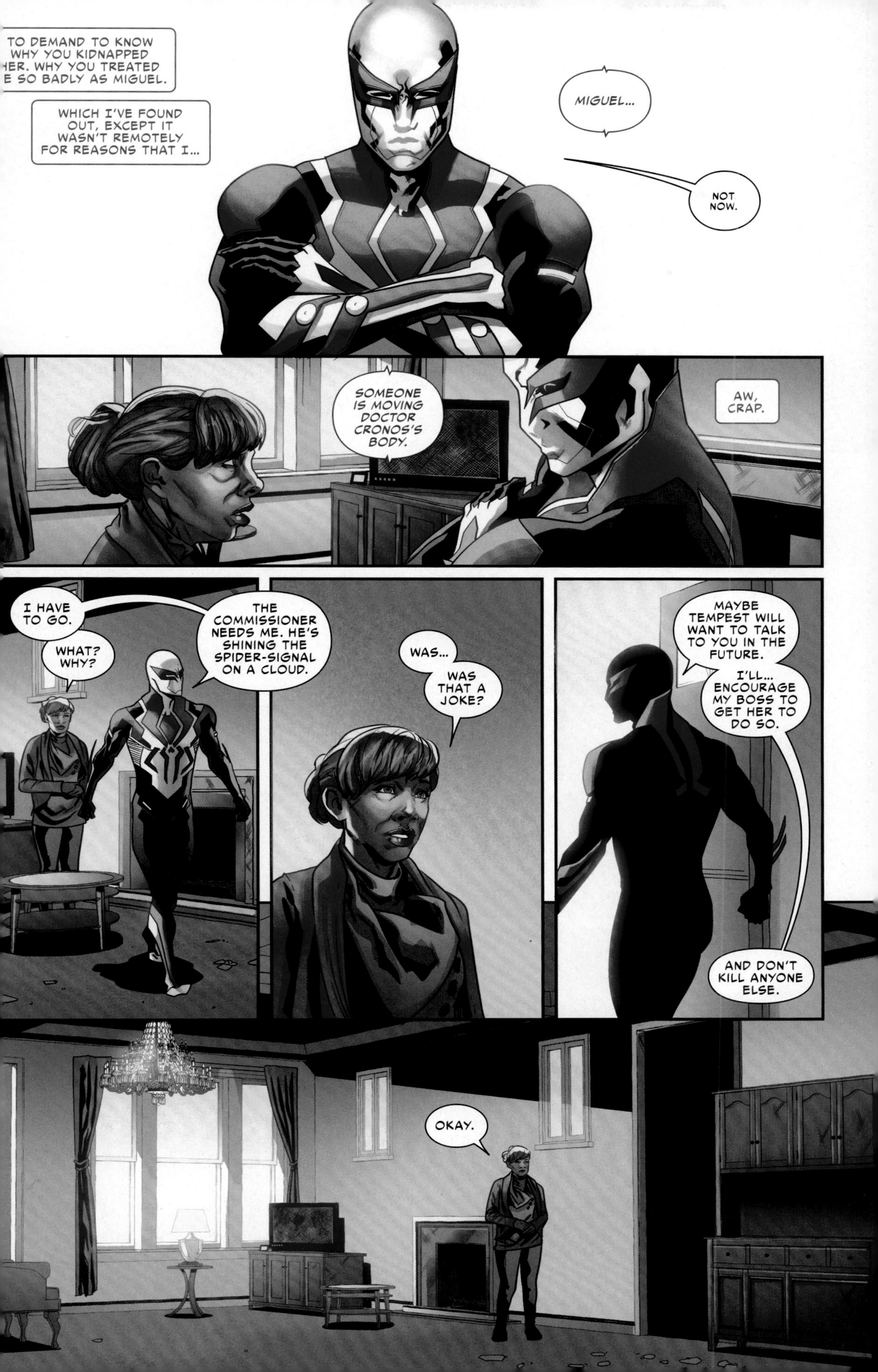
TO DEMAND TO KNOW WHY YOU KIDNAPPED HER. WHY YOU TREATED E SO BADLY AS MIGUEL.
WHICH I'VE FOUND OUT, EXCEPT IT WASN'T REMOTELY FOR REASONS THAT I...
MIGUEL...
NOT NOW.
SOMEONE IS MOVING DOCTOR CRONOS'S BODY.
AW, CRAP.
I HAVE TO GO.
WHAT? WHY?
THE COMMISSIONER NEEDS ME. HE'S SHINING THE SPIDER-SIGNAL ON A CLOUD.
WAS...
WAS THAT A JOKE?
MAYBE TEMPEST WILL WANT TO TALK TO YOU IN THE FUTURE.
I'LL... ENCOURAGE MY BOSS TO GET HER TO DO SO.
AND DON'T KILL ANYONE ELSE.
OKAY.

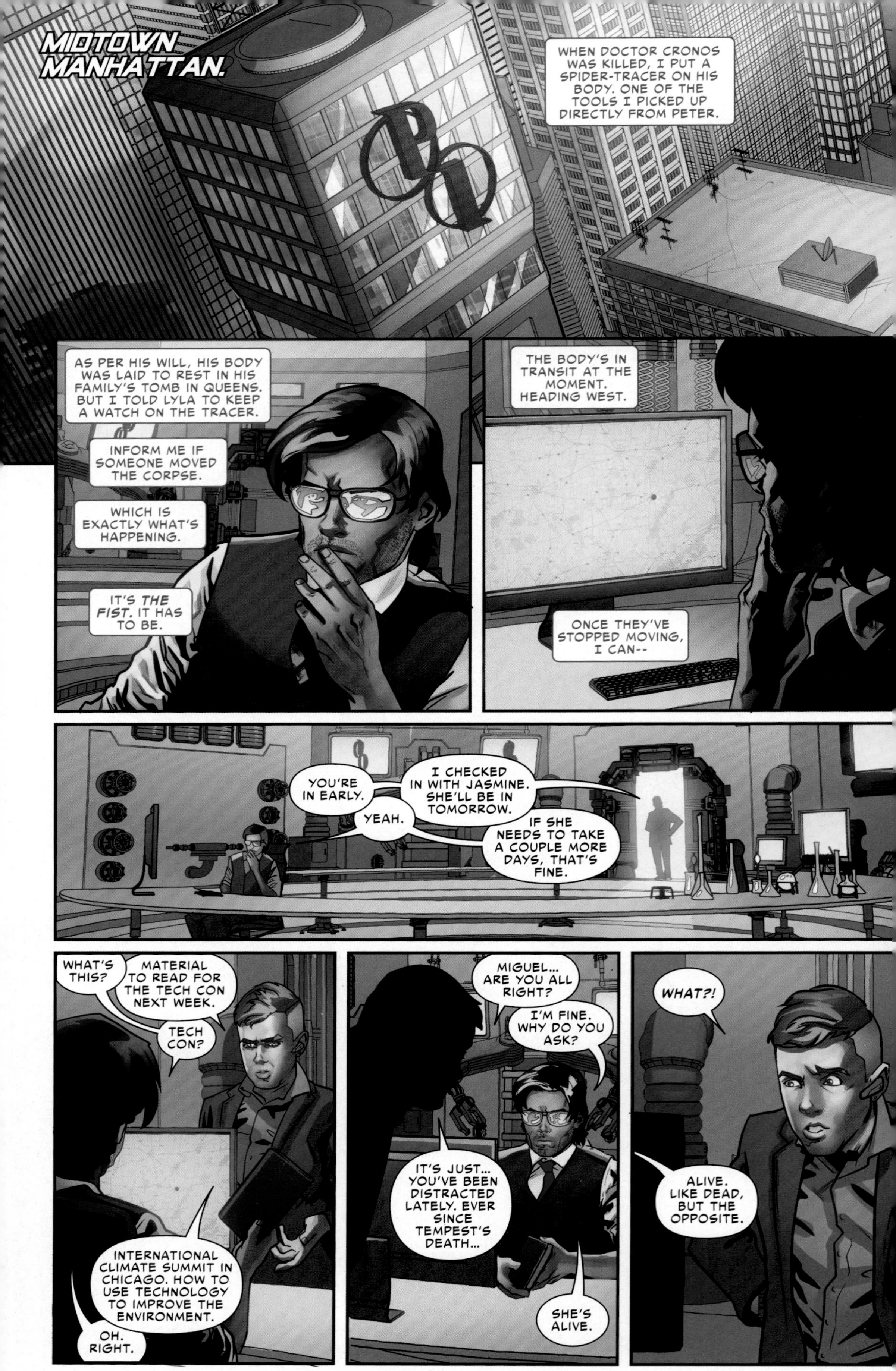
MIDTOWN MANHATTAN.
WHEN DOCTOR CRONOS WAS KILLED, I PUT A SPIDER-TRACER ON HIS BODY. ONE OF THE TOOLS I PICKED UP DIRECTLY FROM PETER.
AS PER HIS WILL, HIS BODY WAS LAID TO REST IN HIS FAMILY'S TOMB IN QUEENS. BUT I TOLD LYLA TO KEEP A WATCH ON THE TRACER.
INFORM ME IF SOMEONE MOVED THE CORPSE.
WHICH IS EXACTLY WHAT'S HAPPENING.
IT'S *THE FIST*. IT HAS TO BE.
THE BODY'S IN TRANSIT AT THE MOMENT. HEADING WEST.
ONCE THEY'VE STOPPED MOVING, I CAN--
YOU'RE IN EARLY.
YEAH.
I CHECKED IN WITH JASMINE. SHE'LL BE IN TOMORROW.
IF SHE NEEDS TO TAKE A COUPLE MORE DAYS, THAT'S FINE.
WHAT'S THIS?
MATERIAL TO READ FOR THE TECH CON NEXT WEEK.
TECH CON?
INTERNATIONAL CLIMATE SUMMIT IN CHICAGO. HOW TO USE TECHNOLOGY TO IMPROVE THE ENVIRONMENT.
OH. RIGHT.
MIGUEL... ARE YOU ALL RIGHT?
I'M FINE. WHY DO YOU ASK?
IT'S JUST... YOU'VE BEEN DISTRACTED LATELY. EVER SINCE TEMPEST'S DEATH...
SHE'S ALIVE.
WHAT?!
ALIVE. LIKE DEAD, BUT THE OPPOSITE.

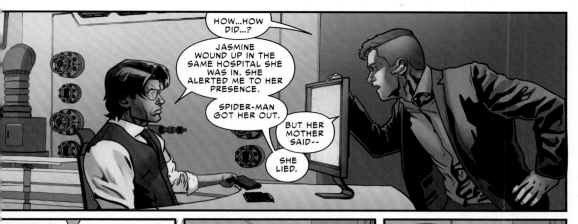

HOW...HOW DID...?

JASMINE WOUND UP IN THE SAME HOSPITAL SHE WAS IN. SHE ALERTED ME TO HER PRESENCE.

SPIDER-MAN GOT HER OUT.

BUT HER MOTHER SAID--

SHE LIED.

I NEED YOU TO PUT THE COMPANY JET ON ALERT.

BECAUSE I ASKED YOU TO, AND YOU WORK FOR ME. I WASN'T AWARE THAT YOU NEEDED MORE OF A REASON THAN THAT.

WHAT? WHY?

WHERE ARE YOU GOING?

WHERE SPECIFICALLY?

OUT WEST SOMEWHERE.

NOT SURE YET. I'LL LET THEM KNOW ONCE I BOARD.

MIGUEL, THIS IS RIDICULOUS--! YOU'RE NOT...

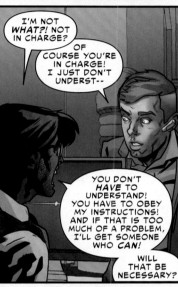

I'M NOT WHAT?! NOT IN CHARGE? OF COURSE YOU'RE IN CHARGE! I JUST DON'T UNDERST--

YOU DON'T HAVE TO UNDERSTAND! YOU HAVE TO OBEY MY INSTRUCTIONS! AND IF THAT IS TOO MUCH OF A PROBLEM, I'LL GET SOMEONE WHO CAN!

WILL THAT BE NECESSARY?

I'LL PUT THE PLANE ON ALERT.

YES, SIR.

THANK YOU. THAT'S ALL.

YEAH. YOU HANDLED THAT GREAT. GOOD MOVE ALL AROUND.

RAUL BUSTS HIS BUTT AROUND HERE. HE GOT HIMSELF ARRESTED TO HELP JASMINE, AND YOU THREATEN TO FIRE HIM.

RAUL...

WHAT?

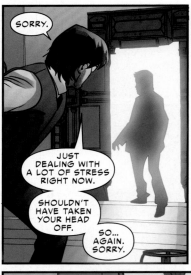

SORRY.

JUST DEALING WITH A LOT OF STRESS RIGHT NOW.

SHOULDN'T HAVE TAKEN YOUR HEAD OFF.

SO... AGAIN. SORRY.

TEMPEST IS ALIVE. YOU SHOULD BE OVERJOYED.

HELL, I'M NOT EVEN SURE WHY YOU'RE HERE AND NOT AT HER BEDSIDE.

GOOD POINT.

WHERE IS SHE?

NOT GONNA TELL YOU. THE FEWER WHO KNOW, THE BETTER. BUT I'LL KEEP YOU APPRISED OF HER CONDITION.

MUCH OBLIGED.

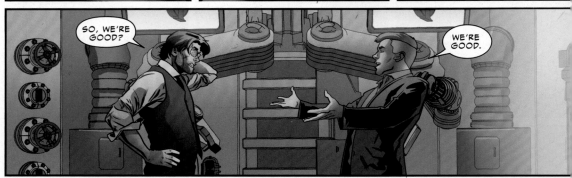

SO, WE'RE GOOD?

WE'RE GOOD.

WHAT ARE YOU DOING?

I...THOUGHT WE WERE GONNA HUG.

NO.

SOOO, I GUESS I READ THAT SIGNAL WRONG.

OH, YEAH. BIG TIME.

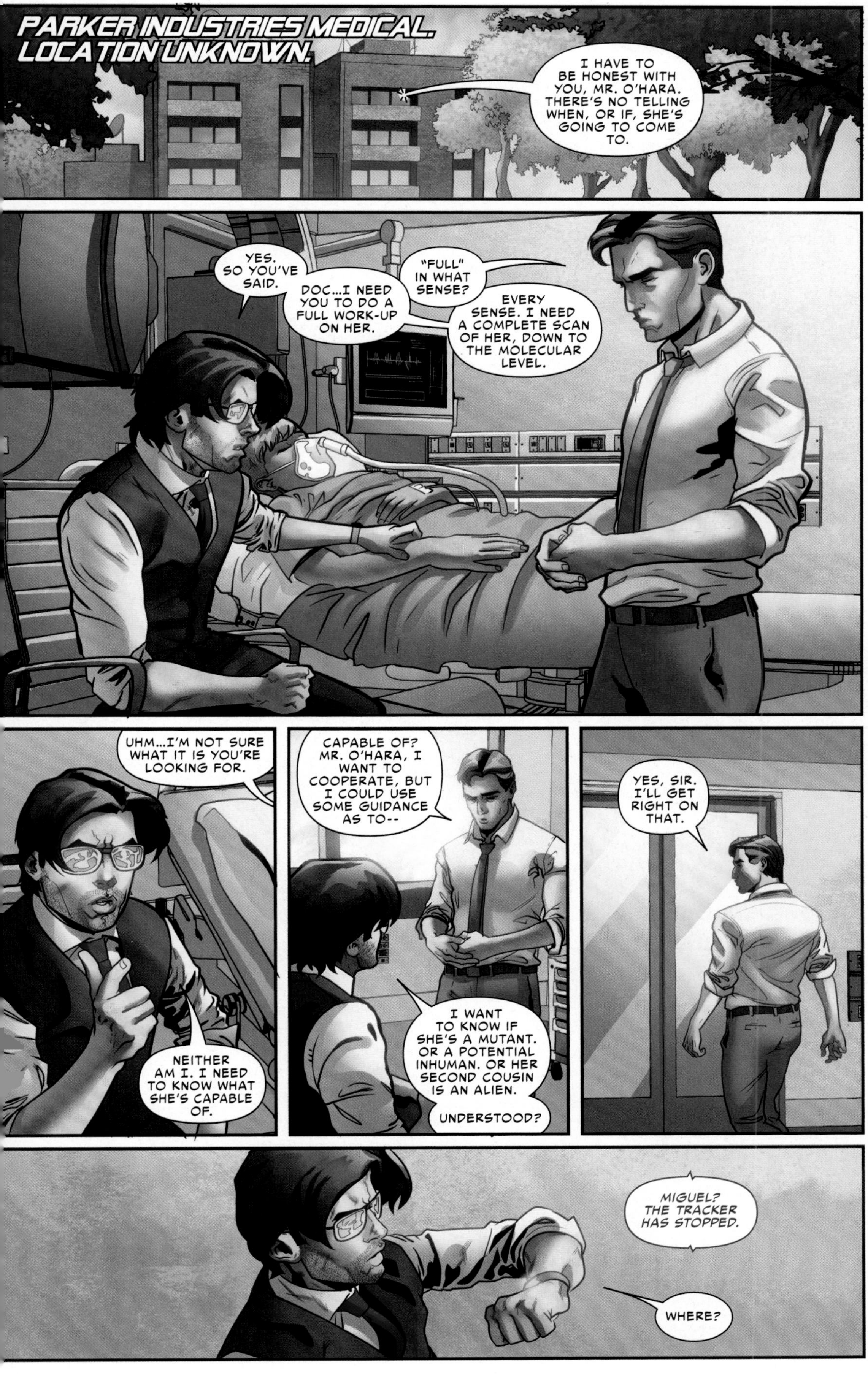
PARKER INDUSTRIES MEDICAL. LOCATION UNKNOWN.
I HAVE TO BE HONEST WITH YOU, MR. O'HARA. THERE'S NO TELLING WHEN, OR IF, SHE'S GOING TO COME TO.
YES. SO YOU'VE SAID.
DOC...I NEED YOU TO DO A FULL WORK-UP ON HER.
"FULL" IN WHAT SENSE?
EVERY SENSE. I NEED A COMPLETE SCAN OF HER, DOWN TO THE MOLECULAR LEVEL.
UHM...I'M NOT SURE WHAT IT IS YOU'RE LOOKING FOR.
NEITHER AM I. I NEED TO KNOW WHAT SHE'S CAPABLE OF.
CAPABLE OF? MR. O'HARA, I WANT TO COOPERATE, BUT I COULD USE SOME GUIDANCE AS TO--
I WANT TO KNOW IF SHE'S A MUTANT. OR A POTENTIAL INHUMAN. OR HER SECOND COUSIN IS AN ALIEN.
UNDERSTOOD?
YES, SIR. I'LL GET RIGHT ON THAT.
MIGUEL? THE TRACKER HAS STOPPED.
WHERE?

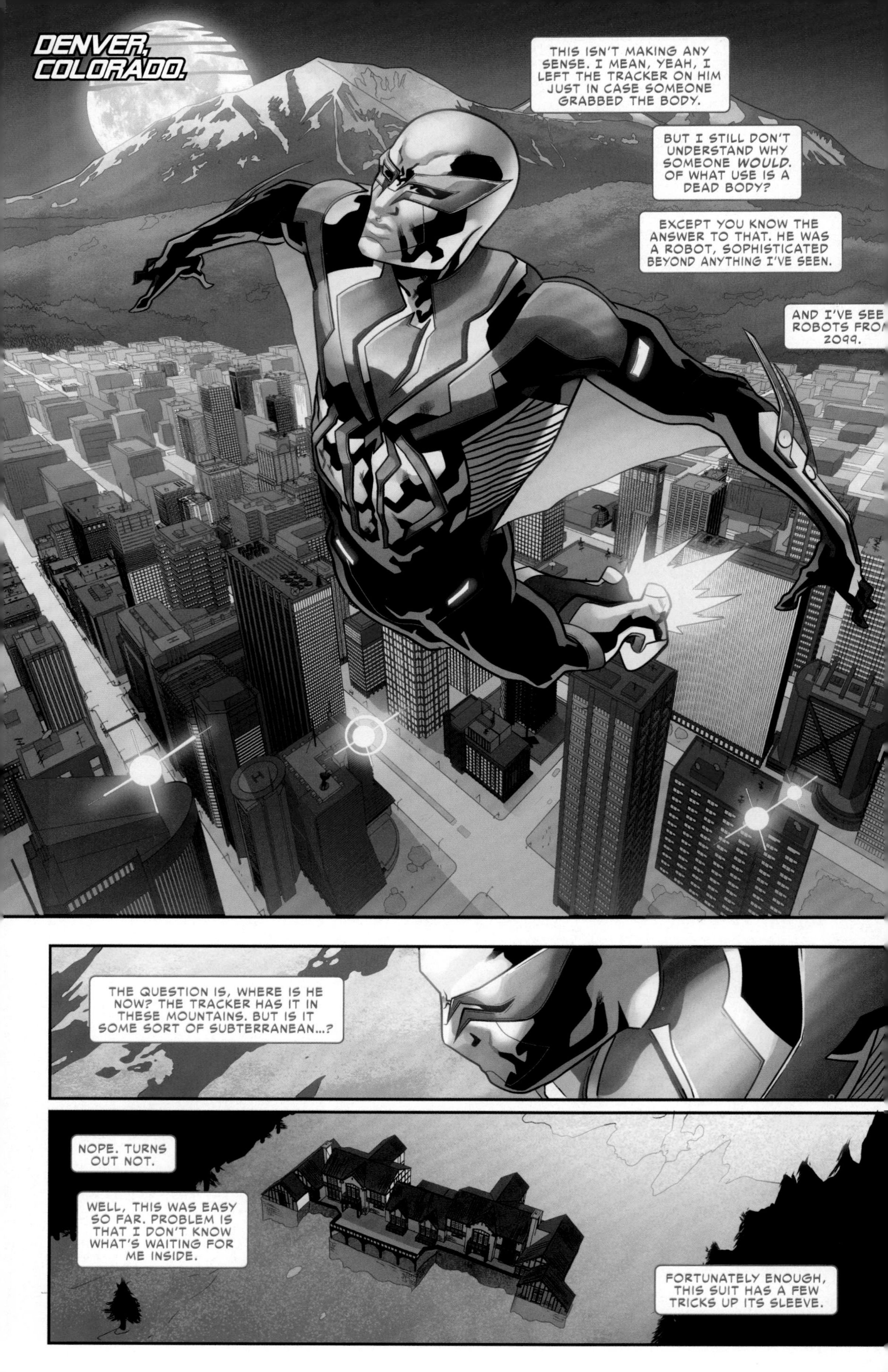
DENVER, COLORADO.
THIS ISN'T MAKING ANY SENSE. I MEAN, YEAH, I LEFT THE TRACKER ON HIM JUST IN CASE SOMEONE GRABBED THE BODY.
BUT I STILL DON'T UNDERSTAND WHY SOMEONE *WOULD*. OF WHAT USE IS A DEAD BODY?
EXCEPT YOU KNOW THE ANSWER TO THAT. HE WAS A ROBOT, SOPHISTICATED BEYOND ANYTHING I'VE SEEN.
AND I'VE SEE ROBOTS FROM 2099.
THE QUESTION IS, WHERE IS HE NOW? THE TRACKER HAS IT IN THESE MOUNTAINS. BUT IS IT SOME SORT OF SUBTERRANEAN...?
NOPE. TURNS OUT NOT.
WELL, THIS WAS EASY SO FAR. PROBLEM IS THAT I DON'T KNOW WHAT'S WAITING FOR ME INSIDE.
FORTUNATELY ENOUGH, THIS SUIT HAS A FEW TRICKS UP ITS SLEEVE.

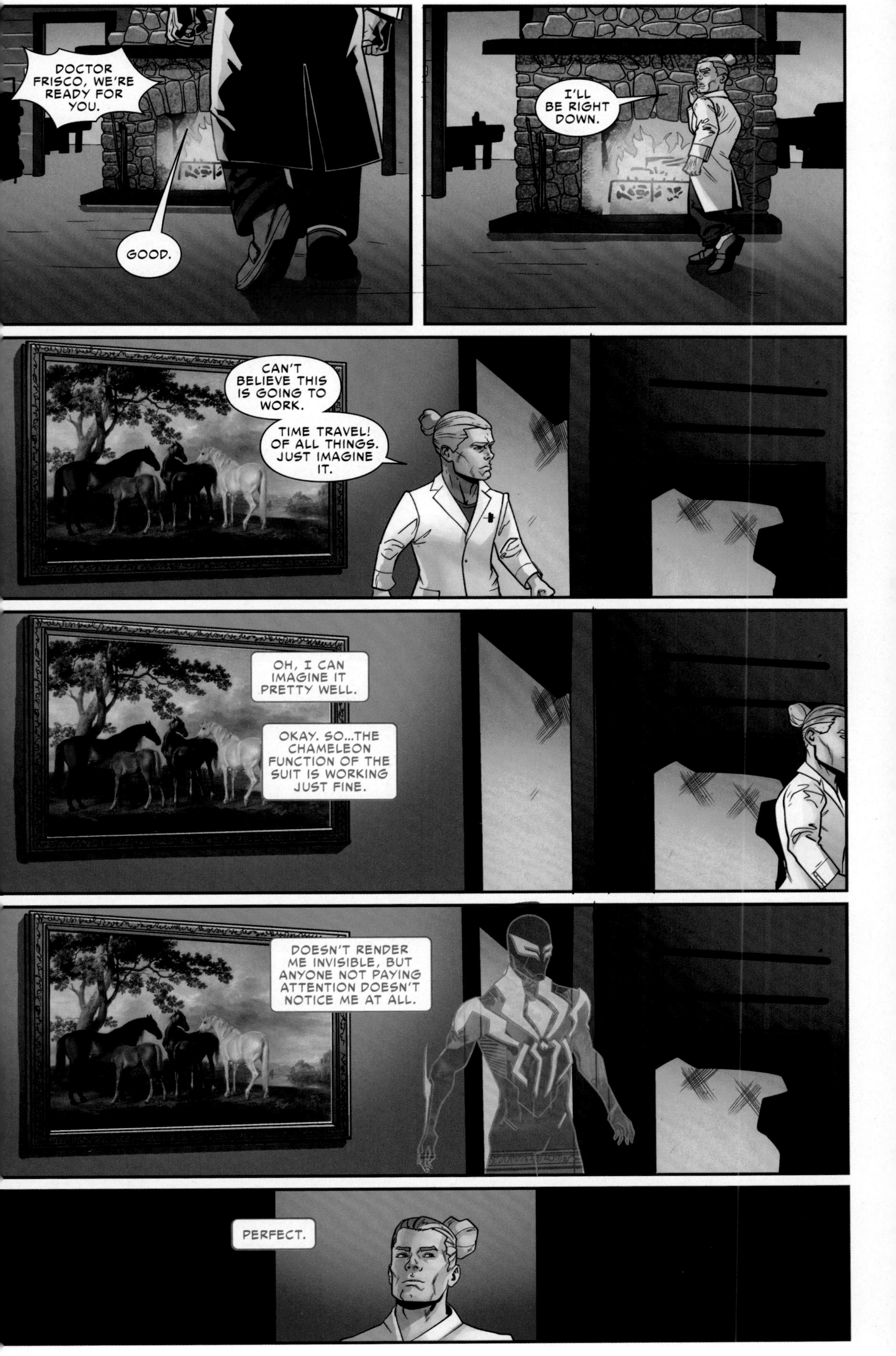
DOCTOR FRISCO, WE'RE READY FOR YOU.
GOOD.
I'LL BE RIGHT DOWN.
CAN'T BELIEVE THIS IS GOING TO WORK.
TIME TRAVEL! OF ALL THINGS. JUST IMAGINE IT.
OH, I CAN IMAGINE IT PRETTY WELL.
OKAY. SO...THE CHAMELEON FUNCTION OF THE SUIT IS WORKING JUST FINE.
DOESN'T RENDER ME INVISIBLE, BUT ANYONE NOT PAYING ATTENTION DOESN'T NOTICE ME AT ALL.
PERFECT.

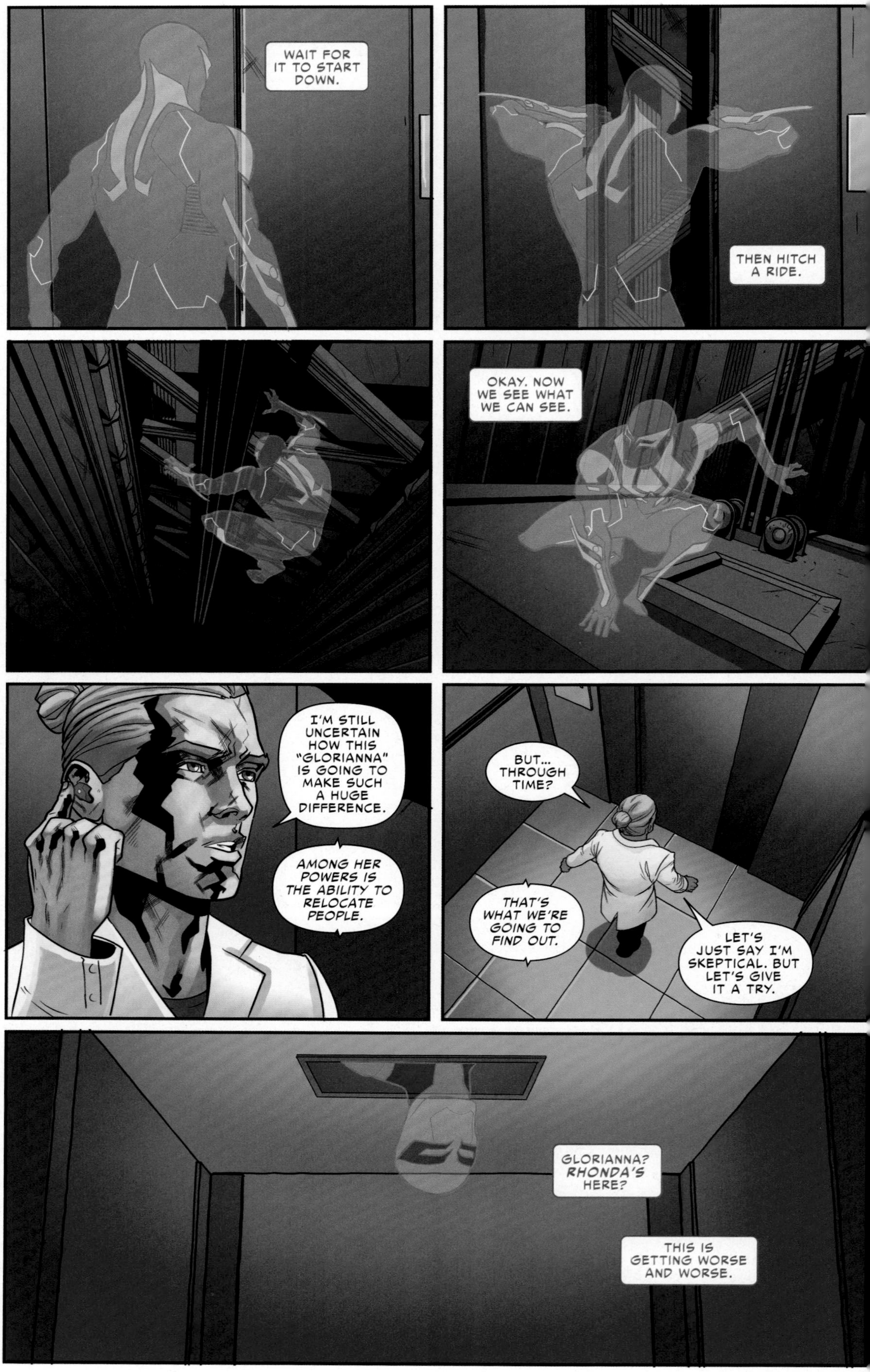
WAIT FOR IT TO START DOWN.
THEN HITCH A RIDE.
OKAY. NOW WE SEE WHAT WE CAN SEE.
I'M STILL UNCERTAIN HOW THIS "GLORIANNA" IS GOING TO MAKE SUCH A HUGE DIFFERENCE.
AMONG HER POWERS IS THE ABILITY TO RELOCATE PEOPLE.
BUT... THROUGH TIME?
THAT'S WHAT WE'RE GOING TO FIND OUT.
LET'S JUST SAY I'M SKEPTICAL. BUT LET'S GIVE IT A TRY.
GLORIANNA? RHONDA'S HERE?
THIS IS GETTING WORSE AND WORSE.

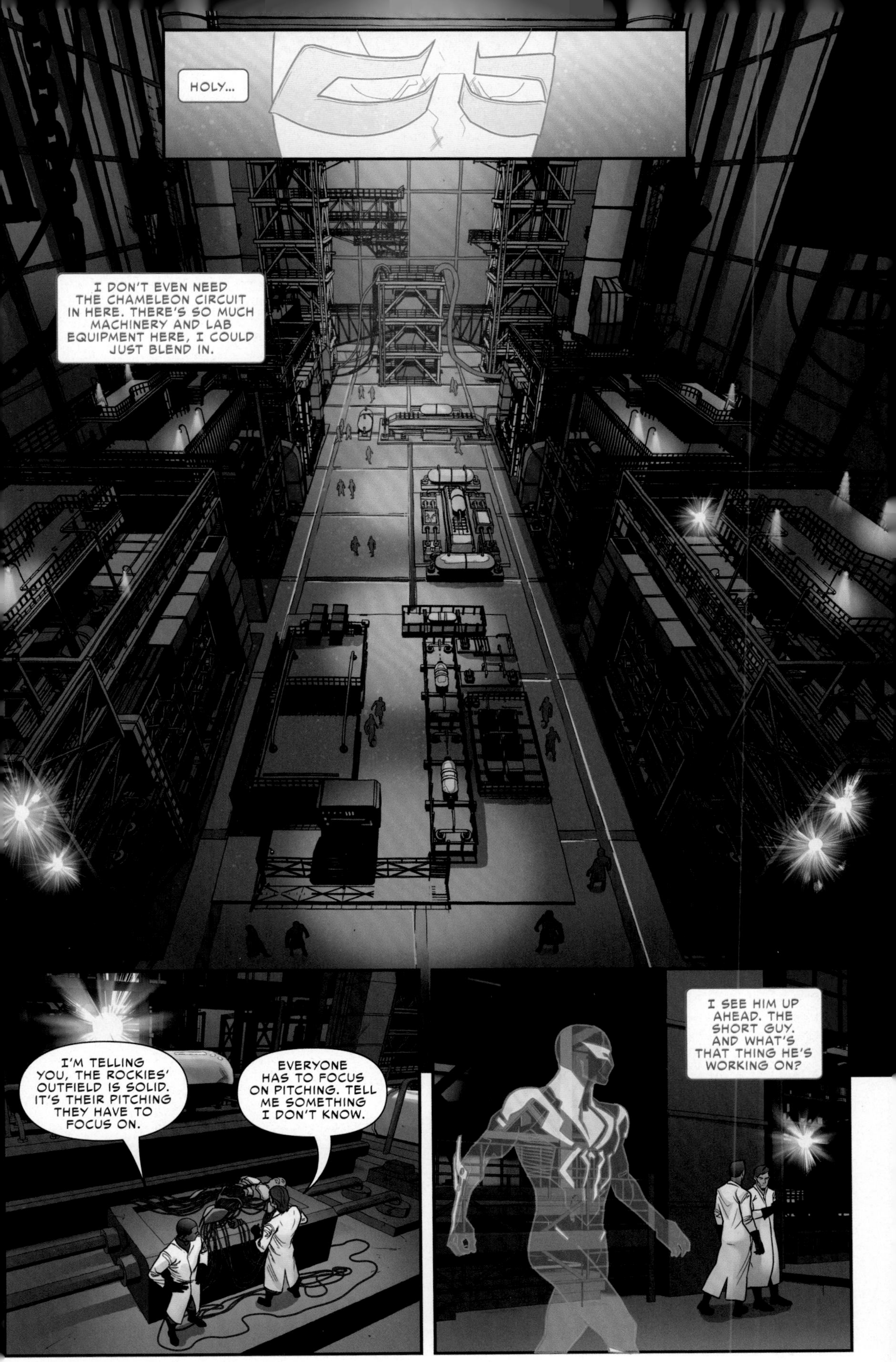
HOLY...
I DON'T EVEN NEED THE CHAMELEON CIRCUIT IN HERE. THERE'S SO MUCH MACHINERY AND LAB EQUIPMENT HERE, I COULD JUST BLEND IN.
I'M TELLING YOU, THE ROCKIES' OUTFIELD IS SOLID. IT'S THEIR PITCHING THEY HAVE TO FOCUS ON.
EVERYONE HAS TO FOCUS ON PITCHING. TELL ME SOMETHING I DON'T KNOW.
I SEE HIM UP AHEAD. THE SHORT GUY. AND WHAT'S THAT THING HE'S WORKING ON?

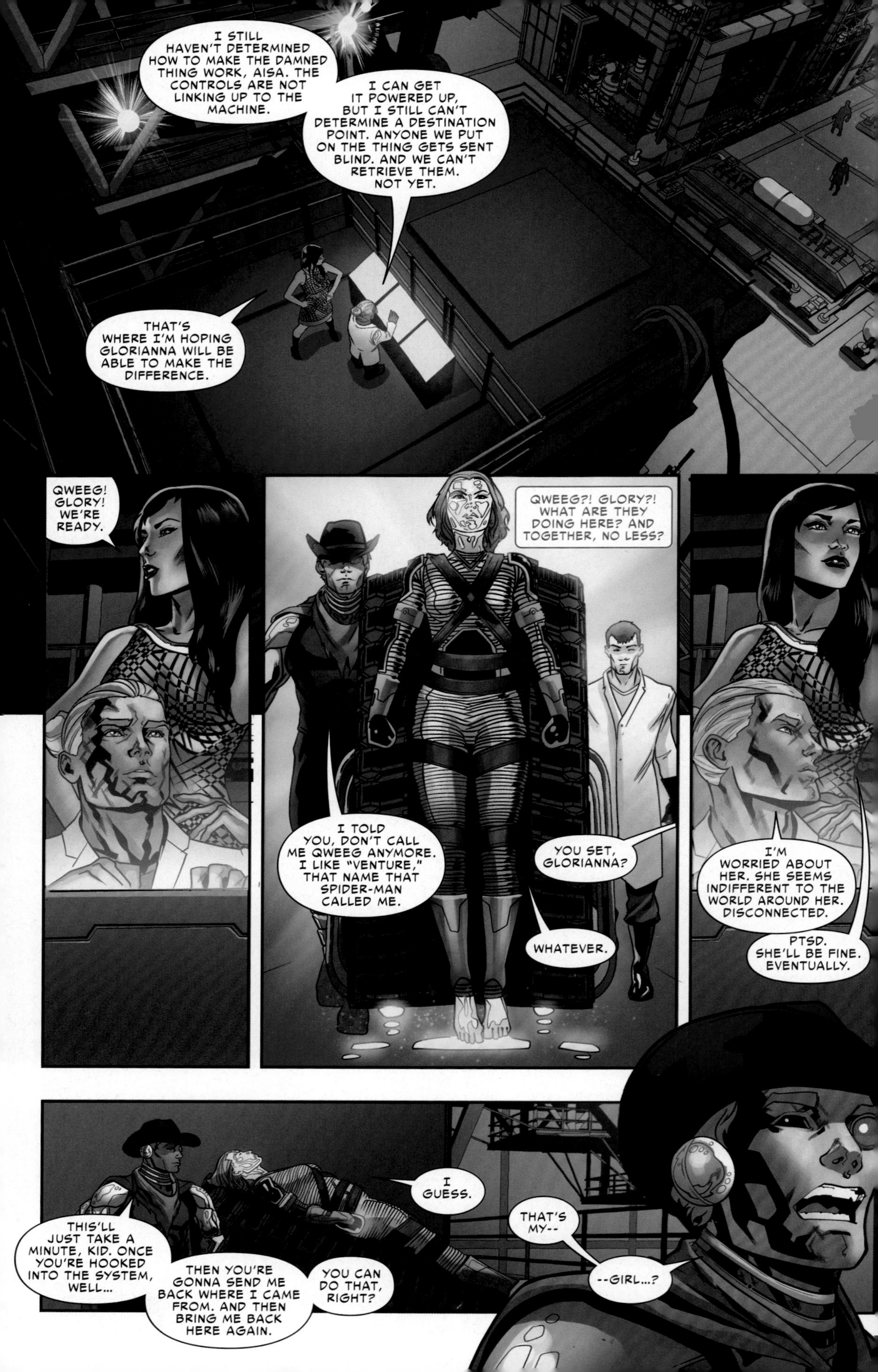
I STILL HAVEN'T DETERMINED HOW TO MAKE THE DAMNED THING WORK, AISA. THE CONTROLS ARE NOT LINKING UP TO THE MACHINE.
I CAN GET IT POWERED UP, BUT I STILL CAN'T DETERMINE A DESTINATION POINT. ANYONE WE PUT ON THE THING GETS SENT BLIND. AND WE CAN'T RETRIEVE THEM. NOT YET.
THAT'S WHERE I'M HOPING GLORIANNA WILL BE ABLE TO MAKE THE DIFFERENCE.
QWEEG! GLORY! WE'RE READY.
QWEEG?! GLORY?! WHAT ARE THEY DOING HERE? AND TOGETHER, NO LESS?
I TOLD YOU, DON'T CALL ME QWEEG ANYMORE. I LIKE "VENTURE," THAT NAME THAT SPIDER-MAN CALLED ME.
YOU SET, GLORIANNA?
WHATEVER.
I'M WORRIED ABOUT HER. SHE SEEMS INDIFFERENT TO THE WORLD AROUND HER. DISCONNECTED.
PTSD. SHE'LL BE FINE. EVENTUALLY.
THIS'LL JUST TAKE A MINUTE, KID. ONCE YOU'RE HOOKED INTO THE SYSTEM, WELL...
THEN YOU'RE GONNA SEND ME BACK WHERE I CAME FROM. AND THEN BRING ME BACK HERE AGAIN.
YOU CAN DO THAT, RIGHT?
I GUESS.
THAT'S MY--
--GIRL...?

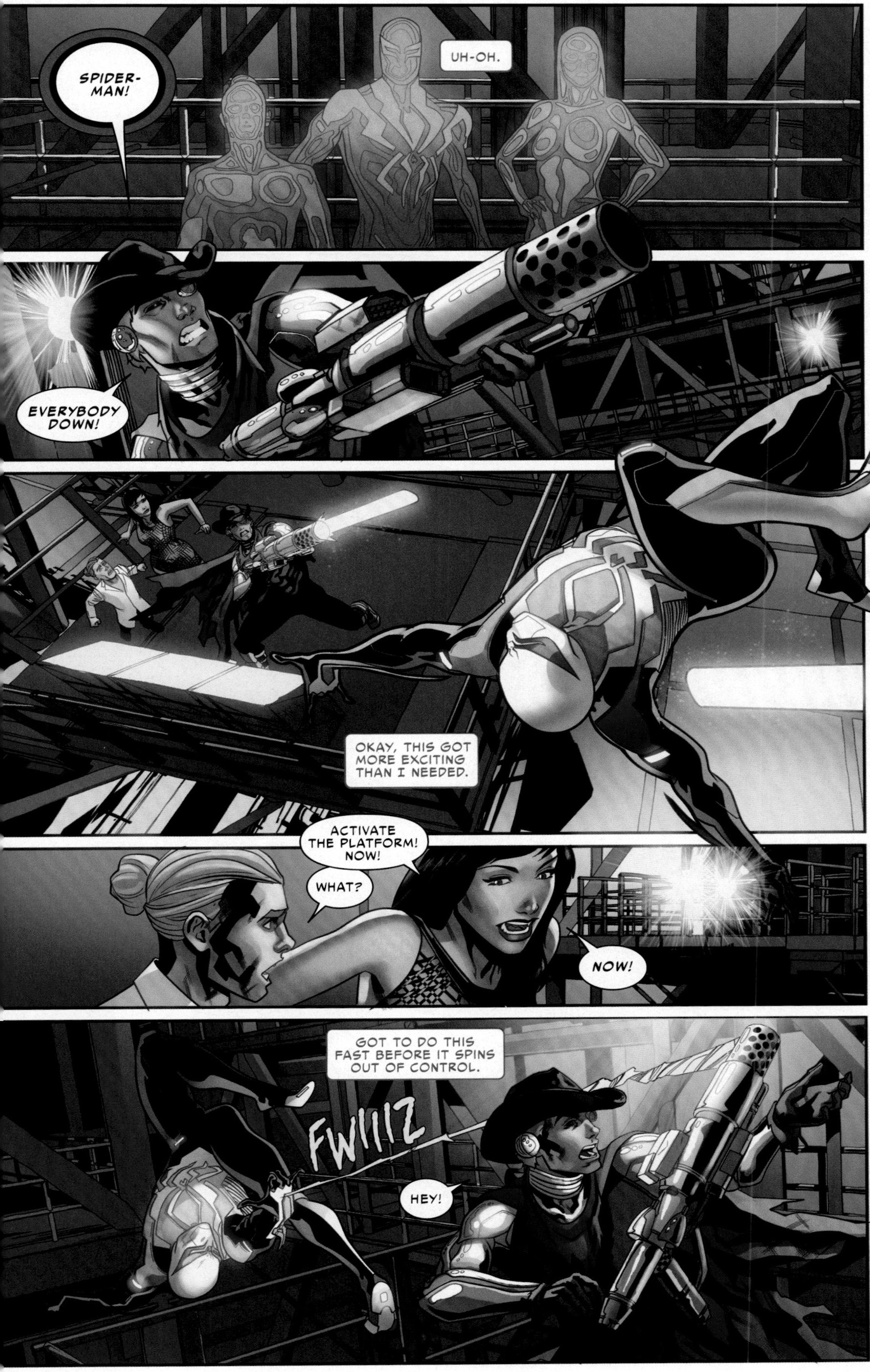
SPIDER-MAN!
UH-OH.
EVERYBODY DOWN!
OKAY, THIS GOT MORE EXCITING THAN I NEEDED.
ACTIVATE THE PLATFORM! NOW!
WHAT?
NOW!
GOT TO DO THIS FAST BEFORE IT SPINS OUT OF CONTROL.
FWIIIZ
HEY!

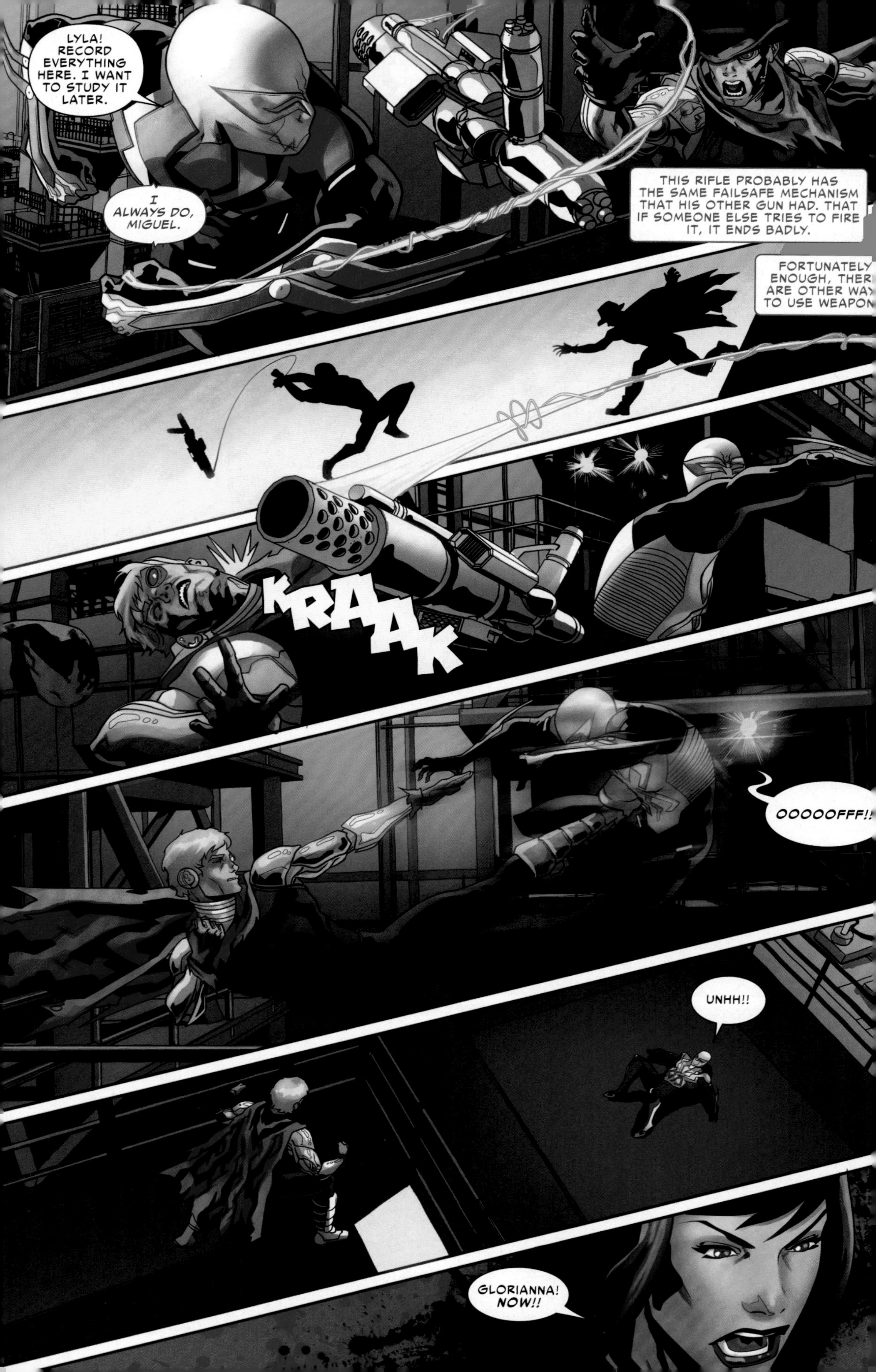
LYLA! RECORD EVERYTHING HERE. I WANT TO STUDY IT LATER.
I ALWAYS DO, MIGUEL.
THIS RIFLE PROBABLY HAS THE SAME FAILSAFE MECHANISM THAT HIS OTHER GUN HAD. THAT IF SOMEONE ELSE TRIES TO FIRE IT, IT ENDS BADLY.
FORTUNATELY ENOUGH, THER ARE OTHER WAY TO USE WEAPON
KRAAAK
OOOOOFFF!!
UNHH!!
GLORIANNA! NOW!!

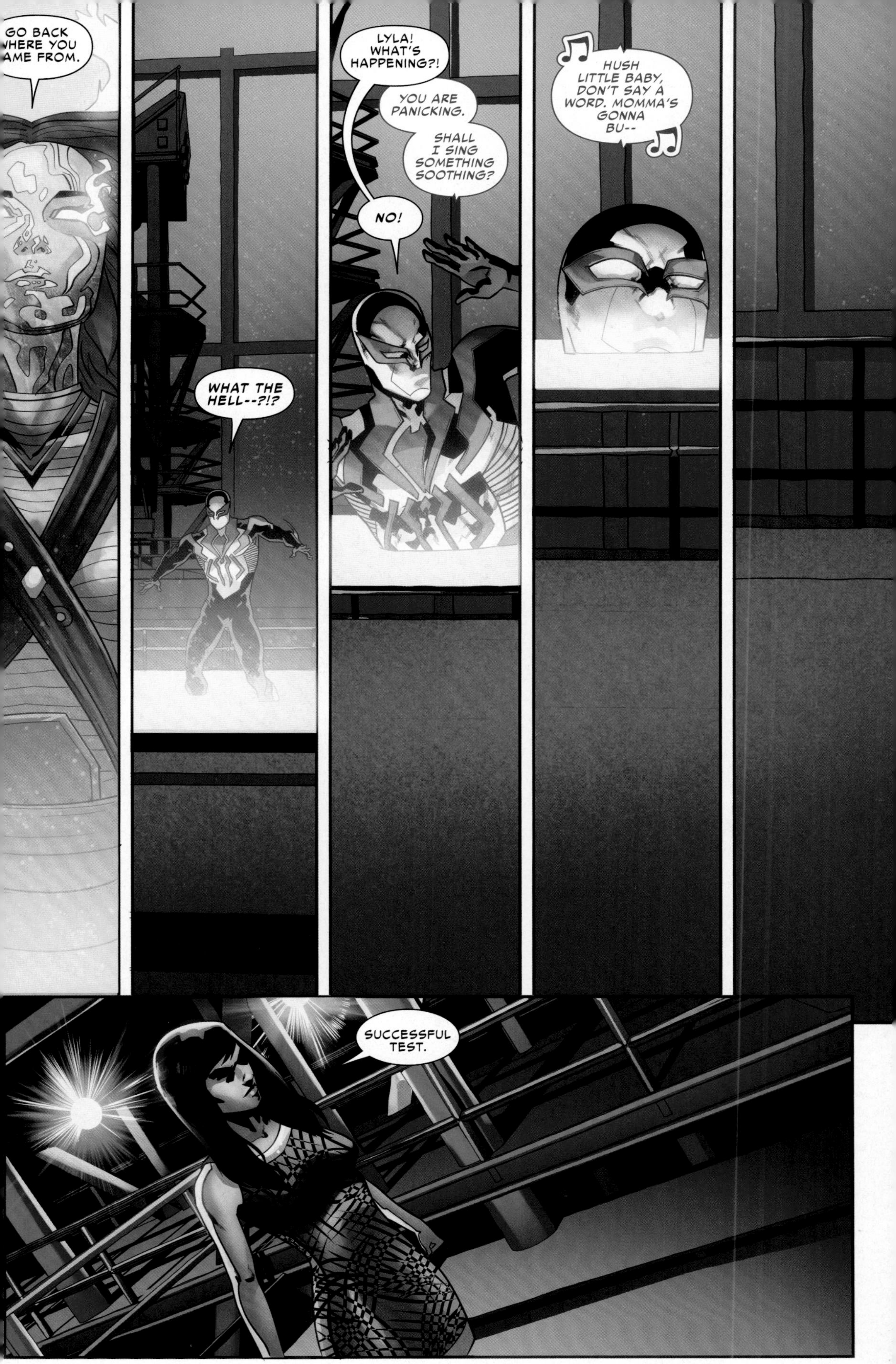
GO BACK WHERE YOU AME FROM.
WHAT THE HELL--?!?
LYLA! WHAT'S HAPPENING?!
YOU ARE PANICKING.
SHALL I SING SOMETHING SOOTHING?
NO!
HUSH LITTLE BABY, DON'T SAY A WORD. MOMMA'S GONNA BU--
SUCCESSFUL TEST.

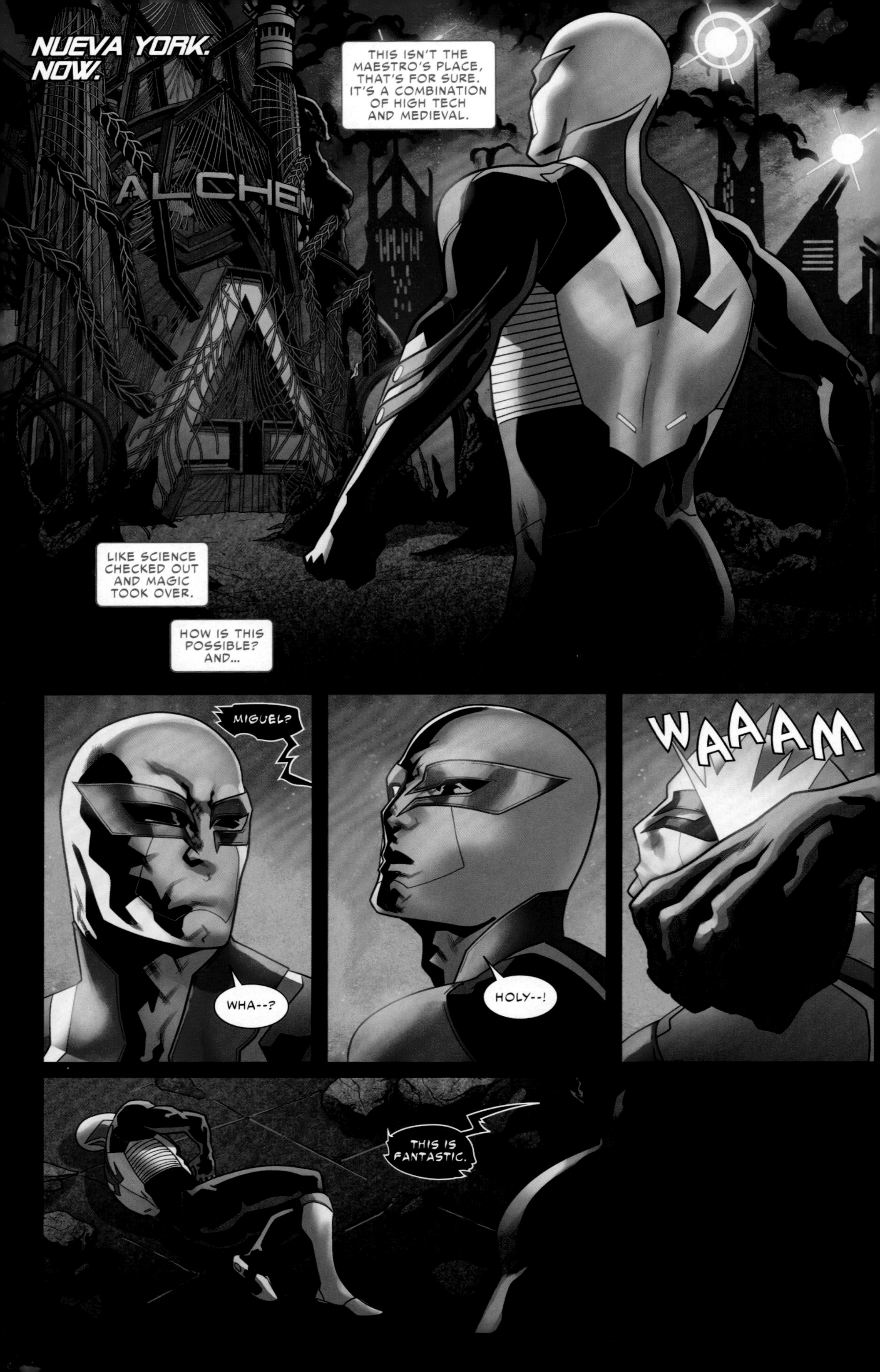
NUEVA YORK. NOW.
THIS ISN'T THE MAESTRO'S PLACE, THAT'S FOR SURE. IT'S A COMBINATION OF HIGH TECH AND MEDIEVAL.
ALCHEM
LIKE SCIENCE CHECKED OUT AND MAGIC TOOK OVER.
HOW IS THIS POSSIBLE? AND...
MIGUEL?
WHA--?
HOLY--!
WAAAM
THIS IS FANTASTIC.

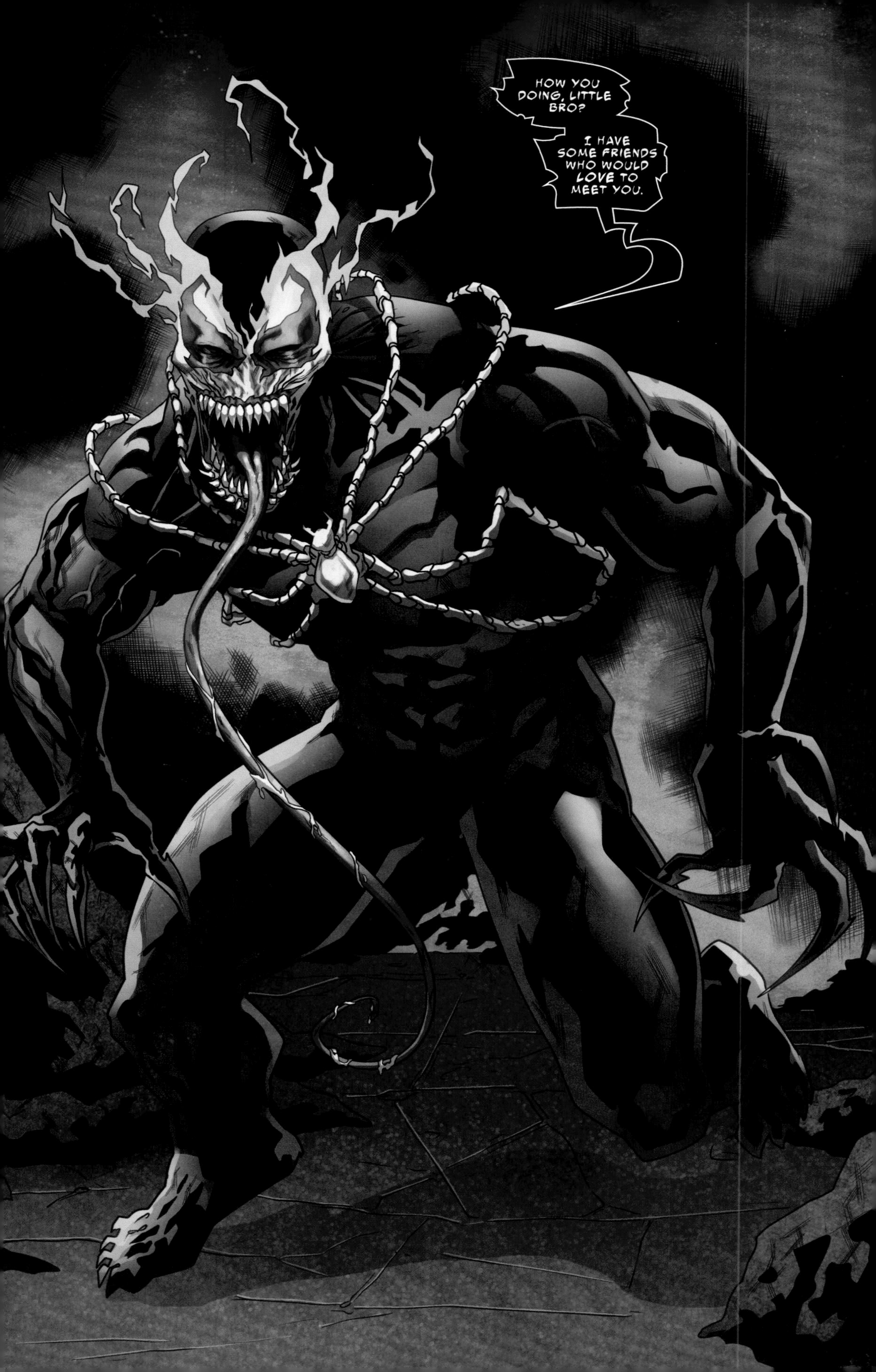
HOW YOU DOING, LITTLE BRO?
I HAVE SOME FRIENDS WHO WOULD **LOVE** TO MEET YOU.

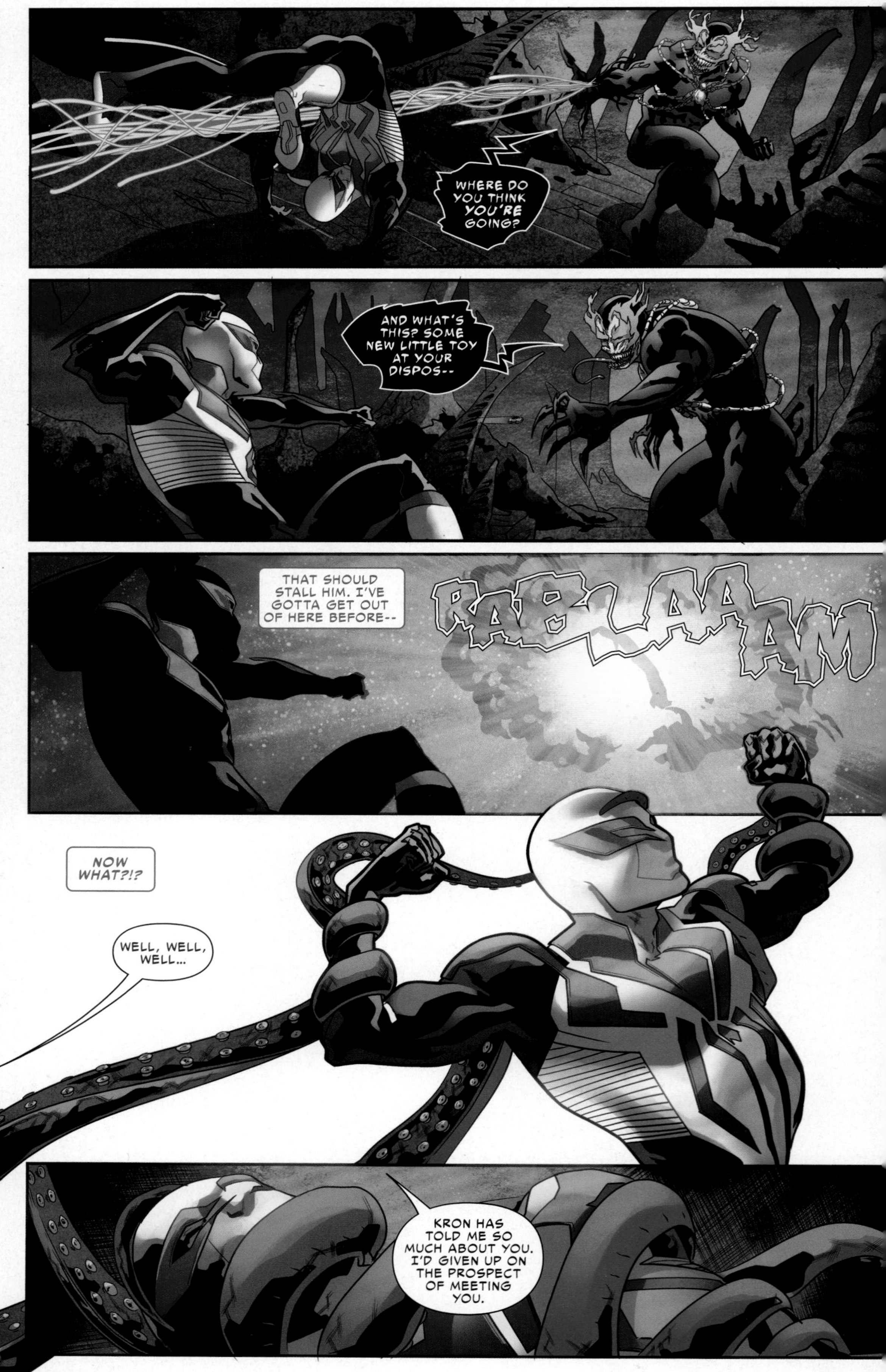
WHERE DO YOU THINK YOU'RE GOING?
AND WHAT'S THIS? SOME NEW LITTLE TOY AT YOUR DISPOS--
THAT SHOULD STALL HIM. I'VE GOTTA GET OUT OF HERE BEFORE--
RABLAAAM
NOW WHAT?!?
WELL, WELL, WELL...
KRON HAS TOLD ME SO MUCH ABOUT YOU. I'D GIVEN UP ON THE PROSPECT OF MEETING YOU.

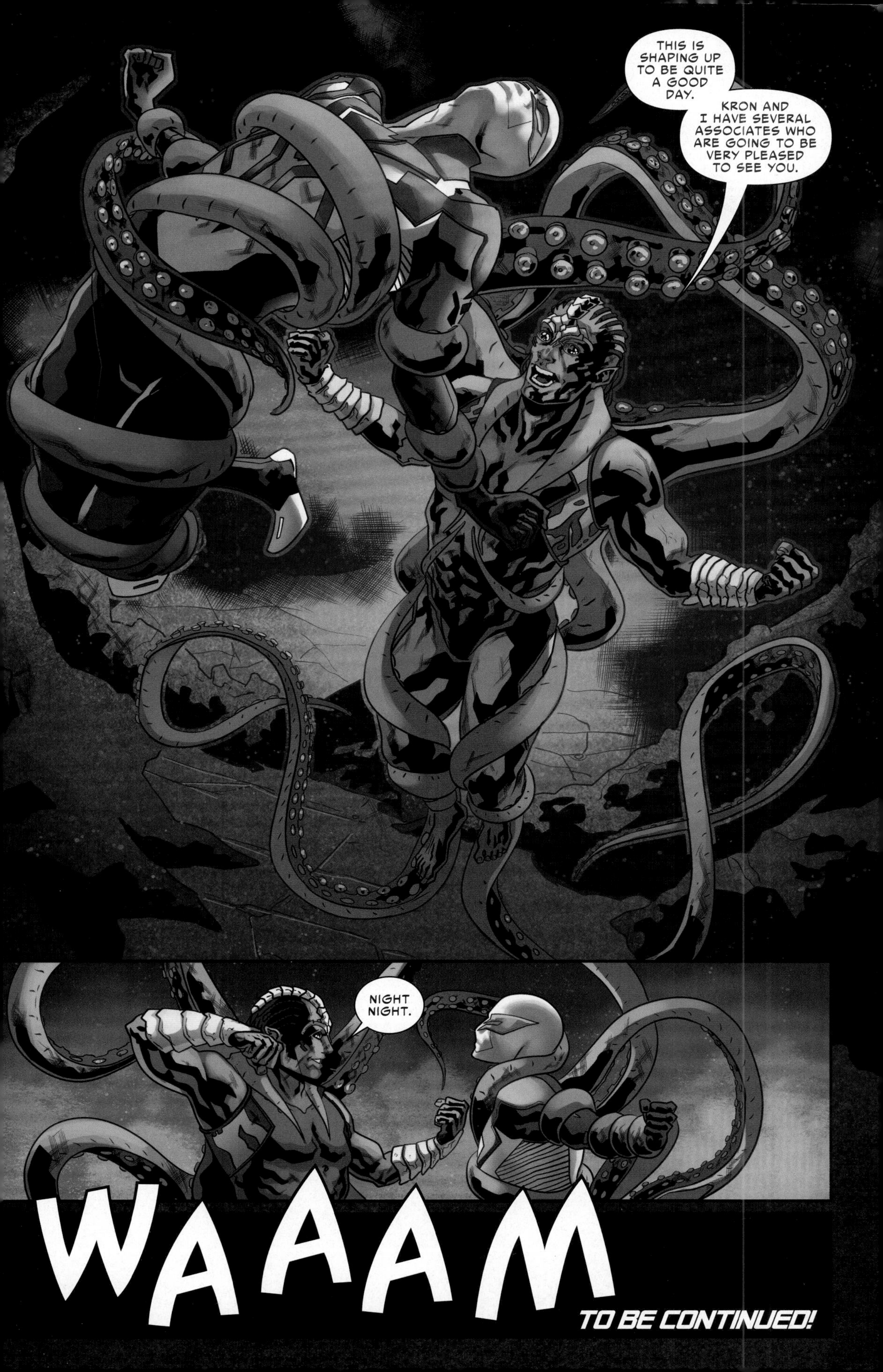
THIS IS SHAPING UP TO BE QUITE A GOOD DAY.
KRON AND I HAVE SEVERAL ASSOCIATES WHO ARE GOING TO BE VERY PLEASED TO SEE YOU.
NIGHT NIGHT.
WAAAM
TO BE CONTINUED!

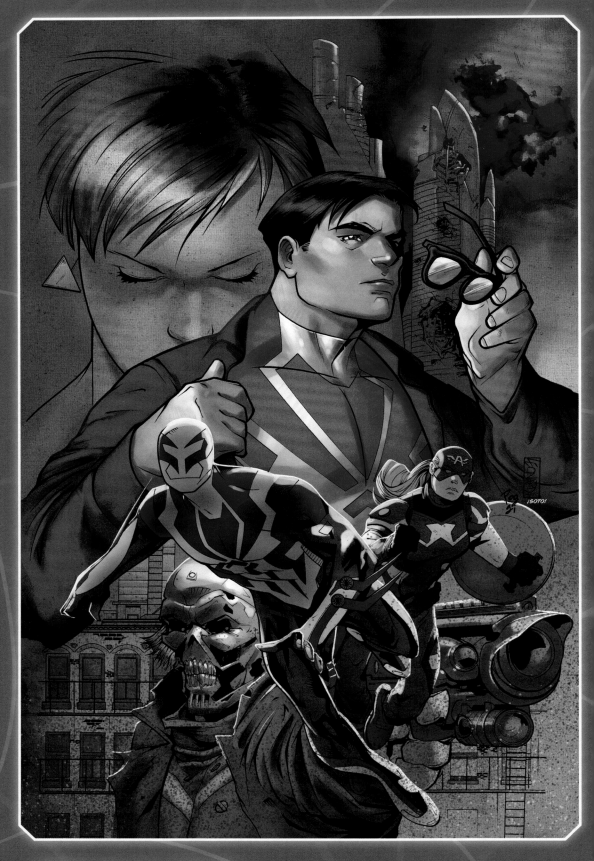

#8 Story Thus Far variant by
RICK LEONARDI & CHRIS SOTOMAYOR

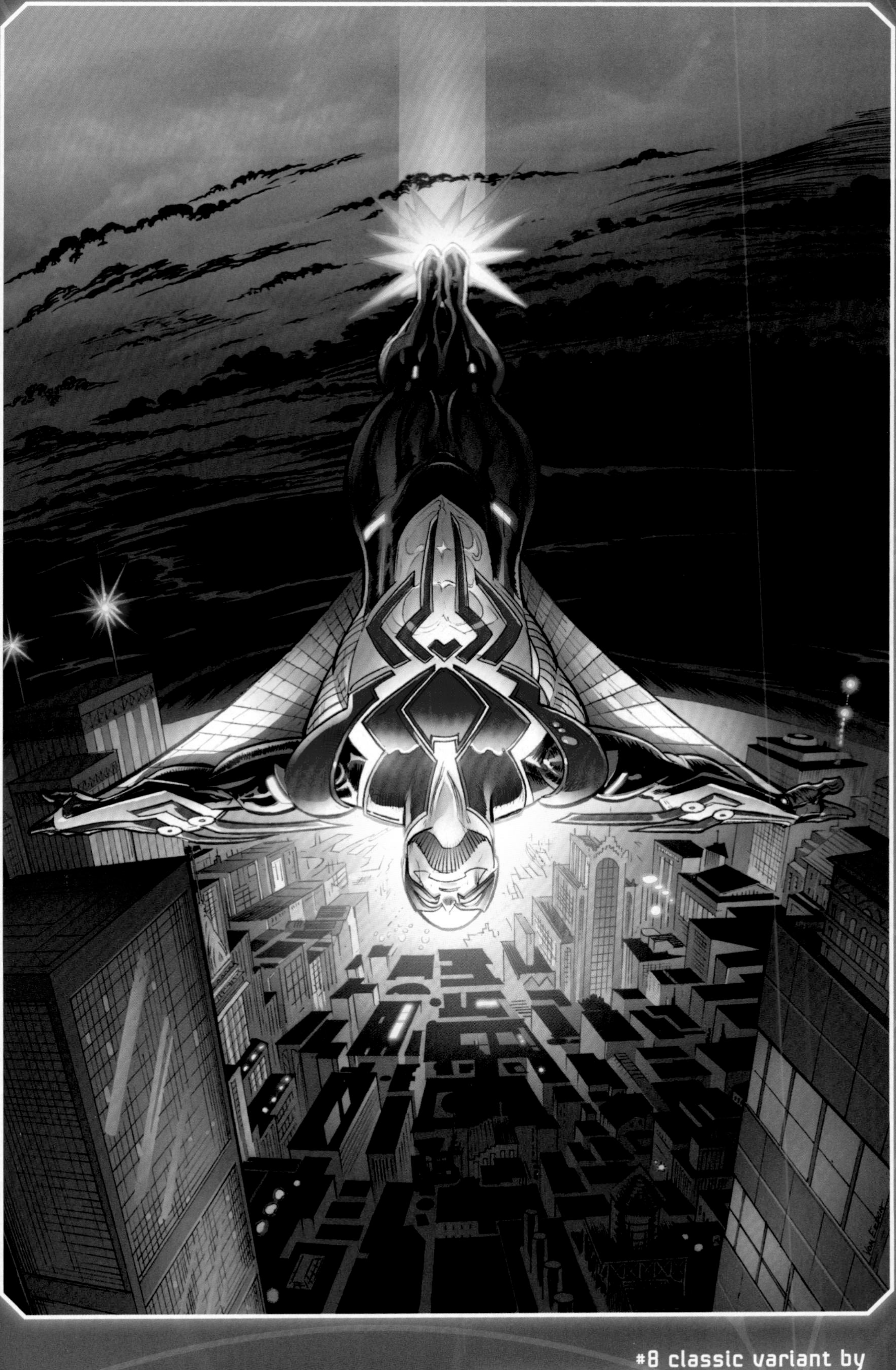

#8 classic variant by
TREVOR VON EEDEN & FRANK D'ARMATA